EXPLORING EMOTION, CARE, AND ENTHUSIASM IN "UNLOVED" MUSEUM COLLECTIONS

COLLECTION DEVELOPMENT, CULTURAL HERITAGE, AND DIGITAL HUMANITIES

This exciting series publishes both monographs and edited thematic collections in the broad areas of cultural heritage, digital humanities, collecting and collections, public history and allied areas of applied humanities. The aim is to illustrate the impact of humanities research and in particular reflect the exciting new networks developing between researchers and the cultural sector, including archives, libraries and museums, media and the arts, cultural memory and heritage institutions, festivals and tourism, and public history.

EXPLORING EMOTION, CARE, AND ENTHUSIASM IN "UNLOVED" MUSEUM COLLECTIONS

Edited by
**ANNA WOODHAM, RHIANEDD SMITH,
AND ALISON HESS**

For Mr and Mrs Browne,
and David Neilson

British Library Cataloguing in Publication Data
A catalogue record for this book is available from the British Library.

© 2020, Arc Humanities Press, Leeds

ISBN (print): 9781641890557
eISBN (PDF): 9781641890564

www.arc-humanities.org

Printed and bound by CPI Group (UK) Ltd, Croydon, CR0 4YY

CONTENTS

SECTION THREE:
EMOTIONAL RESEARCH

ILLUSTRATIONS

ACKNOWLEDGEMENTS

WE WOULD LIKE to thank the AHRC who supported this research and acknowledge the particular early career funding within the "Care for the Future" scheme from which this project benefited. The scheme was designed to allow early career academics the opportunity to work together to conduct small-scale, collaborative, and interdisciplinary research projects. We were also very lucky to be supported by four cultural institutions: the Museum of English Rural Life (MERL), the University of Reading, the Science Museum Group, and the Ironbridge Gorge Museum Trust. We would like to express our sincere thanks to staff at these organizations who helped facilitate the research, often on top of their already stretched workloads. In particular, we thank the Science Museum London, which provided us with the venue for our conference. We believe that this event was the first (of many) conferences to be held in the new Dana Research Centre. We are grateful for the support of staff at Arc Humanities Press, Dymphna Evans—in the early stages of development—and Danièle Cybulskie and others for their assistance in bringing this volume to fruition. We would also like to thank the anonymous reviewer whose comments helped us to clarify the intentions of the book and who provided many insightful suggestions. Finally, we would like to thank all of the presenters and participants at the "Who Cares?" conference and project events in 2015 and the contributors to this volume, which has been several years in the making. We are extremely grateful for your contributions and patience while the volume was taking shape. The editors benefited enormously from their discussions with Helen Peavitt, Jack Kirby, Elizabeth Haines, Nick Wilson, Ollie Douglas, members of the Lock Collectors Association and the Historical Metallurgy Society, and the careful eye of Amy Jane Barnes, to whom we would like to pay special thanks.

INTRODUCTION

ANNA WOODHAM, RHIANEDD SMITH, AND ALISON HESS

Setting the Scene

IT IS A misty November day in Manchester, UK. The fog lingers in the lower yard of the Museum of Science and Industry, the site of a former railway station, as a group of museum staff, expert researchers, and a film crew in scarves and warm jackets walk into the museum's Collections Centre. We are here as part of a research project to talk about how "expert enthusiasts" engage with museum objects. Sometime later, while most of the group is milling around in the open storage, exploring, eagerly taking photographs, and chatting to each other about the objects in front of them, the film crew asks one of the curators to talk on camera about what she thinks is significant about this group's visit. Immediately she replies: "Getting the right people in front of the objects you want answers about ... is kind of invaluable. There's something very special about having the insight of an expert, onsite, with the objects ... and that triangulation that happens."[1] Her comment strikes us as getting to the heart of what this volume concerns, and it gives recognition to the critical, but under-explored, dynamic between collections of "unloved" objects and the groups, individuals, and institutions who actively care for them. This volume asks: (1) What are "unloved" collections and who cares for them? (2) How can considering theoretical concepts of care and emotion help us to understand and interrogate experiences of "unloved" collections? (3) How do different kinds of carers, especially, but not limited to, "enthusiasts," express and share their love for collections in daily practice? (4) And finally, are there ways in which different types of carers can work together collaboratively and creatively to engage others with collections?

The vast majority of museum objects, both in the UK and internationally, sit in storage facilities, which are both costly and chronically underused. They often contain items which are not deemed worthy of display but which are seen as having research potential. On the face of it, keeping an object in storage rather than on public display implies a value judgement that these objects are, for some reason, not of interest to a nonspecialist audience. But in reality, most museum objects will never be included in an exhibition or go on loan, and there are many reasons for this, including pragmatic choices around limited display space. This does not mean, however, that a stored object has no value or relevance but that its significance may be harder to recognize.

Not all of the objects discussed in this volume are in storage, but most would be described by the people who worked with them as "dull." People find this "lack" hard to

---

1 "Energy in Store" project participant, 2017. "Energy in Store" was a follow-up project to the "Who Cares? Interventions in 'Unloved' Museum Collections" research project introduced in this section. See also footnote 50, this Introduction.

articulate, and often such objects are best described as "uncharismatic" in comparison with objects such as the "charismatic" Sultanganj Buddha described by Wingfield.[2] In contrast, the objects discussed in this volume may be unable to "elicit such a degree of human response."[3] However, this is not an issue which only affects museum objects in storage, as for Monti and Keene many displayed objects are also to some extent "silent."[4]

According to Pearce,[5] collections are created by people who care, hence they are, among other things, a manifestation of emotional energy. Sometimes this is easy to understand, but certain collections reflect a singular passion that can be hard to share with a wider audience. Many of the chapters that follow explore the nuances of this specific kind of emotional attachment. Our authors consider: why an object or collection could be deemed "unloved" (as this is far from straightforward), who champions these collections, how they "fell in love" with them, and how we might harness their "enthusiasm" in order to connect with wider audiences. One of the key communities of interest for these collections is not academic researchers but so-called "enthusiasts," people with a detailed knowledge of and a personal passion for certain kinds of objects.

Most analysis of museum interpretation tends to focus on work that engages people in public spaces. Here we aim to take the exploration of emotions, care, and enthusiasm "behind the scenes" and locate these ideas within both seen and unseen museum practices around objects. In doing this we draw on ethnographic, archival, and activist methodologies which seek to explore the spatial, social, and historical dimensions of these practices. By discussing the process of knowledge exchange and the creation of conversations around material things in informal, "behind the scenes," or "raw" museum spaces, recognition can be given to the "lives" of unseen museum collections. Hence this volume goes beyond discussions of curated exhibitions and public spaces, ultimately broadening our understanding of where and how museum-object relationships take place.

In addition to arguments of more theoretical interest, many of the chapters in this volume offer potential practical applications by suggesting strategies for the "reinvigoration" of "unloved" collections. Authors also explore the value of experimentation and of bringing together the voices of academics, enthusiasts, and heritage professionals to consider different viewpoints. We argue that stored collections and traditional communities of interest, specifically enthusiast groups, could be a part of the growing body of research and practice around co-curation and co-creativity. Many of the "enthusiast" collections specialists discussed in this volume are actively engaged in forms of audience development outside of collecting institutions. Examining the politics of their

---

2 Christopher Wingfield, "Touching the Buddha: Encounters with a Charismatic Object," in *Museum Materialities, Objects, Engagements, Interpretations*, ed. Sandra Dudley (London: Routledge, 2010), 53–70.

3 Wingfield, "Touching the Buddha," 55.

4 Francesca Monti and Suzanne Keene, *Museums and Silent Objects: Designing Effective Exhibitions* (Abingdon: Routledge, 2016).

5 Susan Pearce, *On Collecting: An Investigation into Collecting in the European Tradition* (Abingdon: Routledge, 1995).

contribution to the heritage sector and investigating the challenges posed by a need for intergenerational discourse are, we believe, all part of a socially engaged museology. The rest of this introduction frames our approach to these guiding concepts. First of all, we elaborate on what we mean by "unloved" and explain the context around why this term was selected and how we use it. We then set out to position "unloved" collections within a broader framework of stored collections, relating discussion to wider trends in the development and understanding of these spaces. Our approach to emotion, care, and enthusiasm/enthusiasts in the context of "unloved" collections is then introduced, before the final part of this introduction outlines our methodological approach and sets out the structure of the volume.

"Unloved" Collections

The majority of the chapters in this volume have their origins in the "Who Cares? Interventions in 'Unloved' Museum Collections" conference held on November 6, 2015 at the Dana Research Centre, Science Museum, London. The conference marked the culmination of a year-long research project of the same name, funded by the UK Arts and Humanities Research Council (AHRC). Participants were asked to consider what "care" means in relation to museum collections and to explore the emotional aspects associated with stewardship and enthusiasm. They examined the emotional potential of stored, bulky, mundane, "unloved" collections and the place of these collections, and those who care for them, in the future of curatorial and collections management practices.

The term "unloved" was deliberately chosen to provoke discussion, as we were well aware that the vast majority of stored objects are not neglected by their professional custodians and are loved with great intensity by some curators, enthusiasts, and other communities. However, we felt that "unloved" as an idea had a place in our research, as, arguably, for all but a small proportion of the population, stored collections have little or no personal meaning.[6] As introduced above, these objects are hidden from view in museum storerooms, often considered to be unfit for display.[7] Collections knowledge might also be lacking, as curatorial staff no longer always have the expertise and resources to catalogue specialist collections. This is a double bind in which objects are deemed uninteresting and as a result, little research is undertaken to explore their potential significance.

It is clear that "unloved" as a classificatory term implies a number of judgements about the changing values associated with objects. It raises questions about why objects may be "unloved" and how they came to be considered in this way. The objects in this volume became "unloved" for a variety of reasons. This includes their physical and aesthetic characteristics, their status as one of multiple duplicates, the type of history they are connected with (e.g., industrial, working class, rural), changing points of cultural reference for museum visitors, the way they are classified within museum collections, their lack of visibility within a museum, loss of interested champions and research culture, or

---

6 See Martine Jaoul, "Why Reserve Collections?," *Museum International* 47, no. 4 (1995): 4–7.

7 Jaoul, "Why Reserve Collections?," 4–7.

a combination of all or some of the above. To this list we also add a point raised by Simon Knell, who mentions changing historical trajectories, which for some objects results in them becoming "estranged"[8] from the reason why they were collected in the first place. This suggests that simply becoming a museum object is not enough to ensure an enduring sense of purpose.[9] We argue that a greater understanding of these processes may also provide a path towards igniting "love" for them.

Drawing on the work of colleague Hilary Geoghegan,[10] we realized that another potentially fruitful avenue for investigation into "unloved" collections could be in the growing field of research exploring "enthusiasm." Enthusiast groups with an interest in history tend to engage with museum collections, create their own personal collections, and share specialist knowledge among themselves and with the public. This project questioned what care meant for these stakeholders, which emotional states are connected with acts of care, and how enthusiasm for "unloved" objects might be manifested and experienced. It also asked how this extreme form of engagement could be harnessed for wider value.

The original research project centred around three case studies of so-called "unloved objects" that form the focus of three chapters in this volume: the locks and fastenings collection at the Science Museum, London (chapter 1); the Museum of English Rural Life's hand tools collection (chapter 2); and the National Slag Collection at the Ironbridge Gorge Museum Trust (chapter 3). However, as the "Who Cares" conference demonstrated, there was value to broadening this focus to engage with a wide variety of different types of collection, ranging from medical instruments and natural history specimens to textiles and archival material. The contributions in this volume reflect many of the ideas around what the term "unloved" concerns and allow us to critically examine it.

To us, the range of terminology used by the authors here—and by others—to describe the collections that they focus on reveals some of the nuances in approach to this category of object: from "lost objects" to "silent objects"[11] to "uninteresting" and "difficult" objects.[12] These terms convey a range of meanings, which we recognize are not always precise synonyms for "unloved." Yet we suggest that there is a link between them relating to the ease with which it may (or may not) be possible to form an attachment to these objects. Each term, we believe, also indicates the latent interpretive potential of specific objects that do not at first glance appear to have an emotional potency.

---

8 Simon Knell, "Introduction: The Context of Collections Care," in *Care of Collections*, ed. Simon Knell (London: Routledge, 1994), 1–10.

9 Knell, "Introduction," 1.

10 Particularly Hilary Geoghegan, "Emotional Geographies of Enthusiasm: Belonging to the Telecommunications Heritage Group," *Area* 45 (2013): 40–46; and Hilary Geoghegan, " 'If You Can Walk down the Street and Recognise the Difference between Cast Iron and Wrought Iron, the World is Altogether a Better Place': Being Enthusiastic about Industrial Archaeology," *M/C Journal: A Journal of Media and Culture* 12, no. 2 (2009): unpaginated.

11 Monti and Keene, *Museums and Silent Objects*.

12 See Macleod, this volume.

Contextualizing Stored Collections

This volume speaks to the growing interest in the contents and use of museum storerooms. In a time of economic austerity, museums are under increased pressure to demonstrate their wider social value, and stored collections can be seen as an unnecessary luxury. In the UK, a series of reviews and research projects has provided a greater insight into the proportion of museums' collections in storage and the extent to which audiences use these stored objects. It is difficult to be exact, but a DOMUS review (1998–1999) estimated that there were approximately 200 million items in UK collections.[13] However, over half the museums surveyed by Keene and colleagues in 2008[14] had fewer than two visitors a week to their stored collections. Similar issues around lack of engagement with stored objects have been found in more targeted reviews, such as for archaeological archives.[15] This is a potentially serious position for museums linked to neoliberal agendas[16] concerning value versus economic expenditure. As alluded to above, for museums in receipt of public funding, financial investment in storage facilities can be particularly hard to justify in terms of maximum public benefit. There are also arguments emphasizing an ethical and professional duty to ensure the use of stored collections. As Glaister suggests, "If an object sits in a store for ten years, without anyone looking at it, and if it is not published or made available on the internet, can that museum be realizing its responsibilities towards the object and towards the public? If we, as a profession, are merely acting as caretakers and not as collection activists then we are not fulfilling our obligations."[17] Her words hint at an association between professional caring practices in museums and inactivity, a state which she implies fails to keep collections alive and in motion.

Recently, the Mendoza Review has identified storage as an increasing concern for England's museums, an issue that is far from straightforward to resolve, requiring cross-organizational collaboration.[18] Prior to this, in 2002, the Department for Culture, Media and Sport (DCMS) commissioned the consultants PKF to write a report on the costs of

---

13 DOMUS refers to the "Digest of Museum Statistics," a database established by the then UK Museums and Galleries Commission (MGC). See Sophie Carter, Bethan Hurst, Rachael H. Kerr, Emma Taylor, and Peter Winsor, *Museum Focus: Facts and Figures on Museums in the UK*, issue 2 (London: MGC, 1999).

14 Suzanne Keene with Alice Stevenson, and Francesca Monti, *Collections for the People* (London: UCL Institute for Archaeology, 2008); see also Suzanne Keene, *Fragments of the World: Uses of Museum Collections* (Oxford: Elsevier Butterworth-Heinemann, 2005).

15 Rachel Edwards, *Archaeological Archives and Museums 2012* (Society for Museum Archaeology, 2013), http://socmusarch.org.uk/socmusarch/gailmark/wordpress/wp-content/uploads/2016/07/Archaeological-archives-and-museums-2012.pdf [accessed June 29, 2019].

16 Jennie Morgan and Sharon Macdonald, "De-growing Museum Collections for New Heritage Futures," *International Journal of Heritage Studies* (2018): published online.

17 Jane Glaister, "The Power and Potential of Collections," in *Collections for the Future: Report of a Museums Association Inquiry*, ed. Helen Wilkinson (London: Museums Association, 2005), 8–9.

18 Neil Mendoza, *The Mendoza Review: An Independent Review of Museums in England* (London: DCMS, 2017).

storage for the seventeen national museums in the UK.[19] The results of the report are complex. However, the underlying assumption was that storage was costly and that space could be used more efficiently. In the 2015 Autumn Budget Statement, the UK Government announced that it would provide £150 million for new national museum storage and sell Blythe House, a central London facility that had been used as museum storage for national museums in the capital since 1979.[20] Although this decision was driven by a clear economic argument that the income generated from the sale of the site, in its prime West London location, would more than offset the cost of relocating the collections, it also signalled an investment by the UK Government in improving storage facilities for these national museums.

Museum storage is not simply a UK problem, as evidenced by ICCROM's 2016 RE-ORG seminar "Reconnecting with Collections in Storage," which brought together delegates from twenty-eight different countries to discuss the dangers to objects stored in poor conditions.[21] This seminar was in addition to the India-Europe Advanced Network 2014 conference at the Victoria and Albert Museum (V&A)[22] and Brusias and Singh's recent edited volume, which also takes a global approach to the theoretical challenge of museum storage.[23] Hence there is an increased strategic and theoretical interest in the management and physical structures of stored collections.

Suzanne Keene has been one of the few researchers to explore the potential uses of stored collections in contemporary museums.[24] But in academia, the arguments have also recently progressed, for example, in the "Assembling Alternative Heritage Futures" project.[25] The approach of this project speaks to many of the issues discussed here. This volume, therefore, sits within a new wave of research that moves away from discussing the physical requirements and management of museum storage[26] towards examining the emotional experiences of collecting, curating, conserving, and interpreting "unloved" objects.

---

19 This unpublished report was secured by Suzanne Keene, following a Freedom of Information Request, and subsequently critiqued in Suzanne Keene, "Collections in the English National Museums: The Numbers," *Papers from the Institute of Archaeology* S1 (2007): 115–34.

20 HM Treasury, *Spending Review and Autumn Statement 2015* (London: UK Government, 2015).

21 ICOM-CC, *Working Draft Recommendation: Reconnecting with Collections in Storage* (Paris: ICOM-CC, 2017).

22 See: https://arthist.net/reviews/9456/mode=conferences for a report of this conference [accessed November 26, 2018].

23 Mirjam Brusius and Kavita Singh, ed., *Museum Storage and Meaning: Tales from the Crypt* (London: Routledge, 2017).

24 Keene, *Fragments of the World*.

25 See, for example, publications from the "Profusion" strand of this project, such as Morgan and Macdonald, "De-growing Museum Collections for New Heritage Futures."

26 See, for example, May Cassar, *Environmental Management: Guidelines for Museums and Galleries* (London: Routledge, 1994); Suzanne Keene, *Managing Conservation in Museums* (Oxford: Butterworth-Heinemann, 2002); and Freda Matassa, *Museum Collections Management: A Handbook* (London: Facet, 2011).

Framing Emotion and Care in Relation to "Unloved" Collections

The aim of this volume is not simply to look at policy and practice around museum storage but to explore what happens when people who care about stored collections are brought into the research, engagement, and curatorial process. In order to achieve this, our authors have engaged with an emerging body of literature regarding concepts of emotion and care in relation to heritage. While this is not a book on emotion and heritage per se, concepts of care and emotion, particularly at the points of intersection, are central to it. It is well established in arts and humanities research that "heritage" is a highly contested field through which identity is negotiated and shaped.[27] Yet research into the relationship between affect, emotion, and heritage experience is a (relatively) recent development.[28] Researchers argue that, in contrast to earlier ideas of emotion being inferior and in opposition to reason and rationality, or even "dangerous,"[29] emotion is the key to understanding engagement with heritage. As Robinson suggests, "any engagement with the world and its peoples is an emotional engagement, in the sense that we neither read, experience or recall the world and our place within it, solely as fact and without sensation, judgment, consideration of value and processes of evaluation."[30]

We recognize that asking, "who cares?" as per the title of our original research project is also not a straightforward proposition. Our choice of words was again intentional, with the concept of "care" in need of critical exploration in this context. What does care, and what do the emotions that caring concerns, look like for specific communities? Are certain forms of care perceived to be more appropriate than others in a museum? Likewise, we acknowledge that framing the act of caring or not caring as simply one of personal choice does not recognize implicit power structures at play when we discuss museums (see this book for further discussion on these points). Not all individuals and groups are able to "care" equally within these structures.

The term "collections care" is not usually problematized within museum studies, but, taking the approach we have in this volume, "collections care" as a practice becomes a key site for critical exploration. It is often portrayed as the nuts and bolts, day-to-day work which keeps objects safe. However, research into "care" highlights its complex meaning and indicates the need to rethink our approach to it. Conradson,[31] for example, argues

---

27 See, for example, David Lowenthal, *The Heritage Crusade and the Spoils of History* (Cambridge: Cambridge University Press, 1998), and Laurajane Smith, *Uses of Heritage* (Abingdon: Routledge, 2006).

28 Two new major edited volumes were published in 2017 and 2018: Divya P. Tolia-Kelly, Emma Waterton, and Steve Watson, *Heritage, Affect and Emotion: Politics, Practices and Infrastructures* (Abingdon: Routledge 2017), and Laurajane Smith, Margaret Wetherell, and Gary Campbell, *Emotion, Affective Practices, and the Past in the Present* (Abingdon: Routledge, 2018).

29 Laurajane Smith and Gary Campbell, "The Elephant in the Room: Heritage, Affect and Emotion," in *A Companion to Heritage Studies*, ed. William Logan, Máiréad Nic Craith, and Ullrich Kockel (Chichester: Wiley, 2015), 447.

30 Mike Robinson, "The Emotional Tourist," in *Emotion in Motion: Tourism, Affect and Transformation*, ed. Mike Robinson and David Picard (London: Routledge, 2012), 21.

31 David Conradson, "Geographies of Care: Spaces, Practices, Experiences," in *Social & Cultural Geography* 4, no. 4 (December 2003): 451–54.

that practices of care are implicated in the production of social spaces where people are brought together around care-taking tasks such as feeding, washing, teaching, and listening. To this list we also add the social space of the museum. Conradson also notes that in interpersonal terms care can mean the proactive interest in the well-being of another person, we suggest this might include objects and more-than-human subjects as well.[32] However, the things we choose to care for and the practices of care are not neutral. Laurajane Smith's and Emma Waterton's joint work on authorized heritage discourse[33] and Caitlin DeSilvey's[34] work on curated decay, for example, highlight the political nature of decisions around care.

Other recent research has used a broad understanding of "care" in the museum to include the relationship between museums, public health, and social care.[35] For this volume, these debates raise questions around who has the right to care in the space of the museum. Which forms of care are recognized and which are marginalized? And how should museums balance different and sometimes competing forms of care, as seen in Hess's chapter in this volume? We see "care" in museums as going beyond the preservation of objects to include active promotion and research, care for people, and care for communities and places, something Woodall's chapter, which draws on the work of cultural geographer Caitlin DeSilvey,[36] engages directly with. We use the term "care" to explore the sharing of knowledge practices. This includes, as Woodham and Kelleher in this volume suggest, recognizing the political and relational characteristics of the term. Because of their specific institutional and political status and their complicated emotional relationship with the public, "unloved" collections offer a unique opportunity to engage with these different personal and collective definitions of care.

The concept of "care" brings an interesting dimension to the study of emotion in heritage, as its dictionary definitions include a "disquieted state of apprehension, uncertainty and responsibility," "painstaking or watchful attention," and "regard coming from desire or esteem."[37] Within museums we tend to use the term "collections care" to refer to provision of a specific form of guardianship. Objects are cared for in museums with

---

32 Conradson, "Geographies of Care," 451–54.

33 See, for example, Laurajane Smith and Emma Waterton, *Heritage, Communities and Archaeology* (London: Duckworth Academic, 2009).

34 Caitlin DeSilvey, *Curated Decay: Heritage beyond Saving* (Minneapolis: University of Minnesota, 2017).

35 See, for example, Nuala Morse and Helen Chatterjee, "Museums, Health and Wellbeing Research: Co-developing a New Observational Method for People with Dementia in Hospital Contexts," *Perspectives in Public Health* 138, no. 3 (2018): 152–59; Nuala Morse, Krisztina Lackoi, and Helen Chatterjee, "Museum Learning and Wellbeing," *Journal of Education in Museums* 37 (2016): 3–13; Lois H. Silverman, *The Social Work of Museums* (London: Routledge, 2010); and Nuala Morse, *The Museum as a Space of Social Care* (London: Routledge, forthcoming).

36 See, for example, DeSilvey, *Curated Decay*, and Caitlin DeSilvey, "Cultivated Histories in a Scottish Allotment Garden," *Cultural Geographies* 10 (2003): 442–68.

37 Merriam-Webster, "Care," www.merriam-webster.com/dictionary/care [accessed July 5, 2019].

stasis and a more fixed interpretation of preservation in mind.[38] We do not tend to talk about emotional states in reference books on collections care, yet many studies in this volume found that emotion is present in these interactions. The physical and often cognitive "inaccessibility" of many "unloved" collections could make the level of "object-love" that revolves around them seem remarkable. However, the fact that these interactions are more private and the associated knowledge is often highly specialist may be a part of what gives them value for the people who care for them and reduces the value for those without the "right" forms of expertise. This duality offers an interesting lens through which to explore how emotion might imbue daily practices of curation and interpretation, for both professionals and researchers, and to explore curation and collecting as an affective practice.

"Object-love" is a recurring theme of this volume, a term that was introduced by Macdonald in her key work *Behind the Scenes at the Science Museum*.[39] It is used to describe the emotional connection felt by museum staff for objects in their collections.[40] This concept gives visibility to discussions concerning museum workers and their own emotional responses and emotional labour, something that Watson (this volume) argues has traditionally been unacknowledged.[41] Within the museum sector, many professionals give extra time, use their own money, take positions for which they are overqualified, and continue to contribute in retirement. Emotional attachment to work, we suggest, may play a major role in this.

We are reminded by Smith and Campbell of the extent to which emotions are culturally and socially mediated and potentially subject to management and regulation.[42] In relation to this, Geoghegan and Hess have asked what curatorial passion looks like, noting that professional staff often view extremes of emotion as a sign of amateurism.[43] Contributors to this volume, in particular Watson and Church, refer directly to these ideas in relation to the work of museum professionals and archival researchers, prompting us to consider that cultural workers and academics are certainly not excluded from historic (and present-day) practices of "emotion management." These final two chapters of this volume also problematize the idea that academics are objective while enthusiasts are

---

38 See Caitlin DeSilvey, "Observed Decay: Telling Stories with Mutable Things," in *Museum Objects: Experiencing the Properties of Things*, ed. Sandra Dudley (London: Routledge, 2012), 254–68.

39 Sharon Macdonald, *Behind the Scenes at the Science Museum* (Oxford: Berg, 2002).

40 Macdonald, *Behind the Scenes at the Science Museum*; the term is also used by Hilary Geoghegan and Alison Hess, "Object-Love at the Science Museum: Cultural Geographies of Museum Storerooms," *Cultural Geographies* 22, no. 3 (2015): 445–65.

41 For work on emotional labour, see Arlie Russell Hochschild, *The Managed Heart: Commercialization of Human Feeling* (Berkeley: University of California Press, 2012 [1983]), and in the heritage sector, relevant research reports such as Harald Fredheim, Sharon Macdonald, and Jennie Morgan, *Profusion in Museums: A Report on Contemporary Collecting and Disposal* (York: Arts and Humanities Research Council, University of York, 2018), https://heritage-futures.org/profusion-in-museums-report/ [accessed July 9, 2019].

42 Smith and Campbell, "The Elephant in the Room."

43 Geoghegan and Hess, "Object-Love at the Science Museum."

passionate by asking two academic researchers to explore how emotion fits into their research practice with collections.

Heritage sites are particularly intense spaces for "feeling," not least because of the opportunity these locations offer for individual "heritage-making,"[44] referring to the production and reinforcement of our own meanings, value systems, and emotional affiliations, processes which are complex and far from unproblematic. This kind of strong emotional reaction can easily be detected within the study of so-called "difficult heritage,"[45] hence much of the current work on emotion focuses on issues such as memorialization and indigenous rights struggles. However, Smith and Waterton[46] warn us that all heritage is difficult and that we need to explore working class and grass roots heritage alongside nationally and internationally contentious debates. Our interest here is to apply some of these theories to the management of collections and the more mundane behind-the-scenes interactions described in the opening scene of this introduction. For example, many of the contributors to this volume found that, while the term "unloved" was vehemently challenged, they were confused by a lack of extreme emotional response from some research participants.

Smith, Wetherell, and Campbell's recent volume was helpful in this respect by warning against a tendency to focus on extreme emotion.[47] They argue for a theory of affective practice, where emotional engagements with the past in the present are routinely performed and become habitual, positing that "repeated affective practices have a dispositional potential and quality in the sense that they have become canonical and entirely routine for individuals as a result of their personal history and for communities and social groups as a result of collective histories. Affective practices ... wear what could be described as grooves or ruts in people's bodies and minds, just as walking particular routes over the grass year after year produces new paths."[48] It is, however, by exploring what have seemingly become normalized or mundane emotional responses that we can hope to reveal underlying "taken for granted" assumptions about the nature of caring practices in the museum. The focus on emotion in this volume can therefore be seen as a way of shedding light on different understandings of care and the implications these have for future practices around "unloved" collections.

---

44 Laurajane Smith, "Theorizing Museum and Heritage Visiting," in *The International Handbooks of Museum Studies, Volume 1: Museum Theory*, ed. Kylie Message and Andrea Witcomb, series ed. Sharon Macdonald and Helen Rees Leahy (Oxford: Wiley, 2015), 460.

45 See, for example, Sharon Macdonald, *Difficult Heritage: Negotiating the Nazi Past in Nuremberg and Beyond* (London: Routledge, 2009); Sharon Macdonald, "Is 'Difficult Heritage' Still 'Difficult'? Why Public Acknowledgement of Past Perpetration May No Longer Be So Unsettling to Collective Identities," *Museum International* 67, no. 1–4 (2016): 6–22.

46 Smith and Waterton, *Heritage, Communities and Archaeology*.

47 Smith, Wetherell, and Campbell, *Emotion, Affective Practices, and the Past in the Present*.

48 Margaret Wetherell, Laurajane Smith, and Gary Campbell, "Introduction: Affective Heritage Practices," in *Emotion, Affective Practices and the Past in the Present*, ed. Laurajane Smith, Margaret Wetherell, and Gary Campbell (Abingdon: Routledge, 2018), 6.

Enthusiasm and Communities of Care

As well as the role of institutional "care," the chapters in this book consider the communities and individuals who, through their active and often emotional engagement with heritage, care for museum collections. While a range of different "communities" are considered in the following chapters, from academics and artists to museum professionals and other audience groups, a reoccurring "community of practice" across many of the chapters is "enthusiast" groups. To delve into the meaning we wish to convey by using this term, enthusiasts are often the stalwarts of volunteer museums and demonstration sites across the UK and internationally, but arguably they have a complex relationship with the museum profession. We generalize to an extent in this description, but "enthusiasts" often have particular expertise and former or current professional connections to the collections that are the objects of their interest.

This volume partly locates itself within cultural geography, where the study of "affect" has also influenced research into "enthusiasm" and "enthusiasts," although "collectors," "amateurs," and "independent researchers" are also part of this terminology.[49] The terminology associated with this diverse "enthusiast" community can often be patronizing, and the way that this plays out within the museum and heritage sector can be problematic. The etymological origin of the word "amateur" is the Latin *amatar*, referring to one who loves, while the word "curator" means *to tend* or *to care*. However, in daily use, the values attached to each are very different. In an age of increasing specialization and professionalization, the terms *amateur* or *amateurish* can be derogatory and a source of concern for those who worry about things not being "done properly." This complexity is interesting in the museum context because it reveals something, as noted above, about who has the right to "care" for collections and whose knowledge and value systems are, or have been, historically prioritized.

What we care for depends both on wider discourse and on our own personal histories. Professional training may shape what we deem as acceptable practices of care, and different practices of care might sometimes come into conflict in shared spaces. For example, including an object in a museum reminiscence session may embrace new museum outreach practices of care but cause headaches for conservators who wish to protect objects from pollutants and damage, and it may challenge health professionals who wish to protect patients from germs brought in from outside. In this book, many enthusiasts came from professional backgrounds where getting hands-on and fixing

---

49 See, for example, Dydia DeLyser and Paul Greenstein, "'Follow That Car!' Mobilities of Enthusiasm in a Rare Car's Restoration," *The Professional Geographer* (published online, July 2014); Ruth Craggs, Hilary Geoghegan, and Hannah Neate, "Architectural Enthusiasm: Visiting Buildings with the Twentieth Century Society," *Environment and Planning D: Society and Space* 31 (2013): 879–96; Geoghegan, "Emotional Geographies of Enthusiasm"; Geoghegan, "'If You Can Walk down the Street and Recognise the Difference between Cast Iron and Wrought Iron, the World is Altogether a Better Place'"; Richard Yarwood and Nick Evans, "A Lleyn Sweep for Local Sheep? Breed Societies and the Geographies of Welsh Livestock," *Environment and Planning A* 38 (2006): 1307–26; and Richard Yarwood and Jon Shaw, "N-Gauging Geographies: Indoor Leisure, Model Railways and Craft Consumption," *Area* 42 (2010): 425–33.

things to look like new was a source of pride. This may conflict with museological practices of care, which currently focus more on the stabilization of objects than on reconstruction. Some of the enthusiasts in this volume seek to emulate and engage with professionally defined kinds of museum practice, but many also like to "restore" and amass personal collections in a way that is at odds with current museum ethics, collections management, and conservation practice. The creation of collections outside museums by amateurs also creates a potential problem around legacy, as museums are not always able to collect this material due to space constraints and collecting priorities, meaning that collectors may be left with nowhere to place their collections when they give them up or when they pass away.

There are concerns expressed by many enthusiasts in this volume not just regarding the final resting place of their personal collections but also around where the next generation of enthusiasts will come from. As many enthusiasts learned their skills in a late industrial age, it is no longer just through professional apprenticeship that this transfer of "enthusiasm" will take place. Collaboration with professionals (see Hess and Macleod, this volume) around cataloguing and storage might be one way to leave a legacy without donating objects, and public engagement may be another. Despite a slightly "flat" expression of emotional engagement with some objects (as described above), many of the enthusiasts who feature in this volume are excellent communicators and far from the traditional concept of an "anorak." An unexpected finding of the original "Who Cares?" project (see Woodham and Kelleher, and Smith, this volume) was the ability of some enthusiasts to engage a nonexpert, young audience. These chapters draw out that more needs to be done to bring different communities that care (or that may have the potential to care) into contact with one another so as to maximize opportunities for the sharing of enthusiasm.

Discussions around sharing the locus of control in museums also touch upon both conceptual and physical ownership and access to museum spaces, particularly as these spaces have become increasingly professionalized. Some collections were created through "grassroots" initiatives and have continued to "belong" primarily to these communities. However, many collections have become part of larger institutions, and exclusive access to these collections has become harder to obtain. Models like Amberley Museum (mentioned in Smith's chapter in this volume) suggest how space might be created for enthusiasm to flourish. The creation of a new, large-scale museum storage facility as a consequence of the UK Government's sale of Blythe House in central London (as mentioned in this Introduction) also provides an opportunity to consider how new museum storage might be managed, including consideration of the level of access for the various "caring" communities.[50]

---

50 A key finding of the "Who Cares?" project was that museums that wish to develop meaningful and sustained relationships with enthusiast experts may be uncertain of the best methods to successfully achieve this. In order to consider these issues in more detail, a new knowledge exchange project called "Energy in Store" was created in 2017. The project brought together a working group of curators, conservators, enthusiast experts, and academic researchers, all with equal status. The working group undertook a year-long series of visits to the Science Museum sites and storerooms across England, taking part in structured discussions around such issues as collections access, the specific research practices and requirements of this expert enthusiast group, and how their needs can best be catered for in a way that benefits both them and the museum profession.

Many of the chapters in this volume engage with discussions around the role of so-called "nonspecialists" in knowledge production. Graham Black declared that we are now in the "age of participation,"[51] in which audiences expect to be included in knowledge production.[52] There is an urgent need, therefore, to understand the motivations of our core stakeholders, explore the opportunities for diversifying the potential collaborators in producing knowledge around museum collections, and to recognize the institutional power structures that restrict this.[53]

Self in Method: A Note on Our Methodological and Written Approach

Noticeable in many of the chapters in this volume is the presence of the author, as many of us have written in the first person. We were keen to recognize that, as researchers, we are all constituent in the environments in which we operate and which we have written about. The authors, who are academics from a range of disciplinary backgrounds and practitioners, can be seen as both "stepping back from the action" in order to offer a theorization of it and "stepping up" to be an active part of the context. This semi-autoethnographic approach is inspired by David Butz[54] and responds to the point made by Geoghegan and Hess that "there is not enough work within museum studies from an insider's perspective or on the geographies of love based upon the researcher's own feelings."[55]

We asked two contributors (Church and Watson) specifically to reflect on what explicitly engaging with emotions means for their own practice and, more broadly, to reflect on where this leads us. Like Geoghegan and Hess, however, we are aware that using our own experiences to directly inform our work could be criticized for being "self-absorbed indulgence."[56] However, in response to this, we consider this kind of reflexivity to be a strength. Indeed, within ethnographic writing and practice, the concept of positionality and experiments in written form have been common for decades, especially within feminist and queer approaches to methodology.[57] To deny this approach completely also

---

51 Graham Black, *The Engaging Museum* (London: Routledge, 2005).

52 See also Graham Black, *Transforming Museums in the Twenty-First Century* (Abingdon: Routledge, 2011), and Nina Simon, *The Participatory Museum* (Santa Cruz: Museum 2.0, 2010).

53 Bernadette Lynch, "Collaboration, Contestation and Creative Conflict: On the Efficacy of Museum/Community Partnerships," in *The Routledge Companion to Museum Ethics: Redefining Ethics for the Twenty-First Century Museum*, ed. Janet Marstine (London: Routledge, 2011), 146–64; Bernadette Lynch, *Whose Cake Is It Anyway? A Collaborative Investigation into Engagement and Participation in 12 Museums and Galleries in the UK* (London: Paul Hamlyn Foundation, 2011).

54 David Butz, "Autoethnography as Sensibility," in *The SAGE Handbook of Qualitative Geography*, ed. Dydia DeLyser, Steve Herbert, Stuart Aitken, Mike Crang, and Linda McDowell (London: SAGE, 2010), 138–55.

55 Geoghegan and Hess, "Object-Love at the Science Museum," 452.

56 Geoghegan and Hess, "Object-Love at the Science Museum," 453.

57 See Kath Browne and Catherine J. Nash, *Queer Methods and Methodologies: Intersecting Queer Theories and Social Science Research* (London: Routledge, 2016).

risks ignoring what we believe to be a valid data source that adds greater depth and texture to the research. Also, for a collection of chapters that explore the themes of emotion, care, and engagement in particular, it would seem peculiar (to us) if we divorced ourselves from the subjects of the research. After all, it is through our own eyes that we see and make sense of the world.

As academics and professionals working in universities and museums, the authors in this volume are driven by their own research passions and interests in a way that is similar to our "research participants." Does this make us more sympathetic to this kind of work? Perhaps, but it also gives us an insight into this important aspect of heritage practice that we are choosing to embrace rather than ignore. We believe that it is acceptable and even more appropriate for a subject such as this that we do not hide behind the arguments of academic distancing and objectivity when, in reality, this is impossible (and we believe undesirable) to achieve completely.

The Structure of This Volume

Section One, "Enthusiasts and Care for Collections," draws on the work of the original "Who Cares?" project. Alison Hess's chapter focuses on the Science Museum Group's collection of locks and fastenings to explore what new meanings external stakeholders can reveal about this collection and how an appreciation of emotion alters the ways we access these meanings. Hess's chapter also presents a number of challenges to the current interpretation of the collection, which is comprehensive to the point of being repetitive. Its subject matter is fairly mundane and there is also relatively little information on many of the objects within it. While all this seemed to point to the collection being "unloved" by the museum, a long-standing relationship with the Lock Collectors Association revealed that there were those who felt differently. Following this, Rhianedd Smith's chapter discusses the emotional, biographical, and professional ties that connect people to "unloved" objects, exploring emotional responses from donors, collectors, and former users of collections of historic hand tools. The case studies presented by Smith examine how the context and very act of collecting changes the meaning of these objects. Her discussion touches upon loss of meaning and the difficulties of transmitting skills-based knowledge. She argues for recontextualization of this kind of collection, which moves away from an object's typological significance towards an approach that reawakens emotional response. Anna Woodham and Shane Kelleher's chapter then presents the National Slag Collection as a case study of co-management by an external group. The chapter critiques what it means to care in the context of a museum, asking whether these institutions are ready to share this caring responsibility with others. Woodham and Kelleher's discussion examines who the enthusiasts are that co-manage the collection and what characterizes the forms of care they offer. The authors consider whether is it possible for their enthusiasm to be transferred or shared between those who "care" and those who seemingly do not.

The second section, "'Unloved' Collections," asks professionals to examine their work with "unloved" collections and to identify strategies for reviving collections. Here, the three chapters each engage with the question of how museums can approach their collections to signal shifts in value and practice and the strategies needed to successfully reinvigorate collections in order to remain relevant. Alexandra Woodall focuses on what might happen when artists are encouraged to venture into the hidden spaces of museums. Focusing in particular on their interventions with neglected collections, Woodall argues that, rather than being places of unimagined objects, museum storage might instead become a place for imagining (and reimagining) these potential "treasures." By looking at ways in which artists have brought neglected collections to life and building on approaches to museum materialities, Woodall proposes a new type of "material interpretation," in which a delight in rummaging and using neglected collections is seen as transforming museum practice.

Museum practitioner Mark Carnall focuses on the changing use and valuation of natural history collections, where 99 percent of these collections have traditionally been treated as second class, distinct from the top tier of rare specimens or those originating from the collections of famous names. Carnall maps a crisis in the management of natural history collections and trends towards a holistic management of natural history specimens, arguing that a traditional approach that focuses solely on scientific knowledge seems at odds with the cultural role of the museum. The case studies in this chapter, which include "Underwhelming Fossil Fish of the Month" and road-tripping dodo models, argue for the integration of a wide range of different forms of expertise and knowledge in order to raise public interest in natural history collections. These approaches acknowledge personal responses, individual emotions, humour, creativity, and the unique characteristics of social media as platforms through which to connect with audiences.

Finally, in this section Mark Macleod reflects upon the establishment of medical instrument collections and specific challenges to their interpretation. Based on his experience at The Infirmary, Worcester, Macleod considers how, by making use of "expert volunteers" and careful interpretation strategies, the most mundane and impersonal medical objects can be used to engage communities, helping audiences to understand what it means to be human.

In the final section, "Emotional Research," two researchers are asked to explore the role of emotion and care in their practice with collections. Sheila Watson considers the recent turn towards emotion in the way that museums consider their collections. Using personal reflections, Watson focuses on what she calls "lost objects"—objects without any context or with very little—and how these are approached by museum staff as a consequence of this "lost" status. Importantly for this volume, Watson's chapter opens up the debate about how museum professionals can recognize their own emotional responses to these objects. She explores the challenges and pitfalls of acknowledging emotional significance and puts forward an understanding of what this means for cataloguing practices and a more meaningful engagement with these items.

In the last chapter, Francesca Church focuses attention on a different kind of assemblage—archival collections—and, in particular, the layers of care that are bound up in the archival practices of collections-based research. However, as with Watson's chapter, which explores the responses to objects of museum practitioners, Church's chapter also views the (archival) collection from a particular starting point: her own experiences of working as an academic researcher with the Campaign for the Protection of Rural England (CPRE) collection held at the Museum of English Rural Life (MERL). Church's chapter discusses the ways in which researchers "care" in collections-based work through an examination of three specific forms of care: care for the material, care for the researcher, and care through communication. Church's discussion illuminates the relationship between a researcher, their emotionally demanding "care-full" work, and a collection of relatively silent archival objects.

At the end of the volume, Rhianedd Smith and Anna Woodham reflect in a concluding section on the themes that have been drawn through the various chapters in this book, returning to the four questions posed at the start of this Introduction and considering: what next for "unloved" collections?

Bibliography

Black, Graham. *The Engaging Museum: Developing Museums for Visitor Involvement*. London: Routledge, 2005.

———. *Transforming Museums in the Twenty-First Century*. Abingdon: Routledge, 2011.

Browne, Kath, and Catherine J. Nash. *Queer Methods and Methodologies: Intersecting Queer Theories and Social Science Research*. London: Routledge, 2016.

Brusius, Mirjam, and Kavita Singh, ed. *Museum Storage and Meaning: Tales from the Crypt*. London: Routledge, 2017.

Butz, David. "Autoethnography as Sensibility." In *The SAGE Handbook of Qualitative Geography*, edited by Dydia DeLyser, Steve Herbert, Stuart Aitken, Mike Crang, and Linda McDowell, 138–55. London: SAGE, 2010.

Carter, Sophie, Bethan Hurst, Rachael H. Kerr, Emma Taylor, and Peter Winsor. *Museum Focus: Facts and Figures on Museums in the UK*. Issue 2. London: Museums and Galleries Commission, 1999.

Cassar, May. *Environmental Management: Guidelines for Museums and Galleries*. London: Routledge, 1994.

Conradson, David. "Geographies of Care: Spaces, Practices, Experiences." *Social & Cultural Geography* 4, no. 4 (December 2003): 451–54.

Craggs, Ruth, Hilary Geoghegan, and Hannah Neate. "Architectural Enthusiasm: Visiting Buildings with the Twentieth Century Society." *Environment and Planning D: Society and Space* 31 (2013): 879–96.

DeLyser, Dydia, and Paul Greenstein. "'Follow That Car!' Mobilities of Enthusiasm in a Rare Car's Restoration." *The Professional Geographer*. Published online, July 2014.

DeSilvey, Caitlin. "Cultivated Histories in a Scottish Allotment Garden." *Cultural Geographies* 10 (2003): 442–68.

———. *Curated Decay: Heritage beyond Saving*. Minneapolis: University of Minnesota Press, 2017.

———. "Observed Decay: Telling Stories with Mutable Things." In *Museum Objects: Experiencing the Properties of Things*, ed. Sandra Dudley, 254–68. London: Routledge, 2012.

Dudley, Sandra, ed. *Museum Objects: Experiencing the Properties of Things*. London: Routledge, 2012.

Edwards, Rachel. *Archaeological Archives and Museums 2012*. Society for Museum Archaeology, 2013. http://socmusarch.org.uk/socmusarch/gailmark/wordpress/wp-content/uploads/2016/07/Archaeological-archives-and-museums-2012.pdf [accessed June 29, 2019].

Fredheim, Harald, Sharon Macdonald, and Jennie Morgan. *Profusion in Museums: A Report on Contemporary Collecting and Disposal.* York: Arts and Humanities Research Council, University of York, 2018.

Geoghegan, Hilary. "Emotional Geographies of Enthusiasm: Belonging to the Telecommunications Heritage Group." *Area* 45, no. 1 (2013): 40–46.

———. " 'If You Can Walk down the Street and Recognise the Difference between Cast Iron and Wrought Iron, the World is Altogether a Better Place': Being Enthusiastic about Industrial Archaeology." *M/C Journal: A Journal of Media and Culture* 12, no. 2 (2009): unpaginated.

Geoghegan, Hilary, and Alison Hess. "Object-Love at the Science Museum: Cultural Geographies of Museum Storerooms." *Cultural Geographies* 22, no. 3 (2015): 445–65.

Glaister, Jane. "The Power and Potential of Collections." In *Collections for the Future: Report of a Museums Association Inquiry*, ed. Helen Wilkinson, 8–9. London: Museums Association, 2005.

HM Treasury. *Spending Review and Autumn Statement 2015.* London: UK Government, 2015.

Hochschild, Arlie Russell. *The Managed Heart: Commercialization of Human Feeling.* Berkeley: University of California Press, 2012 [1983].

ICOM-CC. *Working Draft Recommendation: Reconnecting with Collections in Storage.* Paris: ICOM-CC, 2017.

Jaoul, Martine. "Why Reserve Collections?" *Museum International* 47, no. 4 (1995): 4–7.

Keene, Suzanne. "Collections in the English National Museums: The Numbers." *Papers from the Institute of Archaeology* S1 (2007): 115–34.

———. *Fragments of the World: Uses of Museum Collections.* Oxford: Elsevier Butterworth-Heinemann, 2005.

———. *Managing Conservation in Museums.* Oxford: Butterworth-Heinemann, 2002.

Keene, Suzanne with Alice Stevenson, and Francesca Monti. *Collections for the People.* London: UCL Institute for Archaeology, 2008.

Knell, Simon, ed. *Care of Collections.* London: Routledge, 1994.

Lowenthal, David. *The Heritage Crusade and the Spoils of History.* Cambridge: Cambridge University Press, 1998.

Lynch, Bernadette. "Collaboration, Contestation and Creative Conflict: On the Efficacy of Museum/Community Partnerships." In *The Routledge Companion to Museum Ethics: Redefining Ethics for the Twenty-First Century Museum*, edited by Janet Marstine, 146–64. London: Routledge, 2011.

———. *Whose Cake Is It Anyway? A Collaborative Investigation into Engagement and Participation in 12 Museums and Galleries in the UK.* London: Paul Hamlyn Foundation, 2011.

Macdonald, Sharon. *Behind the Scenes at the Science Museum.* Oxford: Berg, 2002.

———. *Difficult Heritage: Negotiating the Nazi Past in Nuremberg and Beyond.* London: Routledge, 2009.

———. "Is 'Difficult Heritage' Still 'Difficult'? Why Public Acknowledgement of Past Perpetration May No Longer Be So Unsettling to Collective Identities." *Museum International* 67 (2016): 6–22.

Matassa, Freda. *Museum Collections Management: A Handbook.* London: Facet, 2011.

Mendoza, Neil. *The Mendoza Review: An Independent Review of Museums in England.* London: Department for Culture, Media and Sport, 2017.

Monti, Francesca, and Suzanne Keene. *Museums and Silent Objects: Designing Effective Exhibitions.* Abingdon: Routledge, 2016.

Morgan, Jennie, and Sharon Macdonald. "De-growing Museum Collections for New Heritage Futures." *International Journal of Heritage Studies* (2018). Published online.

Morse, Nuala. *The Museum as a Space of Social Care*. London: Routledge, forthcoming.

Morse, Nuala, and Helen Chatterjee. "Museums, Health and Wellbeing Research: Co-developing a New Observational Method for People with Dementia in Hospital Contexts." *Perspectives in Public Health* 138, no. 3 (2018): 152–59.

Morse, Nuala, Krisztina Lackoi, and Helen Chatterjee. "Museum Learning and Wellbeing." *Journal of Education in Museums* 37 (2016): 3–13.

Pearce, Susan. *On Collecting: An Investigation into Collecting in the European Tradition*. Abingdon: Routledge, 1995.

Picard, David, and Mike Robinson, ed. *Emotion in Motion: Tourism, Affect and Transformation*. Abingdon: Ashgate, 2012.

Silverman, Lois H. *The Social Work of Museums*. London: Routledge, 2010.

Simon, Nina. *The Participatory Museum*. Santa Cruz: Museum 2.0, 2010.

Smith, Laurajane. "Theorizing Museum and Heritage Visiting." In *The International Handbooks of Museum Studies, Volume 1: Museum Theory*, edited by Kylie Message and Andrea Witcomb, series editors Sharon Macdonald and Helen Rees Leahy, 459–84. Oxford: Wiley, 2015.

——. *Uses of Heritage*. Abingdon: Routledge, 2006.

Smith, Laurajane, and Gary Campbell. "The Elephant in the Room: Heritage, Affect and Emotion." In *A Companion to Heritage Studies*, edited by William Logan, Máiréad Nic Craith, and Ullrich Kockel, 443–60. Chichester: Wiley, 2015.

Smith, Laurajane, and Emma Waterton. *Heritage, Communities and Archaeology*. London: Duckworth Academic, 2009.

Smith, Laurajane, Margaret Wetherell, and Gary Campbell, ed. *Emotion, Affective Practices and the Past in the Present*. Abingdon: Routledge, 2018.

Tolia-Kelly, Divya P., Emma Waterton, and Steve Watson. *Heritage, Affect and Emotion*. Abingdon: Routledge, 2018.

Wilkinson, Helen, ed. *Collections for the Future: Report of a Museums Association Inquiry*. London: Museums Association, 2005.

Wingfield, Christopher. "Touching the Buddha: Encounters with a Charismatic Object." In *Museum Materialities: Objects, Engagements, Interpretations*, edited by Sandra Dudley, 53–70. London: Routledge, 2010.

Yarwood, Richard, and Nick Evans. "A Lleyn Sweep for Local Sheep? Breed Societies and the Geographies of Welsh Livestock." *Environment and Planning A* 38 (2006): 1307–26.

Yarwood, Richard, and Jon Shaw. "N-Gauging Geographies: Indoor Leisure, Model Railways and Craft Consumption." *Area* 42 (2010): 425–33.

SECTION ONE

ENTHUSIASTS AND CARE FOR COLLECTIONS

Chapter I

UNLOCKING THE MEANINGS OF COLLECTIONS: EXPERTISE, CARE, AND THE SCIENCE MUSEUM'S LOCKS AND FASTENINGS COLLECTION

ALISON HESS*

THE LOCKS AND fastenings collection at the Science Museum, London is an eclectic collection that maps the evolution of security throughout the ages. It is made up of 497 original pieces, replicas, and scale models. This volume of essays explores the place of "unloved" objects in museum collections, a definition that sits well with the locks and fastening collection. However, there is an intricacy and beauty to this collection (particularly of those examples from the eighteenth century) that sets them apart from some of the other objects discussed in this volume. It is for this reason that locks feature in the collections of both the Science Museum and the Victoria and Albert Museum (V&A), London, where they are appreciated for their design as much as their functionality. Collected by the Science Museum to illustrate a developing technology, the twentieth-century models are the most challenging to display. These later models are much closer to the more familiar padlock, objects where functionality rather than aesthetics was the priority for the designers. The Science Museum acquired these locks in the same spirit, using them to illustrate a gradual evolution of lock design up until the mid-twentieth century. Currently, however, this style of collecting is out of fashion in the professional museum sector, leading to questions about the value of such collections. When the "Who Cares?" project was being developed, the lock collection did seem to be particularly "unloved," as the Locks Gallery had recently been closed and the entire collection was about to be moved into storage.

The Locks Gallery, originally opened in 1972, was located in the basement of the Science Museum. For the latter part of its history, it was located in the Secret Life of the Home Gallery, which presents the history of the development of domestic technology. The museum files that record the development of the gallery show that the curators took inspiration from Vincent Eras's *Locks and Keys throughout the Ages*.[1] In his book on

---

1 Vincent Eras, *Locks and Keys throughout the Ages* (Folkestone: Bailey Bros & Swinfen, 1974), 7.

---

* **Alison Hess** is the Research and Public History Manager at the Science Museum. Alison completed her doctorate on the BBC, interwar radio, and object biographies with the Geography Department at Royal Holloway, University of London, in 2012. Having worked on public-facing projects and exhibitions, in her current role Alison works to shape research at the Science Museum. As well as the "Who Cares?" project, she has been involved in a number of externally funded research projects, and she continues to work on issues related to storage, access, narrative, and material culture.

the social mechanisms that make actors and organizations in the public sphere perform in "civilized" society, Papakostas refers briefly to: "[o]ne book that mixes the professional and collector aspects is Vincent J. M. Eras's beautifully illustrated 'Locks and Keys throughout the Ages' (Eras 1957)."[2] Papakostas also goes on to describe Eras as "the director of a large company that manufactured keys in the Netherlands [and] also became an amateur historian of keys."[3] According to the 1957 edition, Eras was the managing director (and later partner) of Lips' Safe and Lock Manufacturing Company, originally a Dutch company that was later acquired by the Chubb lock company. Like many individuals encountered through the "Who Cares?" project, Eras's professional and personal worlds appear to have become intertwined. In the author's preface of the 1974 edition, he describes his motivations for writing the book: "After 58 years' activity with this firm, I consider it a gratifying task to place on record my experience and through this book save them from oblivion. At the same time an excellent opportunity is presented to show the reader my collection of antique and modern locks—the tangible results of more than 50 years travelling, searching and study in many countries for markets for our products, which collection may be considered unique and as complete as is possible."[4] *Locks and Keys throughout the Ages* was originally published in 1957 by Eras' Company and later republished by Bailey Bros & Swinfen in Folkestone in 1974. Despite the most recent edition being published nearly forty-five years ago (at the time of writing), it is still one of the key references for historians of locks.

Eras's approach to lock history is evident in the style and objects selected for the Science Museum's Locks Gallery. As a gallery leaflet produced at the time of opening describes: "This gallery contains a fine representative collection of locks and is in the basement adjoining the Children's Gallery. The wall cases contain panels showing the whole history of locks. There are examples from all periods, from the ancient Egyptian ones (incorporating the principle used in today's Yale locks) to those of the present day. In the centre of the room are displayed a series of large working models of the different types of lock, so that visitors can work these locks for themselves."[5] At the heart of the gallery was a "full size shop window similar to that in Piccadilly, London occupied by Bramah and Company," famous lock-makers of the nineteenth century. Alongside this was "probably the most famous lock in history," the original Bramah lock that was on display in the shop for fifty years with a reward of 200 guineas to anyone who could pick it. It remained unpicked for sixty-seven years until American locksmith Alfred Charles Hobbs finally managed the feat. The lock is currently on display in the Making the Modern World Gallery of the Science Museum. Since the gallery first opened, exhibition styles have moved towards a more narrative, thematic approach. It is therefore unlikely (unless practice changes again) that a gallery that carefully catalogues and explains one type of technology in such detail will appear in the Science Museum again. While few members

---

2 Apostolis Papakostas, *Civilizing the Public Sphere: Distrust, Trust and Corruption* (London: Springer, 2016), 170–71.

3 Papakostas, *Civilizing the Public Sphere*.

4 Eras, *Locks and Keys throughout the Ages*, 7.

5 The Locks and Fastenings Gallery, Gallery Leaflet, September 2, 1983 (London: Science Museum, London Archives, 1983).

Figure 1.1. Keys in the Science Museum Locks and Fastenings Collection, Blythe House, London. Photograph by Alison Hess.

of the public noted the gallery closure, learning that the locks were no longer on display was a source of disappointment for one particular community: the lock collectors. For these collectors, taking the locks off display showed that the Science Museum had "lost interest in locks." An understandable concern, as it is likely that a large proportion of this collection will remain in storage for the foreseeable future.

Now in storage, the locks remain part of the Science Museum's vast "reserve" or "research" collection, available to view on request by researchers. But how would a researcher use this collection? What would they be looking for? Or, more precisely, how would they look at these objects? Through the example of the locks and fastenings collection (see figures 1.1 and 1.2), this chapter considers how researchers use objects as source material and, in particular, has a focus on the gaze of the expert collector. Often retired and often male, these "enthusiasts," as they are sometimes described, given their passionate interest in a specific subject, offer a narrow but powerful way of looking at objects. This chapter considers this "way of looking"—what it tells us about museum objects (and their researchers) and some of the challenges in capturing this knowledge for museums.

Collecting: Professional and Personal

Research within the museum sector on the challenge of ever-expanding stored collections has found that there are approximately 200 million items in UK collections,

Figure 1.2. Padlocks in the Science Museum Locks and Fastenings Collection,
Blythe House, London. Photograph by Alison Hess.

with more and more added every year.[6] Despite this, Suzanne Keene found in a 2008
survey that half the museums contacted had less than two visitors a week to their stored
collections. In her book *Fragments of the World*,[7] she also suggests strategies for reviving
stored collections, and her collaborative work with Francesca Monti discusses display
techniques for "silent objects."[8] By the time the "Who Cares?" project had begun, the
locks were no longer on display and, having in most cases been donated directly by the
manufacturers, had little in the way of related personal stories to bring them to life.
Nonetheless, models comparable to the Science Museum objects were being actively
collected and coveted by collectors across the country. As Pearce says,[9] collections are

6 Museums and Galleries Commission, *Digest of Museum Statistics (DOMUS)* (London: Museum
and Galleries Commission, 1999); Suzanne Keene with Alice Stevenson, and Francesca Monti,
Collections for People: Museums' Stored Collections as a Public Resource (London: UCL Institute for
Archaeology, 2008).

7 Suzanne Keene, *Fragments of the World: Uses of Museum Collections* (Oxford: Elsevier
Butterworth-Heinemann, 2005).

8 Francesca Monti and Suzanne Keene, *Museums and Silent Objects: Designing Effective Exhibitions*
(Abingdon: Routledge, 2016).

9 Susan Pearce, "A New Way of Looking at Old Things," *Museum International* 51, no. 2 (1999): 12–17.

created by people who care about something. Often, collections reflect a singular passion that is not always easy to understand or share. A passion for collecting or consuming certain kinds of objects may be shaped by unfamiliar or unpopular research and teaching objectives; political, cultural, and historical contexts; or representations of the past. Case studies from the history of collections repeatedly present us with passionate, even monomaniacal, collector-curators who amassed vast collections, stuffing their homes to the rafters.[10] Sloane, Ashmole, and the Tradescants all seem to have been driven by some kind of emotional need to collect. This was not purely an Early Modern or Enlightenment phenomenon. Pitt Rivers amassed not one but two collections in his lifetime, and the title of Yallop's study of Victorian collecting, *Magpies, Squirrels and Thieves*, illustrates the complex and emotional nature of nineteenth-century collecting.[11] Traditionally, museums were also home to impassioned collectors, but changes to collecting cultures caused Knell to argue that the modern museum has moved away from collecting as its primary objective.[12] Former Keeper Robert Bud notes that: "The Museum was formed in a period when theories of progress and evolution were intermingled and Darwin's theory of natural selection and the tree of life provided a context for all discussions of progress. Until relatively recently collections 'valued for their comprehensiveness' continued to be built both by 'acquiring in new fields' and also 'filling gaps.' "[13]

In contrast, today, with financial pressures and limited space, the emphasis is on collecting objects that are unique or that tell a particular story. Knell argues that as the "hard fact" approach to research gave way to postmodernism in the late twentieth century, the culture of museums and collecting also shifted towards meaning-making rather than comprehensive reference collections.[14] In her book *On Collecting*, Pearce stresses that collecting is not confined to museums.[15] Enthusiasm is not just about understanding emotion but is also the practice of accumulating material culture. Collecting happens in informal spaces as well as the formal spaces of museums. Many of the most well-known museum collections originally belonged to individuals who shaped them according to their own classificatory systems and personal passions, as can be seen in the example of Henry Wellcome, whom Larson describes as "a man

---

10 Giuseppe Olmi, Oliver Impey, and Arthur Macgregor, *The Origins of Museums: The Cabinet of Curiosities in Sixteenth and Seventeenth-Century Europe* (Oxford: Oxford University Press, 1985); Pearce, "A New Way of Looking at Old Things"; Jacqueline Yallop, *Magpies, squirrels and Thieves: How the Victorians Collected the World* (London: Atlantic, 2011).

11 Chris Gosden and Frances Larson, *Knowing Things: Exploring the Collections at the Pitt Rivers Museum 1844–1945* (Oxford: Oxford University Press, 2007); Yallop, *Magpies, Squirrels and Thieves*.

12 Simon J. Knell, *Museums and the Future of Collecting* (Aldershot: Ashgate, 2004).

13 Robert Bud, "Infected by the Bacillus of Science: The Explosion of South Kensington," in *Science for the Nation: Perspectives on the History of the Science Museum*, ed. Peter Morris (London: Palgrave Macmillan, 2013), 269.

14 Knell, *Museums and the Future of Collecting*.

15 Susan Pearce, *On Collecting: An Investigation into Collecting in the European Tradition* (London: Routledge, 1995).

who was drawn into the world through his desire for objects."[16] Present-day personal collectors have similar motivations, and untangling these became an important part of understanding the lock collection.

Emotion, Enthusiasm, and Care

What do we feel when we experience heritage and how do we express this? Researchers are opening up the field of affect and heritage.[17] The definition of *enthusiasm* arises from a state of religious frenzy or extreme passion, while the term *enthusiast* has been used since the mid-1980s by sociologists to refer to "organised leisure."[18] This is not a new phenomenon, with research at the University of Oxford exploring the historical dimensions of what is now termed "citizen science."[19] In the days before formal university departments in subjects such as archaeology or natural history, all practitioners were to some extent "amateurs." However, the rise in the formalization of academic disciplines and the professionalization of careers such as archaeologist and curator has altered our understanding of the expert/amateur divide.

The last ten years has seen an increased interest in harnessing the power of citizens or enthusiasts on large research questions.[20] This raises questions about what motivates people to donate their time and spend a lifetime building expertise for not only no remuneration but often at a real cost. The casual application of the term to what might be termed "hobbyists" connotes strength of feeling and a visible performance of emotion. However, research shows that the experience, expression, and interpretation of affect are culturally, historically, and demographically specific.[21] Geoghegan's research into industrial heritage enthusiasm stresses that by focusing on interior mental states we miss the socio-spatial aspects of these practices.[22] Like many "enthusiasts" of the

---

16 Frances Larson, *An Infinity of Things: How Sir Henry Wellcome Collected the World* (Oxford: Oxford University Press, 2009), 3.

17 See Divya P. Tolia-Kelly, Emma Waterton, and Steve Watson, ed., *Heritage, Affect and Emotion: Politics, Practices and Infrastructures* (London: Routledge, 2016); Mike Crang and Divya P. Tolia-Kelly, "Nation, Race, and Affect: Senses and Sensibilities at National Heritage Sites," *Environment and Planning A* 42, no. 10 (2010): 2315–31; and Laurajane Smith and Gary Campbell, "The Elephant in the Room: Heritage, Affect, and Emotion," in *A Companion to Heritage Studies*, ed. William Logan, Máiréad Nic Craith, and Ullrich Kockel (Chichester: Wiley-Blackwell, 2015), 443–60.

18 Hilary Geoghegan, "Emotional Geographies of Enthusiasm: Belonging to the Telecommunications Heritage Group," *Area* 45, no. 1 (2013): 40–46.

19 Sally Shuttleworth and Sally Frampton, "Constructing Scientific Communities: Citizen Science," *The Lancet* 385, no. 9987 (2015): 2568.

20 Geoghegan, "Emotional Geographies of Enthusiasm"; and Hilary Geoghegan, "'If You Can Walk down the Street and Recognise the Difference between Cast Iron and Wrought Iron, the World is Altogether a Better Place': Being Enthusiastic about Industrial Archaeology," *M/C Journal* 12, no. 2 (2009): unpaginated.

21 Catherine Lutz and Geoffrey M. White, "The Anthropology of Emotions," *Annual Review of Anthropology* 15, no. 1 (1986): 405–36; Barbara H. Rosenwein, "Worrying about Emotions in History," *The American Historical Review* 107, no. 3 (2002): 821–45.

22 Geoghegan, "Emotional Geographies of Enthusiasm."

heritage of science, technology, and engineering, most of our participants were male, white British, and retired. They were born before 1950 and had worked in industries that were now on the wane. What did "care" or "love" look, sound, and feel like for them? How was it expressed through relationships with objects, spaces, and people?

Even within literature aimed at the collector there is a fear that enthusiasts might "feel" too much, the assumption being that their innate passion would make them a danger to museum collections or that they might collect or research in a way that is irrational. The case study also sought to explore this perceived emotional dichotomy between the "distanced," "rational" professional and the "impassioned" amateur. We explored how care or love for stored objects might be experienced or expressed by professional museum staff by injecting an emotional response into collections' work through collaboration with experts. In her key work *Behind the Scenes at the Science Museum*, Sharon Macdonald introduced the phrase "object-love" to describe the emotional connection felt by museum staff with objects in their collections.[23] Geoghegan and Hess have also explored the emotional experiences of stored collections by staff and professional researchers at the Science Museum's Blythe House site.[24] The so-called "father of heritage interpretation," Freeman Tilden, argued that his principles "could all be telescoped into one—love."[25] Every collection has a champion, a person or an organization that sees value in objects that others might not recognize, and this case study within the "Who Cares?" project sought to connect with these individuals in the context of a museum storeroom.

The concern that enthusiasts might "feel too much" requires practical consideration when placing them within the environment of the storeroom. Can they get so carried away with their passionate interest in an object that they could do more harm than good? The other side of this passion is that it encourages an interest in an object or collection of objects that might be otherwise overlooked by museum staff in the busy, pressured environment of the institution. However, this chapter will explore whether "object-love" and expertise, as demonstrated by collectors, results in a form of investigation that differs from traditional museum or academic uses of objects. Do our lock collectors "look" at objects in a different way? Do they ask different questions? And are they better placed through the refinement of technical skills gained through practice in their leisure time to answer these questions? All of these questions are important for museums to consider as they increase research access and use of their stored collections.

A Day with the Stored Collections

As discussed in the Introduction to this volume, the original "Who Cares?" project and conference brought together this collection of essays. The collection of locks and fastenings

---

23 Sharon Macdonald, "Behind the Scenes at the Science Museum: Knowing," *Academic Anthropology and the Museum: Back to the Future* 13 (2001): 117.

24 Hilary Geoghegan and Alison Hess, "Object-Love at the Science Museum: Cultural Geographies of Museum Storerooms," *Cultural Geographies* 22, no. 3 (2015): 445–65.

25 Freeman Tilden, *Interpreting Our Heritage*, 4th ed. with an introduction from R. Bruce Craig (Chapel Hill: University of North Carolina Press, 2007), 19.

at the Science Museum formed one of the original case studies. The aim was to introduce members of the Lock Collectors Association to the Science Museum's collection. The
timing seemed ideal given the recent closure of the Locks Gallery. Over twelve months,
this case study involved face-to-face conversations and email exchanges around the subject of the lock collection, finally culminating in a visit to the collection in the Science
Museum storerooms at Blythe House, London.[26] Given the focus of this book on unloved
and stored collections, the remainder of this chapter focuses closely on this one visit to
Blythe House, the Science Museum's object storerooms, contextualizing it with information gathered at the time. The visit offered an opportunity for the two collectors and the
researchers to visit the collection. The aim was to learn more about each other's practice
and the specific challenges in accessing a museum collection of this kind. The Curator of
Consumer Technology, who has oversight of the lock collection, accompanied the group.

The project originally intended to work with the wider Lock Collectors Association,
but following a discussion with the organization's secretary and a restructure of the
organization taking place at the time, we were advised to work with two particular
members instead. This decision took place within the context of project funding that
only lasted one year, resulting in a lack of flexibility in the project's timetable. Our two
members of the Lock Collectors Association were given lists of all the objects in the
collection before the visit. Both the collectors live with their collections, and one aspires
to set up his own lock museum if he can secure the necessary funding or, as he terms it,
"the magic million pounds." He is a passionate advocate for the study of locks and sees
himself as curator and caretaker of his extensive collections, although he was unable to
tell us exactly how many locks he actually owns. In the course of a conversation during
our visit he outlined why the study of locks is so important to him: "By studying locks
you learn everything there is to know about the human animal. Absolutely everything.
As soon as mankind formed into communities, even if those communities started off
being nomadic, the lock appears. It's human nature to be suspicious of our neighbour
… The locksmith is supposed to be the second oldest profession [laughing]."[27] There are
497 individual items listed as part of the locks and fastenings collection and we had
only two hours in which to look at them. From an object list supplied before the visit,
the collectors had selected some items they wanted to see, and we had also identified some mystery objects that the Museum wanted them to help identify. While this
preparation was important, there was also a sense that the whole team wanted to "just
see what was there," with the serendipity of discovery a key part of the excitement of
visiting the collections. The benefit of browsing a collection as a research technique is
rarely acknowledged or successfully duplicated by searching digital databases. Simple
decisions taken by successive curators, conservators, and object handlers and influenced
by the space of the storerooms, the requirements of the object, and the logic systems
applied to different collections all dictate which objects sit in each location.

---

26 Blythe House, London was the location of the locks and fastenings collection at the time of
writing. However, from 2019 the Science Museum will be moving all the Blythe House collections to
a new National Collections Centre near Wroughton, Swindon, UK.

27 Visit to Blythe House, video recording, October 25, 2015.

Recording a visit to the storerooms is therefore not just a case of capturing audio: It is about recording the space, the objects, the visitors, and the interaction between all three. Audio recordings and photographs employed in the course of previous projects only managed to capture a very partial experience. The decision was therefore taken to film the unpacking of the objects as well as the discussion that took place around them. However, filming does create other challenges, not least the participants' awareness that they are being recorded, which in some cases meant that they were more reticent about their practice and in others offered an opportunity to "sell" their particular point of view. All of this needed to be negotiated during analysis of the resulting film. While, in the context of the whole project, the visit was comparatively brief, the rich discussions make it a valuable focus for this chapter.

During the visit we asked our experts to look at a selection of "mystery" objects from the collection. These are items in the storerooms that either do not have an identifying object number or for which there is little related information in the archives. We selected these by finding the objects with the least amount of information about them in our catalogue and in consultation with the curator. Using objects and collections as sources in research is not always intuitive, particularly with examples such as these. Working with people who are tuned in to the qualities of objects is one way around this. In working with the lock collectors, it was not just what they could tell us about the examples we presented them with that was valuable, but the way they looked at them. They paid close attention to the materials the objects were made from, the quality of the joins, and the number of parts used to construct a key. The shape of some of the components is in some cases as good as a signature when identifying a manufacturer.

The lock collectors also demonstrated the techniques used to safely disassemble a lock, revealing the mechanism of one unidentified object in the collection. As an object with little contextual information, the interior revealed that the lock was probably constructed to support a patent application. However, useful as this insight proved, disassembling the lock also raised the difficult issue of how to balance particular research needs with museum conservation procedures designed to protect the object. In the case of these individuals, it was felt that they had the expertise to complete this intervention without any damage to the lock. Access for enthusiasts is often about touch and taking things apart, which often works in opposition to museum practice. Despite this, disassembling the patent lock highlighted the real value of a large, repetitive catalogue collection: Learning to look is also about looking at lots of things. Access to a range of examples of a type of object allows the researcher to identify differences in design, unexpected alterations, makers' marks, or even damage. These subtle differences could point to key moments in an object's design, production, or use. As one collector describes: "a reference collection has every example or even several examples of the same things, so we can actually compare them and do exactly that and get used to the feel of them. It's like down in the Natural History Museum [London] they've got drawers of bones of different species. Lots of different things so you can compare, it's the same thing."[28]

---

28 Visit to Blythe House, video recording, October 25, 2015.

The collector was referring to his own collection in this case, but it is arguably true of any historic museum collection too, independent of the category of object. The "Who Cares?" project was interested in repetitive catalogue collections, and, as with the wider project, this case study demonstrated the need for organizations to be flexible in how their objects are used. This in turn raised questions about how a museum assesses the qualifications of an "independent expert" and ensures that collections continue to be accessible for future generations. In recent years there have been discussions about democratizing heritage, but challenges remain around how we balance the passion of the few with a responsibility to the many.[29]

The focus of a large portion of the storeroom visit remained on the mysterious patent lock, and, with the collectors, we explored in depth the techniques and questions used to understand it. The reason for this strong interest soon became clear as one of our collectors described the tantalizing mystery the object represented when on display in the Locks and Fastenings Gallery: "I've been looking at that for forty years in your cabinets and thinking the description says nothing. Unknown ... its always been ... that's always been in there, so you couldn't see this, for example [indicating an uncovered section of the lock]. Okay, well, I know it's a slider lock but how's it been put together, what's the idea behind it?"[30] As the collector began to carefully undo screws and remove metal plates, the conversation turned to the way the lock had been constructed and the way certain pieces had been marked by the manufacturer. In the phrasing of this conversation it felt at times as if the lock was part of the conversation, an active actor in a dialogue between collector, witnesses, and object:

> COLLECTOR ONE: It says something else just looking at it. The way the casing has been put together with screws on the side. It's [the lock is] screwed together [which] tells me this is not a major production lock.
>
> COLLECTOR TWO: I think it's an experiment ...
>
> COLLECTOR ONE: It is ... it's interesting enough that they've gone to the trouble of marking the screw ... one, two, *three*, four. That probably dates it a bit earlier. That means that it's more handmade rather than machine made ... machine made you'll get consistency of parts and screws.[31]

At this point there was a pause and a decision to be made about whether two screws should be undone. The collectors wanted to push the investigation further and remove a plate within the lock, but the curator must consider the conservation responsibilities of the museum. In taking this decision she must balance her professional role against her personal enthusiasm for the investigation. Does the (admittedly small) chance of harm to the object outweigh the opportunity to increase the curator's and therefore the museum's knowledge of its collection? The decision was taken to proceed, given the

---

29 See, for example, Helen C. Graham, "The 'Co' in Co-production: Museums, Community Participation and Science and Technology Studies," *Science Museum Group Journal* 5 (2016): online.

30 Visit to Blythe House, video recording, October 25, 2015.

31 Visit to Blythe House, video recording, October 25, 2015.

expertise of the lock collectors and that previous permission had been received from conservators: "As long as they can put it back together again!"

The collectors had brought their own tools with them—small screwdrivers and spatulas designed for opening the cases to look for makers' marks and other clues. One of the collectors removes a piece of the lock and says:

COLLECTOR ONE: You can see where it has been bushed.
CURATOR: Can you explain "bushed"?
COLLECTOR ONE: It's where a piece has been put on a stud and then for whatever reason the diameter would need to be bigger, so they've put a bush on it.[32]

Everything was then laid out in a "logical sequence" to aid in the important process of reassembling the lock. Collector Two explained that ordinarily they would photograph the lock before beginning to take it apart, and at this point, he asked permission to do so in the storage area. The question reflects an underlying concern about whether museum regulations are compatible with the collector's usual practices. At every stage they describe the reasoning behind their approach but look to the curator to sanction it. As Collector One said: "We had a debate over whether you would even allow us to do this … half of it is the intrigue and excitement of the day."

As Collector One removed the plate, he reassured us that he was not "hurting" the object, and the curator explained that their approach is not that far from museum practice: "We do something similar when we unpack scientific instruments from boxes in storage because you can guarantee the time has gone by since you unpacked it the box might have warped again."[33] Without makers' marks or other textual sources, one of the key pieces of evidence at the lock collectors' disposal is the material from which is it constructed and the style of the components. This material evidence provides clues to the history of the lock and its previous use. In the case of this patent lock, it hints at a highly competitive industry that was constantly borrowing ideas and developing new technology. Collector Two:

Well, its steel … it tells you the composition and also the fact that you've got sliders rather than levers. It also helps to put it into a period. Basically, lock manufacturers, people who have ideas pinch each other's ideas. They see something that someone else has patented, they like it and then they say let's put it into our lock but in a slightly different format that isn't apparent.[34]

Later, this point was further illustrated as the investigation moved onto another "mystery object," a pair of small chests. The collectors identified that one of the keys accompanying the locked chests was not the original. They reached this conclusion based on the shape of the key and that it was not formed from a single piece of metal.

---

32 Visit to Blythe House, video recording, October 25, 2015.
33 Visit to Blythe House, video recording, October 25, 2015.
34 Visit to Blythe House, video recording, October 25, 2015.

COLLECTOR TWO: Key collectors would get right involved about the knurling. You see, for example, the way that this has got a knurling but it's got a ribbing on it, see? See that you can run your hand across it. A key collector will say I can recognize the manufacturer from these ... from the different knurling and the spacing.

RESEARCHER: That's less reliable ...

COLLECTOR TWO: It's less reliable, of course it is, but I would say a key collector would start off with saying that it's French and they would probably recognize it anyhow.[35]

This conversation also draws out how subjective the value of an object is even within apparently closely related collecting interests. A key collector would start with the key and a lock collector would start with the lock as the primary source of historical information. Both are equally valuable forms of investigation but could potentially produce different interpretations. As well as the differences between collecting disciplines, this desire to dig deeper into the materiality of an object means that a collector also looks for different things from a museum exhibit than might a casual visitor. In this visit to the storerooms, the locks were not being looked at as illustrative of their social history so much as the material clues hidden within them.

RESEARCHER: Do you find going around galleries with locks that you think if somebody was a lock enthusiast who put together this display, they would have done it completely differently?

COLLECTOR TWO: Yes, yes ... [laughing].

RESEARCHER: Because you're saying there is quite a simple change there that would have given you so much more information ...

COLLECTOR TWO: Yes, some of the other locks that you had, you showed them half shot, which you can see half closed. I understand a lot more about this. But because when it arrived in the 1950s, no one really knew what it was. They couldn't write too much about it.[36]

Conclusion

While the aim of the visit to Blythe House was to better understand the approach that collectors take to historic objects, it also demonstrated the power they have to prompt personal recollection. Locks play a hugely significant part in the lives of our participants: They live with them and they care for them. They underpin their social lives and their passion has grown alongside their working lives. In a quiet moment between looking at objects, one of the collectors offered these reflections:

A lot of people do. They get something in their childhood and then they leave it, then as they grow up, you know, get more independence, until the family, the parents of someone says there's this attic full of your old stuff. What do you want to do with it? And people

---

35 Visit to Blythe House, video recording, October 25, 2015.
36 Visit to Blythe House, video recording, October 25, 2015.

collect comics and it's, and I've got a friend who collects comics, and many friends who collect stamps because they rediscovered their boyhood stamp collection in the attic, when maybe their parent passed on or wanted to move home and they developed an interest in that. And now there's a bit more time on my hands.[37]

These comments evidence how expertise can grow out of enthusiasm and the extent to which expertise in museum collections sits on the blurred line between personal and professional worlds. In the case of the collectors, their professional lives as locksmiths are integral to their approach to the materiality of the lock collections. The tools they use and the skill they have in recognizing another craftsperson's work (even from hundreds of years ago) stem from their own lived experience; experience that helps to shape a specific way of looking at collections. The challenge for museum work is how to bring these personal stories and practical experiences together in a meaningful way with objects in museum storerooms. A meaningful visit for these collectors was an opportunity to select objects, view accompanying files, and, importantly, touch and disassemble the object. For the duration of the visit, the museum had to lend the collectors curatorial authority, and this authority (as we have seen) was constantly questioned and referred to by all involved. The authority was hesitantly handed over and gingerly taken on board, with a feeling on the collectors' side that they would "get into trouble" with the higher powers of the museum. The authority was also time limited, restricted to the parameters of this visit, and negotiated with the professional staff of the museum. However, the session itself was hugely informative and allowed the researchers and the curators to fill in some gaps in the official records of the Science Museum.

A final thought for the project comes from the collectors. In a later discussion after the visit, Collector One expressed a keen interest in continuing to care for the Science Museum locks. They were, after all, just sitting in storage, far away from the current exhibition priorities of the museum. Why could he not be an officially recognized external Curator of Locks? He would care for, research, and catalogue and, in return, he would get official institutional recognition, a status that would open so many doors in his pursuit of a great and comprehensive history of the lock. Unfortunately, this has never gone further than a conversation. Can a museum really award one individual curatorial rights and title without advertising and interviewing candidates? Can it really make a role such as this entirely voluntary without appearing to take advantage of the individual involved? There are examples where relationships such as this have worked (Woodham and Kelleher's chapter in this volume describes the productive relationship between Ironbridge Gorge and the Historic Metallurgy Society), but, in these cases, it is a carefully negotiated relationship between a museum and an established society rather than an individual. The example of the imagined Curator of Locks only serves to emphasize the difference in working practice between the amateur and professional worlds of curation, the power and inflexibility of national museums, and the responsibility that access to collections entails.

---

37 Visit to Blythe House, video recording, October 25, 2015.

Bibliography

Bud, Robert. "Infected by the Bacillus of Science: The Explosion of South Kensington." In *Science for the Nation: Perspectives on the History of the Science Museum*, edited by Peter Morris. London: Palgrave Macmillan, 2013.

Crang, Mike, and Divya P. Tolia-Kelly. "Nation, Race, and Affect: Senses and Sensibilities at National Heritage Sites." *Environment and Planning A* 42, no. 10 (2010): 2315–31.

Eras, Vincent. *Locks and Keys throughout the Ages*. Folkestone: Bailey Bros & Swinfen, 1974.

Geoghegan, Hilary. "Emotional Geographies of Enthusiasm: Belonging to the Telecommunications Heritage Group." *Area* 45, no. 1 (2013): 40–46.

——. " 'If You Can Walk down the Street and Recognise the Difference between Cast Iron and Wrought Iron, the World is Altogether a Better Place': Being Enthusiastic about Industrial Archaeology." *M/C Journal* 12 (2009): unpaginated.

Geoghegan, Hilary, and Alison Hess. "Object-Love at the Science Museum: Cultural Geographies of Museum Storerooms." *Cultural Geographies* 22, no. 3 (2015): 445–65.

Gosden, Chris, and Frances Larson. *Knowing Things: Exploring the Collections at the Pitt Rivers Museum 1884–1945*. Oxford: Oxford University Press, 2007.

Graham, Helen C. "The 'Co' in Co-production: Museums, Community Participation and Science and Technology Studies." *Science Museum Group Journal* 5 (2016): online.

Keene, Suzanne. *Fragments of the World: Uses of Museum Collections*. Oxford: Elsevier Butterworth-Heinemann, 2005.

Keene, Suzanne with Alice Stevenson, and Francesca Monti. *Collections for People: Museums' Stored Collections as a Public Resource*. London: UCL Institute for Archaeology, 2008.

Knell, Simon J. *Museums and the Future of Collecting*. Aldershot: Ashgate, 2004.

Larson, Frances. *An Infinity of Things: How Sir Henry Wellcome Collected the World*. Oxford: Oxford University Press, 2009.

Lutz, Catherine, and Geoffrey M. White. "The Anthropology of Emotions." *Annual Review of Anthropology* 15, no. 1 (1986): 405–36.

Macdonald, Sharon. "Behind the Scenes at the Science Museum: Knowing." *Academic Anthropology and the Museum: Back to the Future* 13 (2001): 117.

Monti, Francesca, and Suzanne Keene. *Museums and Silent Objects: Designing Effective Exhibitions*. Abingdon: Routledge, 2016.

Morris, Peter, ed. *Science for the Nation: Perspectives on the History of the Science Museum*. London: Palgrave Macmillan, 2013.

Museums and Galleries Commission. *Digest of Museum Statistics (DOMUS)*. London: Museums and Galleries Commission, 1999.

Olmi, Giuseppe, Oliver Impey, and Arthur Macgregor. *The Origins of Museums: The Cabinet of Curiosities in Sixteenth and Seventeenth-Century Europe*. Oxford: Oxford University Press, 1985.

Papakostas, Apostolis. *Civilizing the Public Sphere: Distrust, Trust and Corruption*. London: Springer, 2016.

Pearce, Susan. "A New Way of Looking at Old Things." *Museum International* 51, no. 2 (1999): 12–17.

——. *On Collecting: An Investigation into Collecting in the European Tradition*. London: Routledge, 1995.

Rosenwein, Barbara H. "Worrying about Emotions in History." *The American Historical Review* 107, no. 3 (2002): 821–45.

Smith, Laurajane, and Gary Campbell. "The Elephant in the Room: Heritage, Affect, and Emotion." In *A Companion to Heritage Studies*, edited by William Logan, Máiréad Nic Craith, and Ullrich Kockel, 443–60. Chichester: Wiley-Blackwell, 2015.

Shuttleworth, Sally, and Sally Frampton. "Constructing Scientific Communities: Citizen Science." *The Lancet* 385 (2015): 2568.

Tilden, Freeman. *Interpreting Our Heritage*, 4th ed., expanded and updated with introduction from R. Bruce Craig. Chapel Hill: University of North Carolina Press, 2007.

Tolia-Kelly, Divya P., Emma Waterton, and Steve Watson, ed. *Heritage, Affect and Emotion: Politics, Practices and Infrastructures*. London: Routledge, 2016.

Yallop, Jacqueline. *Magpies, Squirrels and Thieves: How the Victorians Collected the World*. London: Atlantic, 2011.

Chapter 2

"A HAWK FROM A HANDSAW"†: INVESTIGATING ENTHUSIASM FOR RURAL HAND TOOLS

RHIANEDD SMITH*

Introduction

ONE OF THE rare negative TripAdvisor reviews for the Museum of English Rural Life (MERL) complained that it contained just a "bunch of old tools," which should be thrown in a skip. The author of the review argued that they had expected the Museum to be full of beautiful pieces of furniture and was disappointed by this less glamorous depiction of rural life. The need to balance an audience appetite for rural aesthetics with the complex multifaceted stories of the English countryside is something which shaped debate during the Museum's recent redisplay.[1] As part of this redisplay, the MERL glazed its storage area to make it accessible to the public as part of the overall museum experience. Visitor feedback has been positive, but many have requested further information about stored objects that are now unfamiliar to most of the population. As a university museum, we also find that our students have trouble engaging with our more workaday items and gravitate towards decorative and domestic objects. Increasingly, we find that our visitors and future curators lack a first-hand understanding of the MERL's objects

---

† William Shakespeare, *Hamlet* (1601), Act II, Scene 2. A hawk is the name for a plasterer's tool, a fact which struck me as a useful example of the loss of specialist knowledge. The actual meaning of this line may well have nothing to do with hand tools, but even so, the debate about the line speaks to this chapter's exploration of the loss of everyday knowledge.

1 The Heritage Lottery Fund project "Our Country Lives" (2014–2017) included both a redisplay and an activity programme engaging with new and traditional communities. The Museum of Rural Life, "Our Country Lives," https://merl.reading.ac.uk/news-and-views/tag/our-country-lives/ [accessed July 5, 2019].

* **Rhianedd Smith** is the director of the Heritage and Creativity Institute for Collections and the University Museums and the Special Collections Services Director of Academic Learning and Engagement at the University of Reading. She was principal investigator on the AHRC Care for the Future project "Who Cares? Interventions in 'Unloved' Museum Collections" and co-investigator on the AHRC follow-on funding project "Glastonbury Abbey: Archaeology, Legend and Public Engagement." Rhianedd is based at the Museum of English Rural Life, University of Reading, where she heads an interdisciplinary institute for collections-based research and champions learning with collections as part of the student experience. Her research explores the significance of historic collections in contemporary identity politics, and her doctoral research examined the role of myth and spirituality in the heritage interpretation of medieval monastic ruins.

and issues. The obvious approach might be to turn our back on specialists, but it is argued here that engagement with people who "love" these collections might help us to engage wider audiences.

This chapter explores enthusiasm and expertise for hand tools and questions the place of the Museum of English Rural Life's collection of hand tools in that wider context. The issue of enthusiasm for historic hand tools in the UK is examined through site visits to the Tools and Trades History Society's (TATHS) Museum at Amberley and the Tools for Self Reliance workshop in the New Forest. This investigation of contemporary expertise and enthusiasm is brought together with the research already being undertaken regarding the history and future of the MERL. The chapter ends with an account of an intervention staged at the MERL to explore how expertise and enthusiasm might be transferred between generations. Research into enthusiasm notes the importance of studying networks (which might be in some ways virtual) and real-world spaces in which these individuals come together to share their enthusiasm.[2] Geoghegan and Hess have also experimented with autoethnography and walking tours as ways of trying to capture the experiences of engaging with objects in stored collections and professional and personal responses to collections.[3] This was the inspiration for the mixed methodological approach applied here, which included both personal reflection and more ethnographic techniques.

This volume asks how the theoretical framework of "object-love" and "enthusiasm" can enrich our understanding and identify possible future pathways for ensuring ongoing engagement with these far-from-"unloved" objects. Hence this chapter is organized into two sections, which look firstly at the wider context of "care" for historic hand tools and secondly at the historical and contemporary museum context of care for these collections at the MERL. In this way it suggests two possible future avenues for future research in this field: (1) exploring how physical acts of care and emotion are intertwined with regards to "unloved" collections in "The Third Age," and (2) the need to combine deeper historical perspectives on enthusiasm, intergenerational collaboration, and contemporary experimentation when investigating potential uses of stored collections in museological contexts.

Caring Practices in "The Third Age"

The growing field of literature on "enthusiasm" offers a useful theoretical pathway for examining competing values and practices around engagement with collections.[4]

---

2 Hilary Geoghegan, "Emotional Geographies of Enthusiasm: Belonging to the Telecommunications Heritage Group," *Area V* 44, no. 1 (2013): 40–46; Hilary Geoghegan, "'If You Can Walk down the Street and Recognise the Difference between Cast Iron and Wrought Iron, the World is Altogether a Better Place': Being Enthusiastic about Industrial Archaeology," *M/C Journal: A Journal of Media and Culture* 12, no. 2 (2009): unpaginated.

3 Hilary Geoghegan and Alison Hess, "Object-Love at the Science Museum: Cultural Geographies of Museum Storerooms," *Cultural Geographies* 22, no. 3 (2014): 445–65.

4 Ruth Craggs, Hilary Geoghegan, and Hannah Neate, "Architectural Enthusiasm: Visiting Buildings with the Twentieth Century Society," *Environment and Planning D: Society and Space* 31, no. 5

Research in this field often focuses on amateur or voluntary application of expertise and the motivations and mechanisms that underlie this kind of activity.[5] In the introduction to this volume we asked how a deeper understanding of the concept of "care" might enhance our understanding of both "enthusiasm" and professional practice. Hence the first section of this chapter examines "enthusiasm" for hand tools in a wider context. Research into enthusiasm by authors such as Geoghegan, and DeLyser and Greenstein[6] on "fixing" and "tinkering," suggests that enthusiast collecting draws some of its pleasure from manipulating or altering the object(s) of choice rather than maintaining them as found. Research into practices of care around humans also demonstrates that an emotional connection or "attachment" and physical acts of caring are intertwined.[7]

The hand tools that are the focus of this chapter are defined by their haptic qualities and their context of use, which can make static displays unsatisfying. However, as discussed in the Introduction and Conclusion to this volume, "collections care" standards give primacy to the long-term physical stability of the object, even if this means that it is rarely accessed. Hence the case studies presented here will explore the role of physical activity in emotional engagement with "unloved" objects and examine some of the activities that are seen as essential practices of care by "enthusiasts" and voluntary carers.

This chapter also suggests some ways in which "unloved objects" might be connected to the life cycle, sense of self, forms of labour, personal relationships, and the emotional processing of change. A demographic overview of enthusiasts and collectors suggests that many are in an active stage of retirement from work known as "The Third Age." In her examination of ageing and "work/leisure" in New Zealand, Mansvelt[8] noted that "academic and state discourses of ageing tend to reinforce work and leisure as oppositional categories with 'adulthood' occupying years of productivity (both materially and metaphorically) and old age as years of 'retirement' from productive work, paid employment

---

(2013): 879–96; Dydia DeLyser and Paul Greenstein, "'Follow That Car!' Mobilities of Enthusiasm in a Rare Car's Restoration," *The Professional Geographer* 67, no. 2 (2014): 255–68; Dydia DeLyser and Paul Greenstein, "The Devotions of Restoration: Materiality, Enthusiasm, and Making Three 'Indian Motorcycles' Like New," *Annals of the American Association of Geographers* 107, no. 6 (2017): 1461–78; Geoghegan, "Emotional Geographies of Enthusiasm"; Geoghegan, "'If You Can Walk down the Street and Recognise the Difference between Cast Iron and Wrought Iron, the World is Altogether a Better Place'"; Juliana Mansvelt, "Working at Leisure: Critical Geographies of Ageing," *Area* 29, no. 4 (1997): 289–98, published online, 2005; Richard Yarwood and Nick Evans, "A Lleyn Sweep for Local Sheep? Breed Societies and the Geographies of Welsh Livestock," *Environment and Planning A* 38, no. 7 (2006): 1307–26.

5 See the Introduction to this volume.

6 Geoghegan, "Emotional Geographies of Enthusiasm"; Geoghegan, "'If You Can Walk down the Street and Recognise the Difference between Cast Iron and Wrought Iron, the World is Altogether a Better Place'"; DeLyser and Greenstein, "The Devotions of Restoration"; DeLyser and Greenstein, "'Follow That Car!'"

7 For example, theory and practice around "attachment theory" in adoptive families views embodied acts of play and caring as a key component in building attachment between individuals who are not biologically related. See, for example, Daniel Hughes, *Building the Bonds of Attachment: Awakening Love in Deeply Troubled Children*, 2nd ed. (London: Rowman & Littlefield, 2018).

8 Mansvelt, "Working at Leisure," 289–90.

and active life." The participants in Mansvelt's study said that they did not have time for "real leisure" and equated this with being idle or unproductive. They valued forms of leisure that were productive, or "leisure as work," and resisted stereotypical notions of "old people." The theorization of leisure notes that while modernist perceptions of leisure see it as extra or free time, in late capitalism use of leisure time is a major part of identity formation.[9] Hence practices of care around "unloved" collections may give a valuable insight into sense of self and emotional work among this key demographic. They may also point towards some potential therapeutic outcomes that are experienced through collecting, curating, and crafting historic objects.

Why Hand Tools?

We must begin by addressing this potentially strange subject for an academic paper. Here, historic hand tools refers particularly to those tools related to the countryside; that is, agricultural hand tools and tools related to rural crafts. The fate of rural hand tools is embedded in wider debates, which have their roots in discourse regarding "folk" and the "death of the countryside" in an age of increasing industrialization and urbanization.[10] Hand tools are, in short, tools that rely on the power of the human body rather than power created by animals or the burning of fossil fuels. Large repetitive tool collections have been collected by rural museums, social history collections, and historic tool "enthusiasts."

When these collections were collected in bulk by curators, it was partly with the rationale that they might serve some future research purpose. However, the research landscape has changed and the use of objects or historical approaches in "rural" disciplines such as agriculture is very low. Hence, much like "industrial archaeology,"[11] expert knowledge around these collections often lies outside of the academy. The use of these types of collections for display has also dwindled somewhat, as there is a new focus on narrative in museum interpretation and packed comprehensive displays of technological progress are no longer the order of the day. As audience recollection of these items and of rural living is lost, we can also no longer assume that these items will be recognized, let alone treasured. We are now faced with asking how museums might engage audiences with the workaday aspects of rural culture.[12]

---

9 See, for example, John Kelly, *Leisure Identities and Interactions* (London: George Allen & Unwin, 1983); Lois M. Haggard and Daniel R. Williams, "Identity Affirmation through Leisure Activities: Leisure Symbols of the Self," *Journal of Leisure Research* 24, no. 1 (1990): 1–18.

10 Jonathan Bell, "Making Rural Histories," in *Making Histories in Museums*, ed. Gaynor Kavanagh (London: Leicester University Press, 2005), 30–41; Oliver Douglas, "Folklore, Survivals, and the Neo-archaic: The Materialist Character of Late Nineteenth-Century Homeland Ethnography," *Museum History Journal* 4, no. 2 (2011): 223–24; Alun Howkins, *The Death of Rural England: A Social History of the Countryside since 1900* (London: Routledge, 2003); Gaynor Kavanagh, "Mangles, Muck and Myths: Rural History Museums in Britain," *Rural History* 1, no. 2 (1991): 187–204.

11 Geoghegan, " 'If You Can Walk down the Street and Recognise the Difference between Cast Iron and Wrought Iron, the World is Altogether a Better Place.' " See also Woodham and Kelleher, this volume.

12 Victoria Sekules, *Cultures of the Countryside: Art, Museum, Heritage and Environment 1920–2015* (Abingdon: Routledge, 2018).

The reasons for these tools falling out of common use are complex and prone to sim-plification. Very broadly speaking, the industrial and agricultural revolutions changed the way that raw power was harnessed, with a greater emphasis on fossil fuels, produc-tion line systems, and mass production over time.[13] This meant that agricultural hand tools, which were used for field maintenance and preparation, seeding and weeding, harvesting, and processing the crop, were largely superseded by technologies that required less human labour and that could cultivate larger areas more efficiently.[14] Equally, as industrially produced items became cheaper and cities drew in the potential inheritors of family craft businesses, the range of specialist rural craft knowledge, skills, tools, and workshops also declined. It was in this context that the collections discussed in this chapter first moved out of use and into a collecting context in museums such as the Museum of English Rural Life. Experts at the MERL would stress that this linear narrative of progress is a vast oversimplification which romanticizes the notion of a lost past[15] and would note that versions of some of these tools are still in use today.[16] However, a general population move towards urbanization and the passage of time means that most of these objects will not be familiar to the majority of our visitors. So, what might the world of historic tool collecting and restoration beyond the museum teach us about the potential significance of these objects for contemporary audiences?

The Tools and Trades History Society (TATHS)

The following section of this chapter outlines two case studies, which seek to capture some of the practices that are common to those who are enthusiastic about these types of objects. In order to understand the drivers and mechanisms for contemporary hand tool enthusiasm and expertise, I went on two site visits to organizations devoted to working with historic hand tools: the Tools and Trades History Society and Tools for Self Reliance. In both these case studies, the interviews turned into walking tours, where the author was introduced to different settings in which objects were stored, restored, and displayed. These were not static spaces but working environments, where a volunteer

---

13 This depiction of technological advancement is not without its problems and is critiqued by, for example, David Edgerton, *The Shock of the Old: Technology and Global History since 1900* (London: Profile, 2008) and Felicity McWilliams's current doctoral research at King's College London.

14 Roy Brigden, "Research—Social History," in *Manual of Curatorship: A Guide to Museum Practice*, 2nd ed., ed. John M. A. Thompson (London: Routledge, 2015), 547–53.

15 Dr. Ollie Douglas, curator of the MERL collections and advisor to the "Who Cares?" project, personal communication.

16 For example, the way hand tools have survived in rural life is through "heritage crafts." These have been defined broadly as "Practices which employ manual dexterity and skill and an understanding of traditional materials, designs and techniques in order to make, repair, restore or conserve buildings, other structures, modes of transport, or more general, portable objects." TBR, Department for Business Innovation and Skills, *Mapping Heritage Craft: The Economic Contribution of the Heritage Craft Sector in England* (London: Creative and Cultural Skills, 2012), 6 [Executive Summary, Definition].

and largely retired task force was undertaking skilled labour. Walking through these spaces also served as a mnemonic device, allowing the guide to recall the stories of people who had built or donated objects, displays, and even workshop elements.

The Tools and Trades History Society (TATHS) was founded in 1983 by a committee including eminent enthusiast collectors such as Salaman and Hawley,[17] carpenters and joiners, and also academics and librarians. When they held their first Annual General Meeting at the Victoria and Albert Museum (V&A) in 1984, they had ninety members. The TATHS Library is housed at the Museum of English Rural Life and offers a valuable resource for studying the group dynamics of this enthusiast network. Archival research, via early newsletters, offers an opportunity to gather narratives from collectors who are no longer with us. For example, the newsletter segment "Collectors Cornered" provides accounts from collectors regarding their approach to collecting. Letters pages also offer such gems as the one entitled "Preserving and Displaying a Collection in a Limited Space," which notes that "collections begin in a small way but tend to end up as an unimaginable mass to the detriment of a marriage."[18] The tone of the journal is light; there are jokes and it sometimes uses the regional northern English vernacular. This distinguishes it from an academic journal but, at the same time, there is a strong emphasis on knowledge and research. The ongoing mention of obituaries and illnesses in early newsletters highlights that, even from the start, this group attracted an older demographic. The listed names also show that TATHS had, and still has, a predominantly male membership base.

Like other grass roots organizations mentioned in this book, one of TATHS' major mechanisms for creating a network was through annual meetups and also through the publication of a periodic newsletter. Today, TATHS engages with multiple museum collections but it also has its own object collection, which is displayed at Amberley Museum and Heritage Centre, near Arundel in West Sussex. Amberley Museum (also known as the Amberley Working Museum and Amberley Chalk Pits Museum) was founded in 1979 at an abandoned chalk pit by the Southern Industrial History Centre Trust. Other areas of the site focus on specialist interests as diverse as telecommunications, narrow-gauge railways, and stick-making. In Issue 48 of the TATHS newsletter there is a detailed account of how what began as an informal display by a regional group in Amberley progressed to a permanent location.[19]

Visiting the museum gave valuable insights into how the site has developed since that time. The group not only brought their own collections but also constructed their own premises. The museum buildings are a tribute to the work of multiple communities of specialist collectors and practitioners. The "Hall of Tools" was constructed in 2001 by TATHS members, with a grant from the Worshipful Company of Carpenters. A second

---

17 Chris Green, "Salaman, Raphael Arthur (1906–1993)," in *Oxford Dictionary of National Biography* (Oxford: Oxford University Press, 2004); Simon Barley, "Ken Hawley Obituary," *The Guardian*, August 19, 2014, online. www.theguardian.com/culture/2014/aug/19/ken-hawley [accessed July 5, 2019].

18 Tools and Trades History Society, *TATHS Journal* 4 (1984): 36.

19 Tools and Trades History Society, *TATHS Journal* 48 (1996).

building was added for treadle and hand machines and, in 2014, another building was created from scratch, with the local group clearing the site, pouring the concrete, and even creating a façade which blended in with the period look of the site. While walking around the site, my guide would easily move between pointing out objects, to mentioning the person who had donated and restored them, to referring to the display and the building. Hence, while the historic objects were the focus for the display, the volunteers also clearly took great pride in the work that had gone into the construction of their setting and continued curation.

There are very few members of professional staff for the whole Amberley site, with the museum mainly managed by various volunteer groups. Walking around the site, you are immediately struck by how many of these volunteers are retired men, a point that is not unnoticed by the group themselves. Talking to members of TATHS and demonstrators at other locations around the site, it was clear that they often brought with them skills from various civic occupations, such as engineering, town planning, and the police force. Many also had their own equipment and collections in their garages and sheds at home. When asked about their partners, several noted that spouses spent time looking after grandchildren and/or had their own related hobbies, for example, tools related to textiles. Thus, as with many members of the "Third Age," their "leisure time" was being taken up with largely undocumented labour and other practices of "care."[20]

It should be noted here that TATHS has some very active and well-respected female members, most notably former president Jane Rees, who has published several specialist books[21] and recently featured in a series of videos sharing information about related collections. In her video on "Collecting Tools," Rees notes that people tend to collect today via eBay, specialist auctioneers, and tool fairs.[22] She suggests that the best way to start is by learning about tools via reference books aimed at collectors. She also notes, "I am very limited in what I collect these days. I collect rules which I keep in a chest which I think originally had bird's eggs or butterflies or something like that." She also notes that she keeps some tools in a gentleman's tool chest that she found, by chance, in her family home. This move away from active collecting towards the curation of a smaller collection and sharing information with a wider public emphasizes that it is not only the act of collecting but the process of organizing, displaying, and communicating collections that TATHS members, such as Rees, are passionate about.

While passion for the technical aspects of these objects is clear, there are also haptic, aesthetic, social, and emotional variables that give this activity meaning. The objects are not simply preserved but are actively restored by the group, drawing on shared expertise from past lives in carpentry, mechanical engineering, etc. The group were also enthusiastic about how they presented their collection to the public, constructing displays that placed individual objects together to recreate historic craft workshop scenes or creating

---

20 Mansvelt, "Working at Leisure."

21 Jane Rees, *The Rule Book: Measuring for the Trades* (Mendham: Astragal, 2010).

22 Woodlands TV, "Collecting Tools," www.youtube.com/watch?v=gmHOs5fOPC0 [accessed July 5, 2019].

larger patterns and shapes such as circles and fans of tools. Like all of Amberley, this activity was about making and doing together. In other parts of the site, children were allowed to create tools with volunteers or watch as skills were demonstrated.

Familial and social connections also seemed to be significant. For example, TATHS members talked about individuals with reference to their professional knowledge and identity, for example, "a proper chippy always with a mike in his backpocket" meaning a carpenter who was never without a screwdriver. During my visit, the curator emphasized that labels clearly noted who had donated collections, and they mentioned that family members would come to the museum to see or even participate in the conservation of objects. In discussions at the Science Museum,[23] mentioned in Hess's chapter, members of that enthusiast group also saw the removal of donors' names from exhibition labels as an affront. If we view the act of forming and preserving a collection as a "legacy" rather than as a "hobby," we can understand why such perceived erasure of effort might be so emotionally charged. Thus we see that enthusiasm for tools is not a purely a solitary activity and that through familial relations, networks of fellow enthusiasts, joint projects, and engagement with the public such organizations may seek to share their enjoyment with others. When reading the name of the project, "Who Cares? Interventions with 'Unloved' Collections," my guide went to great lengths to stress that these items were not "unloved" but of great significance, not only to TATHS members but also to members of the visiting public who engaged with them. The strength of reaction to the suggestion that these objects were of no value, and the social interactions on site, demonstrated to me that this was not just about the objects. Past identities and skills, gained through the world of work, were repurposed in this new voluntary setting and were an important part of constructing a sense of self in retirement.

Tools for Self Reliance

This was demonstrated in a slightly different way in another case study. Tools for Self Reliance is an organization that also cares about tools and is increasingly becoming a locus where people deposit unwanted tools. Working in the Museum of English Rural Life, I was familiar with the common occurrence of a relative showing up in a car with granddad's tools and asking if they could donate them to the museum. I had heard about Tools for Self Reliance as an organization to which curators pointed would-be donors when they could not accept their tool collections. This rerouting was seen as an option for objects that lacked the significance to make them suitable for museum accession, while giving families a positive and emotionally satisfying alternative to consigning inherited collections of hand tools to the scrap heap.

Tools for Self Reliance's tagline, "Practical Help for Practical People," again references the thread that runs through this chapter regarding the revaluation of "hands-on" skills and knowledge. The charity's digital "dashboard" notes that it had 750 volunteers, shipped 25,000 tools, and supported 4,053 people between July 2018

---

23 Hess, this volume.

and July 2019.[24] The dashboard outlines the key elements of the charity's voluntary work: the refurbishment of discarded tools, which are sent to Africa to be used in the establishment and support of small and micro businesses. The organization was founded in 1979 and was established formally as a charity in 1980. It is based in Netley Marsh, near Southampton in the UK, and the workshop is a fascinating place to visit. In a series of storerooms and specialist workshops, volunteers studiously "refurbish" old tools to make them fit for contemporary use. Not all of the tools are hand-powered, and the charity is looking at issues around skills and health and safety for refurbishing electrical items. They are also considering issues around electrical supply in rural parts of Sierra Leone, Ghana, Malawi, Tanzania, Gambia, and Uganda.

The volunteers themselves are an interesting community. While they are not all collectors per se, their life stories, motivations, and skills and knowledge are channelled into the refurbished tools. Again, the volunteers are mainly men and mainly retired. Many are former carpenters or have had some other kind of hands-on or industrial career in the past. There are, however, significant numbers of female volunteers, for example, applying the skills developed as factory workers to restore sewing machines. There are also work placements, opportunities for long-term unemployed people, and a supported workshop for young people with disabilities on site. During my visit, my guide pointed out that their philosophy of "countering waste" went beyond the tools themselves to include the potential of the people who received the tools and the skills and knowledge of the retired volunteers who restored them.

In addition to the site in Netley Marsh, there are around fifty regional groups who also collect and restore tools and send them through to depots. There are also a series of partnerships with small NGOs in Africa that identify the recipients of tools and organize "in country" face-to-face training. While Tools for Self Reliance does not hold a museum collection, members are collectors and restorers. Their knowledge of and approach to historic hand tools are quite similar to those of TATHS, and there was a suggestion that there might be some crossover in membership.

Many of the tools have been donated following the death of their former owner. The curator of MERL collections, Dr. Ollie Douglas, and the curator of the TATHS museum both told me that when an object did not fit into the collection, they would suggest Tools for Self Reliance as an alternative to people who were often going through a difficult process of redistributing a loved one's possessions and possibly downsizing a family home. My guide at Tools for Self Reliance mentioned that he had invited the families of donors to events or shared with them photographs of the tools used in their new context. He noted that both the process of donating and that of following the trail of a loved one's possessions to a new life in Africa meant that there were often tears on site. In this way the concept of "care" again went far beyond the object to include the donors, donors' families, volunteers, and eventual recipients.

Thus even for objects that are destined to be thrown away there might be a second life. Both site visits demonstrated that there is an anxiety connected to this act of caring outside of the museum context, which might reflect the very personal nature of the

---

24 Tools for Self Reliance, www.tfsr.org [accessed July 5, 2019].

collecting and the lack of surety regarding long-term care. On talking to collectors as part of this project, it became clear that many fear what will become of their collection following their death. This is, in part, a reflection of the age range of enthusiast collectors and also related to the very real limitations on storage space that prevent many museums from actively collecting (as discussed in the Introduction to this volume). Many such items are mass-produced duplicates of objects in existing museum collections, which are already underutilized. Collectors are aware that museums may have to turn away donations from their families after they are gone.

Applying Concepts of "Enthusiasm" to Rural Collections

The second section of this chapter takes this research inside and "behind the scenes" at the museum, combining a historical and a contemporary look at "enthusiasm" and "practices of care" as they pertain to hand tool collections at the MERL. Drawing on the work of several colleagues with museum archives at the MERL, it suggests ways that concepts of "care" and "enthusiasm" might help us to understand the motivations of early collectors and curators. It goes on to outline some recent projects that have worked in part with stored collections, and finally it outlines an experiment to bring challenges around training and engagement into conversation with specialist knowledge. In this way it intends to suggest possible future methods of engaging different kinds of individuals with these collections and of equipping a new generation of museum professionals with the skills to interpret them.

The role of the enthusiast or unpaid amateur in collecting, research, and preservation is nothing new.[25] In the case of rural research, there have been those who have attempted to collect, preserve, and even revive aspects of "folk" or "rural" culture and ways of life since the nineteenth century.[26] Victorian medievalism drove an interest in collecting and reviving vernacular arts, crafts, and architecture of the British past, and the philosophy of the Arts and Crafts movement also made an explicit link with medieval craftsmanship and handmade items.[27] In museological terms, the creation of the first open-air museum at Skansen, Stockholm, with its reconstructed vernacular buildings and accompanying collection (now in the Nordiska Museet), marked a significant watershed.[28] In the UK, this perceived need for museums to capture rural ways of life resulted in the creation of the National History Museum of Wales,[29] the MERL,[30] and the Scottish Rural

---

25 See, for example, work on nineteenth-century citizen science currently being explored at the University of Oxford, "Constructing Scientific Communities," https://conscicom.org [accessed July 5, 2019].

26 Bell, "Making Rural Histories"; Brigden, "Research."

27 Douglas, "Folklore, Survivals, and the Neo-archaic."

28 Sten Rentzhog, *Open Air Museums: The History and Future of a Visionary Idea* (Östersund: Jamtli, 2007).

29 Rhiannon Mason, *Museums, Nations, Identities: Wales and Its National Museums* (Cardiff: University of Wales Press, 2007).

30 Brigden, "Research."

History Museum. These museums were established in the context of the post–Second World War intensification of farming, with each taking a slightly different approach to display, collecting, and national identity construction.[31] A more grass roots development of regional rural museums followed in the 1960s and 1970s.[32]

In reality these collections have faced similar issues around lack of engagement to those seen elsewhere in this volume. Expert in historic hand tools Chris Green stressed to me that tool collections related to rural industries have tended to be under-researched and less valued as collectors' items by the enthusiast community, with agricultural hand tools (his area of expertise) being particularly underappreciated. Hence these objects are doubly damned in terms of wider value by being both more functional than decorative and more rural than urban. Rurality is also a topic that has garnered slightly less academic interest than other forms of "enthusiasm." A notable exception is Yarwood and Evans's work on the preservation of rare breeds.[33] They argue that specialist rural knowledge might cross the boundaries between enthusiasm and production. As agriculture is an economic activity, knowledge of rare breeds cannot be seen purely as a hobby, but Yarwood and Evans stress that it is a form of capital embedded in social networks and activities and thus open to enthusiast research. Other relevant examples of enthusiast research in relation to rurality include Francesca Church's research on preservationist groups such as the Campaign for the Protection of Rural England[34] and Geoghegan and colleagues' work on environmentalism and citizen science,[35] which also offers an insight into group makeup, motivation, and the spatial dynamics of rurally focused enthusiasm.

The Museum of English Rural Life

So, what was the role of "enthusiasm," amateur and/or professional, in the origins of the MERL? The museum is based at the University of Reading and was officially established in 1950, housed in a Victorian building. The first object (a cow bell) was formally accessioned in 1951. Today, the collection comprises over 30,000 objects representing many aspects of rural life and work. A rich museum archive remains, which casts some light on the development of the collection. The museum was not created in a vacuum, and situating it within its historical context allows us to understand the legacy and wider significance of specific collections. It is unusual in being a university museum on

---

31 Peter Rivière, "Success and Failure: The Tale of Two Museums," *Journal of the History of Collections* 22, no. 1 (2010): 141–51.

32 Brigden, "Research."

33 Yarwood and Evans, "A Lleyn Sweep for Local Sheep?"

34 Church, this volume.

35 Glyn Everett and Hilary Geoghegan, "Initiating and Continuing Participation in Citizen Science for Natural History," *BMC Ecology* 16, supplement 1 (2016): online; Hilary Geoghegan, Alison Dyke, Rachel Pateman, Sarah West, and Glyn Everett, *Understanding Motivations for Citizen Science: Final Report on Behalf of UKEOF* (University of Reading, Stockholm Environment Institute, University of York, and University of the West of England, 2016).

a rural theme, thus muddying the waters between grassroots, academic, and national organizations.

In the 1950s, there were several historians in the Agriculture Department at the University of Reading who pioneered the creation of the museum. It originally started out in a tent, which would visit agricultural shows in a way that echoes the work of enthusiast organizations such as the Tools and Trades History Society. Today, such research would be far more likely to be situated within a university history department, and rural history as a discipline is a niche but fascinating academic field. The creators of the MERL were also connected with the wider academic debate regarding the nature of English rural identity. Just before the MERL was created, its founders were involved in the discussion of a never-realized plan being discussed by the Royal Anthropological Institute; draft maps show an open-air formation similar to Skansen.[36] The MERL's approach was very different to this, in a way that has shaped the nature of its collections and its approach to interpretation today.

There were ongoing tensions about the nature of the museum and its designation as a research organization. The University of Reading's vice-chancellor at the time of the MERL's foundation, Sir Frank Stenton, was a well-respected historian of the Anglo-Saxon period, who himself was a collector of coins and books. His remarks regarding the museum are telling: "My clearest memory of Skansen is of curators walking about in seventeenth-century peasant costumes. I hope we shall not make our people dress in smocks and in clothes tied up at the sagging patches with wisps of straw."[37] Thus he expressed certain distaste around re-enactment, which, it seems, did not correspond with the concept of the museum as a serious research organization.

The first keeper and the main driving force behind the museum, John Higgs, was a lecturer in farm mechanization.[38] Higgs had originally considered an open-air forma-tion, and all three locations of the museum have been situated next to green spaces, which have, at various times, been utilized for modest levels of engagement work and re-enactment. This is an ongoing issue, which the current curator of MERL collections, Dr. Ollie Douglas, is exploring through his own research and practice regarding con-temporary collecting, stakeholder engagement, and intangible heritage.[39] His research suggests that this focus on academic research and the reluctance on the part of early MERL curators to embrace an embodied approach to engaging with collections in an open-air setting may also suggest an anxiety around threats to academic and cura-torial professionalism, a wariness of romanticism and nostalgia, and a desire to create emotional distance. In reality such clean objectivity is never possible, but it offers an interesting lens through which to reflect upon our current professional practice.

---

36 Rivière, "Success and Failure."

37 Oliver Douglas, "'Tied up at the Sagging Patches with Wisps of Straw': Re-enactment, Reconstruction and Performance at the Museum of English Rural Life 1951–1956" (Reading: Museum of English Rural Life, no date).

38 Rivière, "Success and Failure."

39 Dr. Ollie Douglas, personal communication, 2018, and see later reference to projects.

Records show that early curators relied on amateur collectors to donate to the early MERL, and it is also worth reflecting upon how these collections might hold on to older, more emotional, practices of creation and care. The museum's first large acquisitions, made in the 1950s, were from Lavinia Smith and Harold Massingham. Lavinia Smith,[40] a key collector, was an American who moved to the UK to work as a teacher. She lived with her sister, Frances, in the village of East Hendred in Oxfordshire (formerly in Berkshire) until her death in 1944, aged 73. She collected objects from friends and neighbours in the local area, even rescuing some from the village dump. She displayed them in her home, mostly for children from local schools. Photographs show that she took some care with the display of objects and that she turned her house into a museum-like space. When she died, the collection was bequeathed to Berkshire Education Services and then transferred to the MERL. Research is ongoing into her collecting practices and her life story and is yet to be formally published.

We can gain an easier insight into the rationale behind Harold Massingham's collecting through his own writing. Massingham, a prolific journalist on rural affairs, noted that when he travelled around the UK in the 1920s and 1930s, he got into the habit of hunting down traditional craftspeople—"if one or another of them had succeeded in keeping his head above the rising economic waters"—to study their processes and their tools.[41] When cutting ivy in 1937, he fell over a concealed feeding trough and spent two years in hospital. His injury led to amputation. He states when writing about this incident that he was too ill to even note the beginning of the Second World War. When he came out of hospital, "as a form of compensation," he built a "hermitage" in his orchard based on an illustration by Gilbert White (another famous rural amateur). For each object he wrote "an obituary" and included among notes on the object's use a potted family genealogy of the craftsperson. A detailed sketch remains of the hermitage, which shows that it was designed as a kind of twentieth-century "cabinet of curiosities"; a microcosm for capturing a world which he argued he could no longer visit in person. In 1951 Massingham donated around 250 items to the MERL and died the following year.

Thus both collectors collected from a sense of needing to preserve what they saw as a disappearing way of life and a need to communicate with the wider world about this subject. It might be argued that Smith and Massingham collected most heavily during what might be classed as periods when their traditional professional role and activities had been curtailed. Smith and Massingham both also took pleasure in pleasing displays, just like TATHS collectors. Both died childless and their collections were subsequently donated, not to family but to the newly formed MERL. However, Smith and Massingham lived at a specific time when the countryside was changing rapidly and when rural museums were expanding their collections. For contemporary enthusiast collectors, this is not the case, and many are facing the fact that their collections will not survive intact or bear their name after their death.

---

40 Greta Bertram, "East Hendred and the Lavinia Smith Collection," https://blogs.reading.ac.uk/sense-of-place/east-hendred-and-the-lavinia-smith-collection/ [accessed July 5, 2019].

41 Harold J. Massingham, *Remembrance: An Autobiography* (Batsford: London, 1942).

Reviving Collections

The work of Dr. Ollie Douglas and others has sought to investigate the history of the MERL's sub-collections and to explore significance through original collecting context. I would argue that this historical approach is an underappreciated aspect of exploring enthusiasm in museums. However, my particular project also sought to revivify particular classes of objects for uninterested audiences. Talking with enthusiast groups gave me, as an educator working within a rural museum, a greater insight into the ways that I might communicate the significance of these collections with my students. The creation of a collection is an act of de-contextualization, to create a new group around a particular category that is deemed "meaningful" to the collector(s).[42] Tools are, by their very definition, "objects of use." So, what do they mean when they are removed from their original context and become valued for their associational and aesthetic meaning rather than for their ability to perform the task that they were designed for? How might contemporary curators revive these collections, and how might we might we engage the next generation of museum professionals with these challenges?

Fortunately, the museum had recently led a number of funded projects that provided inspiration for exploring these issues. For example, the museum's ambitious Heritage Lottery Fund project, "Our Country Lives,"[43] sought to engage with historic and contemporary communities and biographies in the development of new displays. Another area of activity for the revitalization of open storage has been around heritage crafts.[44] At the Museum of Anthropology at the University of British Columbia, an open storage policy for its "study collection" has been in place for many years[45] as a way of allowing indigenous craftspeople to gain skills from examples held by the museum. The MERL "Stakeholders" project attempted to address a disconnect between collections and people by bringing contemporary craftspeople behind the scenes into the strored collections.[46] This project was funded by the Radcliffe Trust, which funds rural heritage craft initiatives. In a session held in the museum's specially designed open stored and mezzanine study area, established and emerging basket weavers worked together to learn from historic collections. The makers then created items inspired by the collections, which themselves were then accessioned.

---

42 Sharon Macdonald, "Collecting Practices," in *A Companion to Museum Studies*, ed. Sharon Macdonald (London: Wiley-Blackwell, 2007), 81–97.

43 The Heritage Lottery Fund project "Our Country Lives" (2014–2017) included both a redisplay and an activity programme engaging with new and traditional communities. The Museum of Rural Life, "Our Country Lives," https://merl.reading.ac.uk/news-and-views/tag/our-country-lives/ [accessed July 5, 2019].

44 David Viner, *Rural Crafts and Trades Today: An Assessment of Preservation and Presentation in Museums and Archives* (Reading: Museum of English Rural Life, 2007).

45 Michael A. Ames, *Cannibal Tours and Glass Boxes: The Anthropology of Museums* (Vancouver: UBC, 1992).

46 University of Reading, "The Museum of Rural Life: Stakeholders," www.reading.ac.uk/merl/research/merl-stakeholders.aspx [accessed July 5, 2019].

A further project with the Designation Challenge Fund, called "The Museum of the Intangible," sought to explore the potential for the MERL to engage with contemporary debates regarding intangible cultural heritage through holding workshops with a range of practitioners, creatives, policymakers, and academics and through commissioning specific works that seek to record, capture, or evoke aspects of intangible rural culture.[47] The work of Massingham as an author and collector was used as the inspiration for one of these workshops. The ongoing impact of this project will ensure that the museum's connections with heritage crafts and other aspects of intangible cultural heritage will continue. This also highlights the benefits of being a university museum, where the MERL can draw on different kinds of expertise and funding to create a forum for experimenting with methods, theories, and practices.

These projects all included some key features: intergenerational learning, workshops based in the stored collections, and engagement with creative practice. This issue of the transmission of specialist knowledge is no small thing. As curatorial expertise is lost, the task of igniting enthusiasm in nonspecialists becomes more difficult. In the UK, Subject Specialist Networks (SSNs) and initiatives such as Monument Fellowships[48] have been striving to "download" specialist knowledge from the minds of professionals and compile resources that can be utilized by a wider network of museum professionals. For example, at the "Who Cares?" conference, a team from the Social History Curators Group discussed their recent series of tool identification films, "Tools of the Trade," which was funded by Arts Council England and loaded onto YouTube and their firstBASE website.[49] By getting experts to demonstrate the uses of historic tools as part of a craft process, they were able to recontextualize individual objects. TATHS was involved in this process, as were other enthusiast groups and collections.

The MERL has also worked with enthusiast groups such as TATHS and the Road Locomotive Society in order to harness some of this expertise. The Road Locomotive Society was involved in a project working with technical drawings in the MERL archive several years ago.[50] One of my museum studies students volunteered with the group

---

47 The Designation Challenge Fund uses Arts Council England funding to enhance collections which have been formally "Designated" as of national or international significance. "The Museum of the Intangible" project is reaching its final phase at the time of going to print: https://merl.reading. ac.uk/merl-collections/research-projects/making-using-enjoying/ [accessed July 5, 2019].

48 Subject Specialist Networks are networks of people with experience and knowledge of a particular collections-based subject specialism. Members are drawn from relevant membership bodies or from across different groupings of museums. Monument Fellowships are fellowships offered by the Museums Association, UK, to allow retiring members of staff to run workshops and create resources in order to allow their skills and knowledge to be passed on. At the MERL, Jonathan Bell (cited in this chapter) worked on the technical drawings of agricultural machinery firms such as Ransomes, Simms, and Jeffries. Alongside staff and volunteers, the enthusiast group the Road Locomotive Society engaged in this project.

49 See the Social History Curators Group YouTube channel: www.youtube.com/channel/UCK7Q9bUM6i-fPKuS-20B5MA.

50 The £50,000 Heritage Lottery Fund "Heavy Metal" project ran in 2007–2008. University of Reading, "Heavy Metal," www.reading.ac.uk/merl/research/merl-heavymetalproject.aspx [accessed July 5, 2019].

for many hours and was by far the youngest person in the room. She was drawn in part to the project by a family enthusiasm for these materials and also from a desire to gain museum and archive experience. She was much more recently working at Blythe House[51] for the Science Museum, where she was able to apply these skills as a professional. Thus this potential for different generations of amateur and professional to work together suggests a possible model for future engagement.

Creating Spaces for Sharing "Enthusiasm"

Inspired by the work of SSNs and the MERL's wider engagement with creative practitioners, I aimed to stage a small intervention around intergenerational enthusiasm for agricultural hand tools. In my role at the museum, I facilitate student and research engagement with collections. I find that it is difficult for students to connect positively with rural objects, with one student who loved classical art stating quite firmly, "you show me these things and I want to cry." This intervention sought to engage with students as early career museum professionals at the University of Reading. This was approached through a three-stage "intervention":

- an expertise workshop on object identification held in the MERL storage areas with curator Chris Green
- a creative thinking workshop identifying ways to translate this information into an engaging intervention at the Science Museum, London, with social media and "Teens in Museums" expert Mar Dixon, creative writing expert Rebecca Reynolds, and maker Julie Roberts
- a pilot engagement with the wider "Who Cares?" project team, in collaboration with Mar, Julie, and Rebecca at a Science Museum "Late".

At the expertise workshop, participants learnt from the experiences of the MERL Fellow Chris Green, a former curator at St. Albans Museum, where he had worked extensively with the one of the collections formed by the famous (in tool enthusiast circles) collector R. A. Salaman.[52] Chris also has strong connections with many major tool collections, such as that amassed by another famous tool collector, Ken Hawley, at Kelham Island, Sheffield.[53] During his role as curator at St. Albans Museum, Chris had been responsible for the Salaman collection of hand tools, which had long been displayed in a diorama reconstruction of a workshop. It has now been removed from display at St. Albans, but Chris remains an advocate for the value of hand tool collections in a contemporary collecting and display context.

---

51 This is the storage space for the Science Museum, the V&A and the British Museum that is referred to in Hess's chapter and in the Introduction to this volume. It is currently being emptied and stored items are being relocated.

52 Green, "Salaman, Raphael Arthur (1906–1993)."

53 Simon Barley, "Ken Hawley Obituary," *The Guardian*, August 19, 2014: online. www.theguardian. com/culture/2014/aug/19/ken-hawley [accessed July 5, 2019].

In the workshop within the museum's storage areas, Chris gave the attendees guidelines for identifying and interpreting agricultural hand tools. As a MERL Fellow, Chris was attempting to share his knowledge formally through creating the *Historical Dictionary of Hand Tools, Devices and Equipment for General Agricultural Work*. The fact that no such catalogue already existed demonstrated the complexity of the task, the relative lack of interest from enthusiasts and curators in these objects, and the relative de-prioritization of classificatory methods for researching and publishing on such collections. For students in attendance, the session proved extremely useful, with one feeding this discussion into a third-year exhibition on rural communities. This student is now also working as a museum professional on the project to move collections belonging to some of the National Museums out of their central London facility, Blythe House.[54]

Following this session, we held a creative thinking workshop at the MERL, in which we worked with early career museum professionals to interpret historic hand tools for a wider audience. This was to be put into action at a Science Museum "Late" on the subject of "Craving" (see also Woodham and Kelleher, this volume). With the workshop participants, we discussed Chris's guidance and identified some key messages that we thought would appeal to attendees at the event. I had really been drawn towards the idea of "hard graft" and "human stories" in conversations with Chris and the enthusiasts and was able to suggest this to students as a "way in" to unfamiliar objects. Hence the group decided that a key message would be emphasizing what it means to be created and powered by human hand. The very materiality of hand tools holds evidence of a relationship with the human body. In scale and ergonomics, they are designed to fit around the human body and enhance its ability to perform certain tasks. In this way, they hark back to the very earliest stone tools used to cut, break, and butcher. They also bear witness to the crafting of the initial construction and years of human intervention, with worn-down handles, symbols of individual ownership burned or carved into them, and evidence of reuse and recycling. We even looked up the calorific outputs for specific tasks undertaken with hand tools in comparison with contemporary exercise regimes. Online advice about using free weights suggested that the sheer act of lifting, let alone wielding and moving these objects, could build muscle and burn calories.

Another element that came out when viewing the TATHS museum at Amberley and attending the "slag workshop" (Woodham and Kelleher, this volume) was that "unloved objects" could be beautiful. The most collected items, according to TATHS newsletters and discussions with contemporary collectors, are woodworking tools. These are often made of high-quality wood with brass fittings and are, in their own right, aesthetically pleasing. Hence I was able to encourage students to engage the public with the crafting, materials, and aesthetic qualities of the objects by designing creative tasks around these objects. A creative writing expert (Rebecca Reynolds) and textile- and paper-maker (Julie Roberts) were employed by the project to help with the "interventions" identified in the project's name.

---

54 For further discussions on the move from Blythe House, see the Introduction to this volume and the chapter by Alison Hess.

In researching enthusiasm for hand tools, I had become aware of the strength of online communities for enthusiasts; for example, the TATHS Facebook page represents a lively digital "space" in which dispersed communities might "meet." As part of the project, Mar Dixon was brought in for her skills as a social media consultant who has worked with young people, to create a "Teens in Museums" manifesto. During the workshop, the group came up with the idea of experimenting with Twitter accounts and hashtags and playing with the idea of boredom. Active pride and engagement with things which other people see as boring is a part of contemporary "nerd culture" and can be seen through the success of initiatives such as "The Boring Conference" or the MERL's 2018 viral Twitter campaign around photographs of historic livestock.[55] It was decided that each student would approach members of the public and ask them to pick a card from a deck and then "bore them" with facts. The members of the public could then vote in pen on the back of the students' t-shirts for the most boring of the three case study collections outlined in the "Who Cares?" project.

Finally, we drew on the desire to touch and to craft/create, which seemed to represent key practices of care for so many enthusiasts. Members of the public were given access to a handling table where they could examine objects in detail. They were also asked to donate real items or concepts of things to a small art installation called "The Museum of Unloved Things" and contribute poems about objects on display. This was a playful and engaging approach, with the emphasis shifted from more traditional approaches to transmitting information. On the night, our table was packed, and we left with a variety of contributions from engaged visitors. This section ends with just one of those encounters.

For the tool collection, one of the most moving episodes during the "Late" was the British Sign Language (BSL) tour facilitated by a BSL translator. Like other visitors that night, the group were fascinated by our accounts of these objects. One of the members of the BSL tour returned later, using his phone to show us videos of his own work in 3D printing. This twist on the transmission of subject-specific knowledge and the use of a technology that captured process was for me particularly enlightening. Hence, by creating these spaces where different kinds of expertise could come together, we were able to explore new ways of working for both our own practice and for future generations of museum professionals.

Conclusion

As with the other chapters in this book, the purpose here has been to use contemporary research into "enthusiasm" and "care" as a lens through which to explore the kinds of collections, collecting, and collectors that are rarely the subject of detailed museological study. In this chapter, a historical approach has been combined with elements of contemporary ethnography and professional practice in order to explore

---

55 *The Times*, April 13, 2018, www.thetimes.co.uk/article/big-thinking-museum-of-english-rural-life-finds-the-secret-of-success-is-a-huge-exmoor-horn-sheep-6tvrml6sr [accessed July 5, 2019]. See also Carnall, this volume, on uses of social media around concepts of "boring."

different ways that we might imagine the care of "unloved" collections. From a personal perspective, this project allowed me to reflect upon my practice as somebody engaged in heritage interpretation and educating the museum professionals of tomorrow. I realized that, as a museum professional with expertise in education, interpretation, and communities of interest, I had sometimes unconsciously looked down upon objects that seemed to have been collected with little or no thought towards their eventual use. This project allowed me to re-engage with more specialized forms of knowledge and to appreciate the power of intergenerational conversations in drawing out meaning and building emotional engagement. In the future, I want to give my students more opportunities to explore, discuss, and "play" with collections. The visits and the infectious enthusiasm of TATHS and TFSR were key to this. Hence it might be that only through re-engaging with our own sense of "object-love" can we engage others with collections.

There were two other areas of investigation outlined at the beginning of this chapter that are worthy of further brief discussion. The first was around understanding the place of collecting and curating in the lives of "Third Age" communities. Talking with enthusiast experts provided an invaluable insight into the life histories and practices of care that gave these objects significance for these individuals. It also highlighted the need for greater understanding of emotion among this demographic group. During the course of this project I was struck by the growth in the UK of "shed" groups, where retired men work together on shared craft projects for therapeutic outcomes and with a specific focus on suicide prevention.[56] This is beyond the subject of this paper, but it suggests that research into enthusiasm for historic objects might provide a valuable route into understanding the place of crafting and collecting in the emotional health of an ageing population.

Secondly, I asked how we might understand contemporary and historical museum practices through the lens of "enthusiasm." This research brought home to me the extent of both the expertise and the knowledge that lies within "amateur" groups and the need to put this activity into a historical context. Refocusing our historical lens from star pieces in public galleries towards less high-profile objects is a useful exercise that a truly critical approach to heritage should embrace. Taking a historical perspective helps us to understand the shifting value judgements that have shaped the biographies of these objects and to uncover silenced stories which might allow us to interpret these objects in new ways. As amateur collections come into larger institutions their significance changes and there may be clues to reviving them in their deeper histories. This long view approach also forces us to reflect upon our own professional practices and to ask hard questions about why we have these objects and what we might be doing to silence them or bring them to life.

With respect to practices of care within museums, work with enthusiasts emphasized the importance of active physical practices of care in emotional engagement with these collections. Creative and tactile engagement also seemed to be a key element in sparking

---

56 The Men's Sheds Association, https://menssheds.org.uk/latest-news/ [accessed July 5, 2019].

an interest when transferred to students and visitors at the "Late." Hence we may need to challenge traditional "hands-off" approaches to collections management and engage with our sense of play in order to engage new audiences for these collections. Other chapters in this book (Hess, and Woodham and Kelleher) have suggested that enthusiasm might also be harnessed through collections knowledge development and through engaging the public. This chapter suggests that these activities might be connected in the training of the next generation of museum professionals as a way of breaking down professional barriers around practices of care.

Finally, talking with enthusiasts emphasized the urgent need for intergenerational collaboration and highlighted the threat to the passing on of collections knowledge. Chris Green told me in an interview at the beginning of the project that, in order to gain knowledge, you "just have to see a lot of things." The collectors and enthusiasts discussed in this chapter expressed respect for experience built up over a lifetime and have attempted to preserve and celebrate this. They argued that the object itself is not enough and that the passing on of knowledge is also important. However, the context in which they gained this experience has gone and knowledge-holders themselves are dying out. Our interventions, as part of this project and the wider work of the MERL, attempted to bring together different generations. In this way we have tried to make enthusiasm "infectious" and to share knowledge acquired over decades. It remains to be seen how enthusiast communities engage the next generation and whether museums could play some collaborative role in this process.

Bibliography

Ames, Michael A. *Cannibal Tours and Glass Boxes: The Anthropology of Museums.* Vancouver: UBC, 1992.

Barley, Simon. "Ken Hawley Obituary." *The Guardian,* August 19, 2014, online. www.theguardian.com/culture/2014/aug/19/ken-hawley [accessed July 5, 2019].

Bell, Jonathan. "Making Rural Histories." In *Making Histories in Museums,* ed. Gaynor Kavanagh, 30–41. London: Leicester University Press, 2005.

Bertram, Greta. "East Hendred and the Lavinia Smith Collection." https://blogs.reading.ac.uk/sense-of-place/east-hendred-and-the-lavinia-smith-collection/ [accessed July 5, 2019].

Brigden, Roy. "Research—Social History." In *Manual of Curatorship: A Guide to Museum Practice,* 2nd ed., edited by John M. A. Thompson, 547–53. London: Routledge, 2015.

Craggs, Ruth, Hilary Geoghegan, and Hannah Neate. "Architectural Enthusiasm: Visiting Buildings with the Twentieth Century Society." *Environment and Planning D: Society and Space* 31, no. 5 (2013): 879–96.

DeLyser, Dydia, and Paul Greenstein. "The Devotions of Restoration: Materiality, Enthusiasm, and Making Three 'Indian Motorcycles' Like New." *Annals of the American Association of Geographers* 107 (2017): 1461–78.

——. " 'Follow That Car!' Mobilities of Enthusiasm in a Rare Car's Restoration." *The Professional Geographer* 67 (2014): 255–68.

Douglas, Oliver. "Folklore, Survivals, and the Neo-archaic: The Materialist Character of Late Nineteenth-Century Homeland Ethnography." *Museum History Journal* 4, no. 2 (2011): 223–24.

———. "'Tied up at the Sagging Patches with Wisps of Straw': Re-enactment, Reconstruction and Performance at the Museum of English Rural Life 1951–1956." Reading: Museum of English Rural Life, no date.

Edgerton, David. *The Shock of the Old: Technology and Global History since 1900.* London: Profile, 2008.

Everett, Glyn, and Hilary Geoghegan. "Initiating and Continuing Participation in Citizen Science for Natural History." *BMC Ecology* 16, supplement 1 (2016): online.

Geoghegan, Hilary. "Emotional Geographies of Enthusiasm: Belonging to the Telecommunications Heritage Group." *Area* 45, no. 1 (2013): 40–46.

———. "'If You Can Walk down the Street and Recognise the Difference between Cast Iron and Wrought Iron, the World is Altogether a Better Place': Being Enthusiastic about Industrial Archaeology." *M/C Journal: A Journal of Media and Culture* 12, no. 2 (2009): unpaginated.

Geoghegan, Hilary, Alison Dyke, Rachel Pateman, Sarah West, and Glyn Everett. *Understanding Motivations for Citizen Science: Final Report on Behalf of UKEOF.* University of Reading, Stockholm Environment Institute, University of York, and University of the West of England, 2016.

Geoghegan, Hilary, and Alison Hess. "Object-Love at the Science Museum: Cultural Geographies of Museum Storerooms." *Cultural Geographies* 22, no. 3 (2014): 445–65.

Green, Chris. "Salaman, Raphael Arthur (1906–1993)." In *Oxford Dictionary of National Biography.* Oxford: Oxford University Press, 2004.

Haggard, Lois M., and Daniel R. Williams. "Identity Affirmation through Leisure Activities: Leisure Symbols of the Self." *Journal of Leisure Research* 24, no. 1 (1990): 1–18.

Howkins, Alun. *The Death of Rural England: A Social History of the Countryside since 1900.* London: Routledge, 2003.

Hughes, Daniel. *Building the Bonds of Attachment: Awakening Love in Deeply Troubled Children,* 2nd ed. London: Rowman & Littlefield, 2018.

Kavanagh, Gaynor. "Mangles, Muck and Myths: Rural History Museums in Britain." *Rural History* 1, no. 2 (1991): 187–204.

Kelly, John. *Leisure Identities and Interactions.* London: George Allen & Unwin, 1983.

Macdonald, Sharon. "Collecting Practices." In *A Companion to Museum Studies,* edited by Sharon Macdonald, 81–97. London: Wiley-Blackwell, 2007.

Mansvelt, Juliana. "Working at Leisure: Critical Geographies of Ageing." *Area* 29, no. 4 (1997): 289–98. Published online, 2005.

Mason, Rhiannon. *Museums, Nations, Identities: Wales and Its National Museums.* Cardiff: University of Wales Press, 2007.

Massingham, Harold J. *Remembrance: An Autobiography.* Batsford: London, 1942.

Rees, Jane. *The Rule Book: Measuring for the Trades.* Mendham: Astragal, 2010.

Rentzhog, Sten. *Open Air Museums: The History and Future of a Visionary Idea.* Östersund: Jamtli, 2007.

Rivière, Peter. "Success and Failure: The Tale of Two Museums." *Journal of the History of Collections* 22, no. 1 (2010): 141–51.

Sekules, Victoria. *Cultures of the Countryside: Art, Museum, Heritage and Environment 1920–2015.* Abingdon: Routledge, 2018.

TBR, Department for Business Innovation and Skills. *Mapping Heritage Craft: The Economic Contribution of the Heritage Craft Sector in England,* 6 [Executive Summary, Definition]. London: Creative and Cultural Skills, 2012.

Tools and Trades History Society. *TATHS Journal* 4 (1984): 36.

Viner, David. *Rural Crafts and Trades Today: An Assessment of Preservation and Presentation in Museums and Archives*. Reading: Museum of English Rural Life, 2007.

Yarwood, Richard, and Nick Evans. "A Lleyn Sweep for Local Sheep? Breed Societies and the Geographies of Welsh Livestock." *Environment and Planning A* 38, no. 7 (2006): 1307–26.

Chapter 3

WHAT'S IN A NAME?
THE ETHICS OF CARE AND
AN "UNLOVED" COLLECTION

ANNA WOODHAM* AND SHANE KELLEHER†

Introduction

> I think the greatest challenge is getting the National Slag Collection ... used [...] if by the time I die, nobody still uses it, then I do wonder, well, what was the point? That would be my deepest regret.[1]

Not all museum objects are created equally, and we live in a world where judgements about the value of a museum object can be made in a split second, often grounded in how it looks.[2] Some museum objects will become iconic star items and others will not,

---

[1] "Who Cares?" research participant no. 1. Interviewed by Anna Woodham, July 10, 2015. Participant names have been replaced by numbers throughout in order to maintain anonymity.

[2] Francesca Monti and Suzanne Keene, *Museums and Silent Objects: Designing Effective Exhibitions* (Abingdon: Routledge, 2016).

---

* **Anna Woodham** is a lecturer in Arts and Cultural Management in the Department of Culture, Media, and Creative Industries at King's College London. Her research focuses on exploring the role of museums and heritage in a changing world. Anna comes from a policy and museum practice background and previously worked at the Department for Culture, Media and Sport (DCMS), which co-funded her PhD research on social inclusion and the geography of school visits to museums. This research looked at the social impact of taking school children from some of the most deprived areas of England to museums and considered the importance of recognizing museums' geographic reach and spatial relationship to audiences. Prior to starting her PhD, Anna worked in the museum sector, including posts at the Fitzwilliam Museum in Cambridge and the British Dental Association Museum among others.

† **Shane Kelleher** has been the Staffordshire County Archaeologist since January 2018, having moved there from the Ironbridge Gorge Museum Trust, where his most recent role was as the Historic England–funded Industrial Heritage Support Officer for England. During the period of research discussed in this volume, Shane was the Museum Archaeologist/Archaeology and Monuments Officer at the Ironbridge Gorge Museum Trust. This role saw him lead on archaeological matters for the museum, including advising on the management, interpretation, and conservation of the historic buildings and monuments in the museum's care; curating the museum's archaeological collections, including the National Slag Collection; and running Ironbridge Archaeology, the museum's archaeology unit. Shane previously worked as a project manager and historic buildings specialist at the University of Birmingham. He is also a specialist lecturer at Birmingham School of Architecture and Design, Birmingham City University, on aspects of conserving the historic environment, and he is an Honorary Research Associate at the Department of Classics, Ancient History and Archaeology at the University of Birmingham.

Figure 3.1. The National Slag Collection. Photograph by Anna Woodham.

regardless of what value and significance they have or represent. This is certainly true of the National Slag Collection (NSC), which forms the focus of this chapter. The NSC is a stored research collection of hundreds of specimens of industrial slag that contributes to our understanding of historic metalworking processes from the Iron Age to the modern day. The collection is owned by the Ironbridge Gorge Museum Trust (IGMT), based at the Ironbridge Gorge World Heritage Site (Shropshire, UK) and co-managed by the Historical Metallurgy Society (HMS), a model of shared collections management that we will return to later in this chapter.

The NSC's public image is compounded by a variety of factors. Slag is a waste product from the smelting of metal ore. It consists of chemical deposits from a process that helped to shape the modern world and is often found spread across postindustrial landscapes. Slag is hard to categorize. It sits in between the human and the natural. It is human made but not human fashioned, a product of chemistry and experimentation rather than worked on and "crafted," as some of the other collections mentioned in this volume are. Formed as part of an industrial process, slag is hard for many to relate to, and people possibly also find it hard to understand its value. As a stored collection (see figures 3.1 and 3.2), the NSC is unlikely to rank highly on the list of "must-see" objects in any behind-the-scenes tour (unless it is for its novelty value). However, we argue that this collection offers a valuable case study specifically because of these ambiguities,

Figure 3.2. Rehousing the National Slag Collection. Photograph by Anna Woodham.

allowing us to consider the implications for the management of this "waste product" and other similar collections.

As the title of this chapter suggests, slag also suffers from the less than salubrious connotations of the word, in English at least, inducing sniggers in many, but also creating genuine issues for family-friendly museum interpretation. As a core audience,[3] museums have a responsibility to consider the most appropriate ways of communicating with family groups. Exhibiting slag is, of course, possible, but it may require some additional thought. The negative light that slag is seen in is further intensified by its association with the Aberfan disaster of 1966.[4] The disaster was caused by the collapse of a colliery spoil tip rather than a slagheap as was erroneously reported.[5] Indeed, the undesirable and unwarranted reputation of the name "slag" led to a failed proposal at the Seventh

---

3 See Graham Black, *Transforming Museums in the Twenty-First Century* (Abingdon: Routledge, 2011).

4 The Aberfan Disaster on October 21, 1966 was a result of a landslide caused by a collapsed spoil tip. The landslide destroyed much of Pantglas Junior School and other buildings in the village, and 116 children and twenty-eight adults lost their lives. See Tony Austin, *The Story of a Disaster* (London: Hutchinson, 1967).

5 See, for example, contemporary reporting in *The Guardian*, "Disaster at Aberfan," October 22, 1966, www.theguardian.com/theguardian/1966/oct/22/fromthearchive [accessed July 9, 2018].

Global Slag Conference in Helsinki to change the name to something with fewer negative connotations.[6]

Despite these problems, slag is an interesting and often beautiful material that can tell us a great deal about the process of historic industry, in particular the smelting of metals such as iron, copper, lead, and tin. For one of the authors of this chapter, it has been an area of research interest throughout much of their archaeological career. The potential for slagheaps to improve their public image is also being investigated by researchers exploring how to capture atmospheric carbon dioxide,[7] perhaps offering the potential for slag to positively reframe its association with polluting industrial processes.

In this chapter, we consider what it means to love and care for the NSC.[8] After introducing the IGMT context and discussing our theoretical understanding of "care," which is, in particular, informed by political scientist Joan Tronto's theories of care, we consider who the enthusiasts are that co-manage the NSC and what characterizes the particular form of care that they give. Finally, we ask whether it is possible for their enthusiasm to be transferred or shared between those who "care" and those who seemingly do not. We conclude by considering what a project like this could this mean for museums with similar collections. Are there lessons to be learnt from the co-management model used at the IGMT that can encourage museums to look again at the latent potential of the perceivably "unloved" collections in their care? Using semi-structured interviews with members of the HMS, observations of a joint workshop between the HMS and the Ironbridge Young Archaeologists' Club (IYAC), and finally observations made at a Science Museum London "Late" event,[9] we consider the emotional affiliations between these objects and people.[10]

The IGMT, Industrial Archaeology and the National Slag Collection

Industrial archaeology is a subject that has been forged by enthusiasm and nonprofessional engagement.[11] In the UK, a post–Second World War modernization and building

---

6 See Global Cement, "The Trouble with 'Slag,'" www.globalcement.com/magazine/articles/634-the-trouble-with-slag [accessed July 9, 2018].

7 Robin McKie, "Can Slag Heaps Help Save the Planet?" *The Guardian*, April 23, 2017, www.theguardian.com/science/2017/apr/23/can-slag-heaps-help-save-the-planet-carbon-dioxide-capture-climate-change [accessed July 9, 2018]. Please note that, as mentioned above, slagheaps and spoil tips as terms are often used interchangeably but are not the same.

8 This research was conducted as part of the AHRC-funded project "Who Cares? Interventions in 'Unloved' Museum Collections."

9 Science Museum "Late" is the name given to the monthly after-hours evening events held at the museum. See www.sciencemuseum.org.uk/visitmuseum/plan_your_visit/lates [accessed July 6, 2018].

10 Hilary Geoghegan and Alison Hess, "Object-Love at the Science Museum: Cultural Geographies of Museum Storerooms," *Cultural Geographies* 22, no. 3 (2015): 445–65.

11 See Hilary Geoghegan, "'If You Can Walk down the Street and Recognise the Difference between Cast Iron and Wrought Iron, the World is Altogether a Better Place': Being Enthusiastic about Industrial Archaeology," *M/C Journal: A Journal of Media and Culture* 12, no. 2 (2009): unpaginated; Kenneth Hudson, *World Industrial Archaeology* (Cambridge: Cambridge University Press, 1979);

boom was accompanied by a corresponding desire to preserve the abandoned ruins of Britain's industrial past.[12] The IGMT itself partially owes its existence to grass roots interest in the preservation of industrial heritage[13] and is seen as one of the primary incubation spaces for industrial archaeology in the UK.[14]

At the IGMT, a strong relationship has always existed between enthusiasts and heritage professionals, and it has been at the forefront of research into and the teaching of industrial archaeology.[15] The IGMT has a long-running partnership with the University of Birmingham,[16] meaning that it has been able to contribute to postgraduate and other programmes in industrial archaeology and heritage management. Reinforcing its connection to volunteer-led action, the IGMT has also recently set up a new Ironbridge Archaeology Volunteer Group,[17] which has been involved in a number of recording, conservation, and monitoring projects in and around the Ironbridge Gorge World Heritage Site.

When it comes to industrial heritage, Ironbridge Gorge has pedigree. The area, which is now often referred to as the "Birthplace of Industry," became a conservation area in 1971, four years after the founding of the Ironbridge Gorge Museum Trust. It was declared a World Heritage Site in 1986.[18] The first International Congress on the Conservation of Industrial Heritage (TICCIH) was held at the site in 1973.[19] The IGMT was founded to preserve and interpret the remains of the Industrial Revolution in the six square miles of Ironbridge Gorge. It is an independent educational charity that encourages visitors to be involved in and support its conservation work through admission charges, trading, and associated commercial activities. The IGMT manages

---

Marilyn Palmer, "Industrial Archaeology: A Thematic or Period Discipline," *Antiquity* 64, no. 243 (1990): 275–82; Marilyn Palmer and Peter Neaverson, *Industrial Archaeology: Principles and Practice* (London: Routledge, 1998).

12 Angus Buchanon, "The Origins and Early Days of the AIA," *Industrial Archaeology News* 169 (2014): 2–4.

13 Cossons notes that the saving of Abraham Darby's "Old Furnace," Coalbrookdale, Shropshire, in 1959 had "repercussions that have resonated across the intervening half century" in that they "influenced directly and indirectly, the setting up of the Ironbridge Gorge Museum … created an understanding that the formative years of what has been called the Industrial Revolution marked an important moment in global history," xiii. Neil Cossons, "Foreword," in *Footprints of Industry: Papers from the 300th Anniversary Conference at Coalbrookdale*, ed. Paul Belford, Marilyn Palmer, and Roger White (Oxford: BAR British Series 523, 2010), xiii–xiv.

14 Catherine Beale, *The Ironbridge Spirit: A History of the Ironbridge Gorge Museum Trust* (Ceredigion: Ironbridge Gorge Museum Trust, 2014).

15 Shane Kelleher, "From 'The Most Extraordinary District in the World' to 'Not All the World but a Very Poor Bit of the Fag End of It': Archaeology at the Ironbridge Gorge World Heritage Site," *Museum Archaeologist* (forthcoming).

16 Beale, *The Ironbridge Spirit*.

17 See Shane Kelleher, "Industrial Archaeology at the IGMT: Past, Present and Future," *Broseley Local History Society Journal* 32 (2013): 18–32.

18 Catherine Clark, *Ironbridge Gorge* (London: English Heritage and Batsford, 1993).

19 See The International Committee for the Conservation of Industrial Heritage (TICCIH), "Homepage," http://ticcih.org/ [accessed July 6, 2018].

thirty-five historic sites (including five scheduled ancient monuments) within the world heritage site of Ironbridge Gorge, ten of which are museums. Across these museum sites, the IGMT also houses a large collection relating to the industrial past. The collection includes aspects that have been designated of national and international significance, including, among other collections, the archives and memorabilia of the Darby Family and the Coalbrookdale Company; the Elton Collection of prints, drawings, books, and ephemera; and the George Maw Geological and Mineral Collection, comprising specimens from all over the world. As with all museum collections, only a small percentage of the collection is on public display and there are, of course, some areas of the collection the significance of which is harder to communicate to a general audience than others. This includes the NSC. As mentioned above, the NSC is co-managed by the HMS, one of several special interest groups that have archives/collections deposited at the museum and which regularly use the museum space.[20] This relationship means that the IGMT can benefit from the expertise, knowledge, and time provided by the HMS members, particularly the members of the HMS Archives and Collections Committee, while the collection is stored safely at the IGMT. The management of the collections, which includes provisions for public access, and the control of new acquisitions are covered by a memorandum of agreement between the HMS and the IGMT, and a member of museum staff is always a member of the HMS Archives and Collections Committee.

Founded originally as the National Metallurgy Group in 1963, the HMS focuses on the conservation and research of the history of metals and associated materials and is an international forum for the promotion of understanding and research in historical metallurgy. It has in the region of 500 members globally. The HMS Archives and Collections Committee has responsibility for managing two key groups of material, the NSC and the Tylecote Slag Collection (TSC), formed from the collection of archaeometallurgist Ronald F. Tylecote.[21] Both collections are stored by the IGMT, but whereas the NSC is an "open collection" wholly owned by the IGMT but managed jointly with the HMS,[22] the TSC is a "closed collection" owned and managed by the HMS.[23] The NSC originated from the private collections of several members of the HMS or was collected during the field visits that took place during HMS conferences. Substantial quantities of material were also deposited in the late 1970s and early 1980s by Leo Biek of the Ancient Monuments Laboratory, part of the then Department of the Environment's Directorate of Ancient Monuments and Historic Buildings (now Historic England).[24] The NSC is arguably not just a record of historic slag specimens but also a biographical collection, telling the story of the Society and its past and present members. The slag specimens cannot be

---

20 Kelleher, "Industrial Archaeology at the IGMT."

21 See University of Oxford, "HMS Metallographic Collections Catalogue," http://tylecote.arch. ox.ac.uk/ [accessed July 11, 2018].

22 A collection which may be added to.

23 A collection which can no longer be added to.

24 Historic England is the public body responsible for protecting the historic environment of England and is funded by the UK Government Department for Digital, Culture, Media and Sport (DCMS). See Historic England, "Homepage," https://historicengland.org.uk [accessed July 12, 2018].

separated from their paper archive and other supporting collections of, for example, books, papers, and glass negatives; one part of the collection helps to give meaning to the other. This may seem like an irrelevant detail, but, as we shall see later in this chapter, it is these human stories that help give slag a greater relevance for nonexperts.

As an example of the co-management activity in action, the HMS has already undertaken a programme of cataloguing and repackaging the NSC specimens in the collection in accordance with modern archiving standards. Following this work, a simple PDF catalogue of the NSC was produced and can be downloaded from the HMS website.[25] The completion of this project has largely been achieved through the volunteer time of members of the HMS Archives and Collections Committee and regular "Slag Study Days," coordinated and run by the HMS, held at the IGMT and open to members and other interested participants. During past Slag Study Days, participants, not all of whom are experts in historic metallurgy, have helped with the reboxing of the NSC and collections and archives documentation, overseen by HMS Committee members. By improving the documentation and storage of the collection, it will then be easier to appreciate what it comprises and its significance. The IGMT is highly supportive of this work, as it understands that this is a project that the museum would have limited resources and capacity to achieve by itself. The co-management of collections is an idea that we will now go on to consider in more conceptual detail.

Defining Care in the Museum

Museum collections are rarely approached in relation to the spaces, systems, and individuals who care for them, and the form of care found, predominantly behind the scenes, in the museum remains underexplored.[26] Before returning to the focus of this chapter—the NSC—this section asks what an "ethics of care" may look like in the museum space, drawing particularly on the work of political scientist Joan Tronto and others.[27]

According to Tronto, care can be defined very broadly as "a species activity that includes everything we do to maintain, continue, and repair our world so that we may live in it as well as possible."[28] This includes care of our bodies, ourselves, and our environment, which, we argue, includes the material objects that contribute to our understanding of the world. It may feel as though caring is a neutral act, but it is a complex process involving the identification, understanding, interpretation, and meeting of particular care needs. Although it may not be immediately obvious, caring is, in some senses, a political process relating to unequal access to power. It concerns decisions

---

25 See The Historical Metallurgy Society, "National Slag Collection Catalogue," http://hist-met.org/images/pdf/nsc2.pdf [accessed April 2, 2018].

26 As explored in Geoghegan and Hess, "Object-Love at the Science Museum."

27 Joan C. Tronto, *Who Cares? How to Reshape a Democratic Politics* (Ithaca: Cornell University Press, 2015); Joan C. Tronto, *Caring Democracy: Markets, Equality and Justice* (New York: New York University Press, 2013).

28 Tronto, *Who Cares?*, 3.

about "who does what"[29] to whom and, therefore, whose understanding of the world is prioritized.

An essential aspect of an ethics of care is to recognize that "all human beings need and receive care and give care to others … It is as important to realize that we are receivers as givers of care, acted upon as well as agents."[30] Receiving as well as giving care is a potentially difficult realization, particularly in relation to maintaining the balance of power by individuals, groups, and organizations that may not see themselves as either requiring or, indeed, giving care. However, this two-way process is arguably an important part of how "care" functions both in and outside of the museum context.

It is reasonable to consider a museum as an organization we would associate with care. Museums "take care" of the objects in their ownership, preserving collections on behalf of their public(s). The responsibility to care for collections appears in various definitions of "museum," for example, the UK Museums Association, which considers museums as institutions that "safeguard" and "hold in trust" their collections.[31] The requirement for boards of trustees to "care for" the objects in their collections can also be found in national legislation for certain museums.[32] This is indicative of the prominent association of care and caring with the responsibilities and organizational requirements of a museum. Interestingly, "care" in the context of the sources mentioned above is associated more with the contents of the museum rather than the people who use, visit, and work in these organizations, a point that we will return to below.

"Care" is also traditionally given to museum objects by those who are authorized to do so, such as conservators, curators, collections managers, and experts who have reached a certain level of professional practice. Volunteers, communities, and other specialists who are not paid employees of the museum are increasingly part of this caring landscape, and, as we have seen in the case of the IGMT, care via volunteer-led action may have predated the official organizational structures of the museum. A broader shift towards co-management of collections, between professional and "external" groups and individuals, can be seen in current museum practice, where museums transition from being the ultimate stewards of the objects in their possession towards a position of "shared guardianship."[33] This practice is, as Marstine (2017; 2015 with Dodd and Jones) argues,[34] a relational activity, which prioritizes the object-generated relationships

---

29 Tronto, *Who Cares?*, 11.

30 Joan C. Tronto, "Interview with the Critical Ethics of Care Foundation," October 16, 2009, https://ethicsofcare.org/joan-tronto/ [accessed July 9, 2018].

31 See Museums Association, "What Is a Museum?," www.museumsassociation.org/about/frequently-asked-questions [accessed July 12, 2018].

32 See legislation.gov.uk, "National Heritage Act 1983," www.legislation.gov.uk/ukpga/1983/47/introduction [accessed July 12, 2018].

33 Janet Marstine, *Critical Practice: Artists, Museums, Ethics* (Abingdon: Routledge, 2017).

34 Marstine, *Critical Practice*; Janet Marstine, Jocelyn Dodd, and Ceri Jones, "Twenty-First Century Museum Ethics: A View from the Field," in *International Handbook of Museum Studies: Volume 4: Museum Practice, Critical Debates in the Museum Sector*, ed. Conal McCarthy, series ed. Sharon Macdonald and Helen Rees Leahy (Chichester: Wiley, 2015), 69–96.

among and between people. Care, with this relational definition, can be considered as "a process: it does not have clear boundaries. It is open-ended [...] a matter of various hands working together (over time) towards a result. Care is not a transaction in which something is exchanged [...] but an interaction in which the action goes back and forth."[35] Arguably, using this definition, care in a museum context goes beyond being just about objects—as the definitions discussed above might lead us to believe—towards a concern for the relationship between people around objects.

Meyer raises some useful additional discussions about how care in the museum also concerns the maintenance of different kinds of relationships rather than being simply about authorized professionals caring for objects. In the Luxembourg Museum of Natural History where his research was based, Meyer recognizes that knowledge creation is actually a co-production between amateurs and professionals. "Among the scientific collaborators of the Museum there are all sorts of people: a bank employee ... a school teacher ... a young student ... In short, many of the Museum's collaborators are people whose profession or day job does not bear a direct link with their active scientific interests."[36] He argues that the boundary between these groups is not very well defined, as, through collaborations of various kinds, "amateurs come to belong to the world of the professional too."[37] In relation to the IGMT and HMS case study, where the IGMT owns the collection but its management is shared between the museum staff and a learned society, the HMS, we can see a clear parallel with this description.[38] However, whereas museum professionals have to work to contracts, deadlines, strict working rules, etc., these "strong ties" to the organization do not fit within the amateurs' knowledge economy, which is, in contrast, typified by "weak ties."[39] Weak ties describe relationships that are potentially more fragile, less formalized, and in need of continuous maintenance. In Meyer's example, it is recognized by the professional museum staff that scientific knowledge production is a collaborative endeavour, thus "caring," in this context, also includes caring for the "weak ties" formed with these collaborators and ensuring, as it is in the best interests of the museum, that they continue. As one participant indicated, "contact care is very important."[40]

This example again reinforces the idea that care in a museum context goes far beyond ensuring the ongoing survival of the museums' physical collections; it also includes nurturing connections between groups and individuals. However, far less attention has been paid by researchers to exploring these kinds of relationships, particularly

---

35 Annemarie Mol, *The Logic of Care: Health and the Problem of Patient Choice* (London: Routledge, 2008).

36 Morgan Meyer, "Caring for Weak Ties: The Natural History Museum as a Place of Encounter between Amateur and Professional Science," *Sociological Research Online* 15, no. 2 (2010): section 1.4.

37 Meyer, "Caring for Weak Ties," section 1.5.

38 It is important to emphasize that "amateurs" are interpreted here as referring to those who are not paid employees rather than people lacking in skills and expertise of various kinds.

39 Mark S. Granovetter, "The Strength of Weak Ties," *American Journal of Sociology* 78, no. 6 (May 1973): 1360–80.

40 Morgan Meyer, "On the Boundaries and Partial Connections between Amateurs and Professionals," *Museum and Society* 6, no. 1 (2008): 48.

collaborative caring practices and processes in the area of collections management.[41] Where discussions of what we might term "collaborative collections management" do exist,[42] they point towards a range of tensions and challenges as well as positive outcomes that are worthy of investigation in the future.[43]

We hope that the above discussion has highlighted a number of key questions, particularly whether there are better ways for a museum to care. Do we currently recognize a museum as being both an agent and a receiver of care? Arguably not, with the dominant mode of caring in a museum being one-directional, from the organization to the object or from the organization to the public. What this section argues for is the recognition that care and caring for collections can be a collective, shared, and multidirectional practice: "caring is sharing." However, in order to achieve this distributed sense of care, certain obstacles need to be overcome. We will examine these in the concluding part of this chapter. The chapter now returns to the NSC—to exploring the people that care for this collection and how the "Who Cares?" project engaged new audiences in the process of caring.

The Enthusiast-Professional

As part of the "Who Cares?" project, interviews were conducted with key members of the HMS Archives and Collections Committee, with the aim of understanding what had inspired the members to get involved with the Society and the NSC and how they viewed the collection in terms of its significance and relevance beyond the HMS. As we argue above, this is a niche collection, not necessarily with wide appeal, so we wanted to find out why the members of the HMS care and how this care is manifested.

The interviewees recognized that the NSC was primarily a reference collection and that it would be unlikely that specimens from it would be placed on display either in the IGMT's museums or elsewhere. They were realistic about the appeal of the collection to nonspecialists, but this did not mean that the HMS members felt that the collection was lacking in significance. A core aspect of why they care is to help raise the profile and general awareness of the collection, even though the NSC is never likely to have the same level of visibility as some of the IGMT's collections.

A level of professionalism was also important to the HMS members. We understand that, typically, enthusiasts demonstrate a high degree of knowledge and expertise about a specific collection, and all of those we spoke to were dedicated to making sure that the

---

41 Collections management can be considered as a broad and fluid area of museum work that is traditionally associated with "the physical care and documentation of collections." See Anne Fahy, "Introduction," in *Collections Management*, ed. Anne Fahy (London: Routledge, 1995), 2.

42 This term is used here to refer to collections management work that involves a degree of participation from individuals, groups, and communities that are not paid employees of the museum.

43 Of relevance to the context explored in this chapter, see, for example, the restoration of the Pegasus computer at the Science Museum by members of the Computer Conservation Society in Doron Swade, "Founding and Early History of the CCS," *Computer Resurrection: The Bulletin of the Computer Conservation Society* 68 (Winter 2014/15): unpaginated.

NSC was well managed to accepted museum standards. Their co-management relationship with the IGMT enabled this to happen, as did the skills of key members of the HMS Archives and Collections Committee, who were active or former professionals in the museum and heritage sector. Interestingly, their enthusiasm for this collection could not be categorized as an "irrational passion," as is associated with some collectors.[44] None of those interviewed, for example, actually had personal collections of industrial slag. One reason given for this was rather pragmatic; they can "see the difficulty it creates."[45] Having sorted through boxes of slag that make up the NSC in their recently completed documentation project, lessons had been learned, for example, not to pick up slag, as there is a risk of forgetting where it has been found and thus being unable to trace its origins. Context is everything with this collection. Slag is also (relatively) easy to come by in industrial landscapes. One interviewee mentioned picking up a lump of slag on a walk, turning it over in their hands and considering taking it home for a moment, but then putting it back on the ground and making the decision instead to leave it where it was.

What characterized the members of the HMS we engaged with was a particular form of enthusiasm. They are what we might, perhaps, term "enthusiast-professionals." All of those we interviewed had personal connections to historic and contemporary metalworking, either through current or prior employment in engineering and the metalworking industries or, as mentioned before, had connections to heritage bodies and agencies. Involvement with the HMS, its Archives and Collections Committee and, by extension, the NSC was one way of continuing to make use of their skills and knowledge and to perform a sense of duty towards this professional area.

One participant saw their involvement in the management of the NSC as aiding others to make more use of it rather than any strong desire to feed their own passion for these objects: "I don't really see my role as a researcher, I see my role as facilitating other people doing research."[46] This attitude could be described as distanced, "platonic," and professional, expressing a desire to see the collection used and valued by others (see also the quotation with which this chapter opened). This, and other similar points raised by participants, stands in contrast to ideas about enthusiasts as being obsessive and less than rational.[47] In general, we argue that HMS members would not recognize themselves in this description. However, to say that the members of the HMS we interviewed had no emotional attachment to the NSC would also be inaccurate, as confirmed by the following participant:

> If it was just professional [interest] then I probably wouldn't be involved. I would ... get enough of that in my day job. I don't need to spend more time doing it at the weekend and actually ... one of the biggest steps forward that have been made with the collection was spent by me at my own expense getting some combinations and transport and bullying

---

44 See, for example, Werner Muensterberger, *Collecting: An Unruly Passion, Psychological Perspectives* (Princeton: Princeton University Press, 2014).

45 "Who Cares?" research participant no. 1. Interviewed by Anna Woodham, July 10, 2015.

46 "Who Cares?" research participant no. 2. Interviewed by Anna Woodham, July 10, 2015.

47 Hilary Geoghegan, "Emotional Geographies of Enthusiasm: Belonging to the Telecommunications Heritage Group," *Area* 45, no. 1 (2013): 40–46.

[people] to spend a week working on the collection … So that's definite passion, that's definite interest in it and as of itself and that runs in parallel with my own professional interest. I think I always get excited about opening boxes of slag![48]

Overall, the members of the HMS who took part in this project prompted us to reflect in a more nuanced sense about who heritage-enthusiasts are, the reasons why they care, and how this care is manifested. As Geoghegan considered and is certainly apparent in this case study, "enthusiasm is felt at a variety of intensities."[49]

Caring with Others

One of the key aims of the "Who Cares?" project was to experiment with new ways of working with stored collections, particularly collections that were unlikely to feature in a museum, gallery, or exhibition but that were, nevertheless, valued and loved by specific groups. Arguably, the long-term sustainability of collections such as these relies on finding ways of making these "unloved" collections meaningful to different audiences. In order to understand how the enthusiasm and knowledge of specialists could be captured to inspire nonspecialists and vice versa, we ran an interactive workshop session that brought together members of the HMS Archives and Collections Committee and an example of a nonspecialist audience, the Ironbridge Young Archaeologists' Club (IYAC), a club for young people aged eight to sixteen who are interested in archaeology.[50] Both of these groups share an interest in exploring the past; however, the latter was unlikely to have heard of, experienced, or been interested in industrial slag. Bringing together these groups also gave us the opportunity to explore "care" across an intergenerational context. There is increasing interest in strengthening intergenerational relationships as societies face rapidly changing demographic contexts.[51] Opportunities to connect older and younger generations in a meaningful way are seen to offer a number of societal and individual benefits, including the sharing of skills and knowledge.[52] Museums are considered by some to be "one of the most important venues" for intergenerational learning,[53] which, it is important to note, can go beyond learning across the generations in family groups.

---

48 "Who Cares?" research participant no. 1. Interviewed by Anna Woodham, July 10, 2015.

49 Geoghegan, "Emotional Geographies of Enthusiasm."

50 The Young Archaeologists' Club (YAC) is a network of clubs across the UK administered by the Council for British Archaeology and run by volunteers, often with the assistance of paid staff from host organizations, such as the Ironbridge Gorge Museum Trust. See Young Archaeologists' Club (YAC), "Homepage," www.yac-uk.org/ [accessed July 6, 2018].

51 Sacha Vieira and Liliana Sousa, "Intergenerational Practice: Contributing to a Conceptual Framework," *International Journal of Lifelong Education* 35, no. 4 (2016): 396–412 at 396.

52 Angela M. La Porte, ed., *Community Connections: Intergenerational Links in Art Education* (Reston: National Art Education Association, 2004).

53 Museums Association, *Department for Innovation, Universities and Skills: Informal Adult Learning—Shaping the Way Ahead* (Museums Association online, June 2008), section 3, www.museumsassociation.org/policy/01062008-informal-adult-learning-shaping-the-way-ahead [accessed July 17, 2018].

The session organized as part of the current project coincided with an HMS slag study day so that there were other HMS volunteers working on documenting parts of the NSC archive in the same room. This also tested whether the physical and conceptual space could be shared by both groups and potentially repeated in the future. In this sense, the idea of "weak ties," as introduced above, could describe the relationship, potentially, not just between the IGMT and the HMS but also between the HMS and the IYAC. Could HMS members decide to invest in maintaining an ongoing relationship with the IYAC? Would they see this as part of their "caring" role?

For the HMS and, no doubt, other similar organizations, there are benefits and challenges to building connections between generations. The HMS recognizes the need to run "outreach activities" to reach out to new audiences and has actively conducted such activities in the past.[54] However, the fact that the members of the Archives and Collections Committee are all volunteers means that there is not always the time or resources to undertake a sustained programme of activities. The HMS committee members are mainly retired individuals, and they recognize the need to recruit the younger generation in terms of the ongoing sustainability of the society. One participant told us about this in relation to the recruitment of two new (younger) members of the Collections and Archives Committee: "We just grabbed them both and went, 'would you like to be on the committee?' ... And fortunately they said yes!"[55] Our discussion revealed a difficult situation in that the HMS appreciates that there needs to be a way of recruiting "new blood," but this is difficult to do in a sustained way due to the volunteer-led nature of the Society. While there is no way to predict whether making stronger connections with the IYAC (and/or other youth groups) would provide this, we wondered if it might be a worthwhile strategy to invest in, to try to ensure that care for the NSC and the HMS's other collections can continue into the future.

The workshop conducted as part of this piece of research began with the authors providing an introduction to the project and an explanation about the format of the session. Members of the HMS and the IYAC then introduced themselves. The HMS cohort had been briefed not to mention anything about slag at this point. The IYAC members were then given a variety of different lumps of slag to look at and examine. They were not told what these objects were and, using only their imaginations, they were encouraged to create their own museum labels with some very interesting results (see figures 3.3 and 3.4). Aliens, volcanoes, lava, planets, and space were among the recurring themes that the IYAC members associated with the slag specimens, perhaps not surprisingly, given the "otherworldly" look of slag.

The second part of the session involved two short talks by the HMS members. One gave an introduction to how slag is formed and the other talked about how to find and collect slag based on his own experience. The IYAC members then "interviewed" him, posing their own questions about his methods and motivations around collecting slag. The session concluded by pairing members of the IYAC and the HMS together to write a second museum label that more "accurately" described the slag specimens. We then

---

54 "Who Cares?" research participant no. 3. Interviewed by Anna Woodham, July 10, 2015.

55 "Who Cares?" research participant no. 3. Interviewed by Anna Woodham, July 10, 2015.

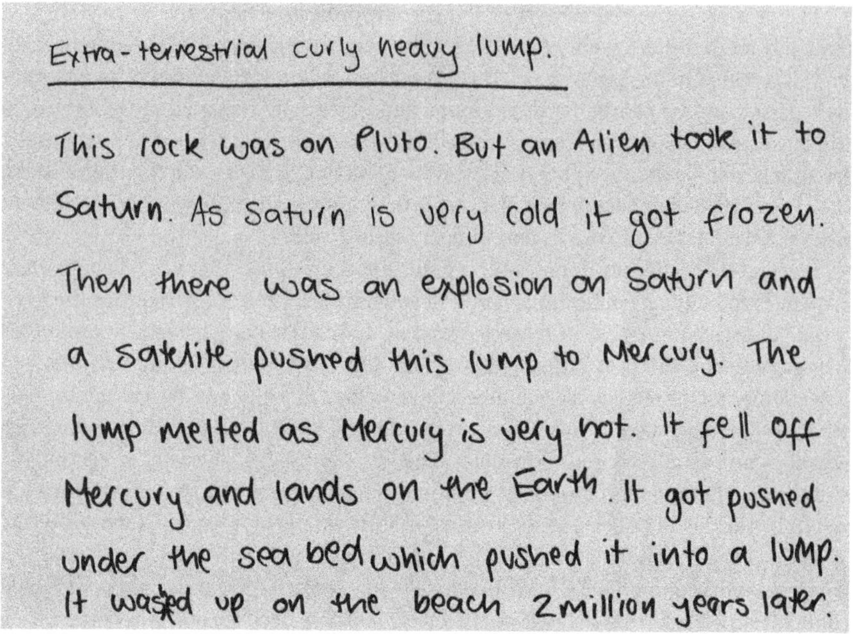

Extra-terrestrial curly heavy lump.
This rock was on Pluto. But an Alien took it to
Saturn. As Saturn is very cold it got frozen.
Then there was an explosion on Saturn and
a satelite pushed this lump to Mercury. The
lump melted as Mercury is very hot. It fell off
Mercury and lands on the Earth. It got pushed
under the sea bed which pushed it into a lump.
It washed up on the beach 2million years later.

Figure 3.3. Example of the IYAC "alternative" museum label by Olivia, aged 9. Photograph by Shane Kelleher.

mice
This piece of slag is made cheese stone
and all the holes were made by mice, they
used to live there, but have now moved out.

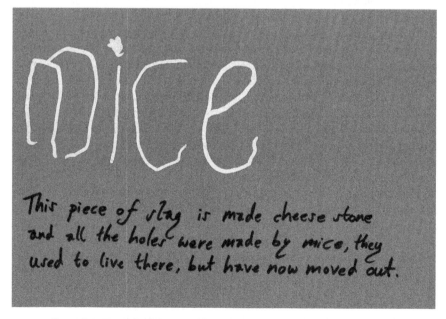

Figure 3.4. Example of the IYAC "alternative" museum label by Aurora, aged 3 (written with help from Aurora's mum). Photograph by Shane Kelleher.

displayed the "real" and "alternative" museum labels together with the slag specimens in a mini "exhibition." The stories that some of the young people created as part of their alternative labels prompted reflection upon the role that the imagination plays in museum interpretation and how uninspiring some real museum labels are! Is there a place in museum interpretation for fantasy, we wonder? It also led to an important finding: Challenging the imagination can be used as one strategy to bring "unloved" objects to life and to stimulate others to care for them.

It was also interesting to note that it was not just the fantasy aspects of the activity that the IYAC found of interest. An observation that all of the "Who Cares?" project research team made about the session was how engrossed the IYAC members were by hearing the two HMS volunteers speak. One of the volunteers was used to communicating to different audiences and explaining complicated scientific processes in a straightforward way. The second volunteer spoke to the young people simply about their own experiences of collecting slag in the field. Their talk was brought to life because of the elements of storytelling and recollection used. Drawing on memory and personal experience using narrative techniques is often used to engage museum and heritage site visitors with objects.[56] However, in the case of the NSC, and to the best of our knowledge, this "less-visible" stored collection has never been given the opportunity to be connected to personal memories in quite this way before.[57] Without conducting a longitudinal study, which was out of the scope of the "Who Cares?" project, the long-term impact of this joint session remains unknown. However, based on feedback received, the IYAC leaders thought that the experience would stay with the IYAC members for a long time to come.

Caring after Hours

The final part of our study took samples from the NSC on a journey from their "behind-the-scenes" storeroom location in Shropshire to a Science Museum "Late" event in London. "Late" events take place in the evening outside usual museum opening hours and are increasingly common in museums as they consider ways to broaden their appeal.[58] At the Science Museum, the audience for these free science-themed events are "independent adults," who are typically aged between eighteen and thirty-five.[59] The visitors come along to socialize and take part in a range of special activities held in the

---

56 In relation to the interpretation of Industrial Heritage, see, for example, Michael Pretes, "Touring Mines and Mining Tourists," *Annals of Tourism Research* 29, no. 2 (2002): 439–56.

57 See also Watson, this volume.

58 Paul Barron and Anna Leask, "Visitor Engagement at Museums: Generation Y and 'Lates' Events at the National Museum of Scotland," *Museum Management and Curatorship* 32, no. 5 (2017): 473–90.

59 Scott Mckenzie-Cook, "Lates at the Science Museum," *CultureHive* 2 (2013): 2. www.culturehive.co.uk/wp-content/uploads/2013/11/Lates-at-the-Science-Museum.pdf [accessed July 6, 2018].

museum's galleries.[60] They are popular events, with around 4,700 people attending on the night we participated.[61]

During the event, visitors were able to handle the slag specimens, see the IYAC's "alternative" and "real" museum labels, hear the top ten slag facts, and vote on their favourite "unloved" collection in a light-hearted competition between the NSC, the Science Museum's locks and fastenings collection (see Hess, this volume), and the Museum of English Rural Life's (MERL) hand tools collection (see Smith, this volume). Each of the collections took on a social media persona and campaigned via Twitter[62] as well as inside the Science Museum galleries. The NSC was victorious, winning the title of "most loved unloved collection."

The activities at the Science Museum "Late" were designed to be fun and enjoyable rather than necessarily serious and didactic. Nevertheless, we wanted to raise awareness of the range of museum collections that visitors do not usually get to see and to bring this collection to a different audience group, encouraging them to engage with it in a memorable way. Two creative practitioners, Rebecca Reynolds and Julie Roberts, helped us to do this on the night. With Rebecca's help, visitors to the "Late" event were encouraged to write poems and creative writing focused on the different "unloved" collections (see below).

> Humorous heritage
> with incredible history
>
> —
>
> So strange but we love you
> Lying there, you look lost
> All of the life has been sucked out of you
> Going unnoticed in our rural landscape … always
>
> —
>
> If I say slag then what comes to mind?
> I bet it's not metal,
> I bet it's not iron
> But history's cool and slag is cool too
> So come over and learn while you can![63]

Some of the poems written during the "Late" event make reference to the less salubrious connotations of the word "slag." This we mentioned at the start of this chapter as something that may make it tricky for museums to use this collection in family-friendly interpretations. However, at a night-time event aimed at adults, the fact that the term "slag" induced laughter actually became a strategy to draw visitors into exploring the

---

60 Mckenzie-Cook, "Lates at the Science Museum."

61 C. Gregory, personal communication, 2015.

62 The three "unloved" collections used the Twitter accounts @WhoCares_slag, @WhoCares_locks, and @WhoCares_tools, run by social media consultant Mar Dixon.

63 Examples of three poems written by anonymous visitors to the Science Museum "Late" event on September 30, 2015.

collection. Using humour as a way into the collection may be seen as a crude instrument by some. However, at this particular event, where we knew that visitors were highly likely to make the association themselves, it made sense to work with it rather than ignore the connotation. The poems above indicate that, for some visitors at least, the wider cultural and historical value of the collection was clear to them.

Being able to take advantage of the "Late" to bring out the NSC from behind the scenes, for a different audience to engage with it, was an opportunity that we could take advantage of, in part, because the NSC is fairly robust in nature and the specimens are small in scale, making it an appropriate collection to be handled and used in this way. In other words, the relative mobility of the collection made it possible to open it up to those who were able to care about the collection and make it visible to people who may otherwise have never come across the NSC. In terms of practical arrangements, the choice of samples took into consideration any handling hazards, such as sharp or rough edges. An assessment had been made in advance for the HMS-IYAC workshop and the same samples were also used for the "Late" event. The authors[64] transported the collection, with permission from the IGMT and the HMS, by train from Shropshire to London. In terms of collections management processes, and for insurance purposes, the samples were deemed to be on loan to the Science Museum for one evening and paperwork was completed accordingly. For a higher-value collection (in financial terms) or one that was fragile or presented serious handling issues, such an activity would have been much harder to organize. Alongside these pragmatic factors, the willingness of the IGMT and the HMS to allow this activity to take place was crucial. In fact, we argue that a can-do attitude (once all the potential risks have been considered) is a critical ingredient when considering how to extend the reach of collections. Outlining the methods used to achieve this, this section has provided an insight into the processes of care involved in making this collection visible for one evening only. We consider that the poems written at the "Late" show a different and valid form of "caring about" these objects, which goes beyond the physical boundaries of the IGMT or the care of the amateur/enthusiast-professionals discussed above.

Conclusion: Museums and an Ethics of Care

An outcome of conducting this research and summarizing it in this chapter has revealed a fascinating social world that exists around even the most challenging of collections and the extent to which such a collection is cared for. We have also posed some strategies for bringing a collection like the NSC to the attention of different groups using, for example, humour and the imagination, the idea being that finding a route in for different individuals could lead to more lasting engagement, not just in terms of ensuring the survival of the collection but in terms of building sustainable "caring" relationships. Building on and maintaining these relationships, though, presents some challenges, not least because of the commitment and potential resourcing implications that this may require. However, while we do not believe that the ultimate goal of a museum object needs to be inclusion

---

64 One of whom was an IGMT employee at the time of the research.

in an exhibition or display, during the process of planning and carrying out this project at the IGMT, the visibility of the NSC was raised internally within the museum to the degree that there are now some specimens from it on permanent display in the Museum of Iron. Whether this was due directly to the "Who Cares?" project or just the timing of the project coinciding with the redisplay of this museum, we would not like to say!

The key theoretical debate that this chapter engages with is around exploring what it means to co-manage a stored museum collection. The HMS and IGMT model works very well, with the NSC, the museum, and the HMS all clearly benefiting from the relationship, which is set out in their memorandum of understanding. However, this success is due, in part, to the boundary between professional and amateur being rather difficult to tease apart in this case. Therefore, the care offered by the HMS aligns very closely to what would be expected if the collection was not co-managed or co-managed by a group that had very different ideas about what caring looked like. However, to our understanding, this model of co-management still appears to be relatively rare in the museum world, and it would be beneficial to understand whether it could go further still, either here or in other examples. What would this look like, we wonder? Perhaps the "Who Cares?" project has, to an extent, hinted at this. For example, drawing on Helen Graham's suggestions for a co-productive museum, being one that "recognises the pluralities of 'co' of which it and the world is comprised."[65] This project has shown that, at its very least, a "co" does exist in the example of the NSC and that "co" takes a number of different forms. The task now, for museums generally, is to fully engage with the idea that caring for collections and caring well can be achieved in a shared and distributed way and to experiment with this process. Using an ethics of care, in particular, underscores the importance of museums to an extent letting go and appreciating that care is a multidirectional process.

Bibliography

Austin, Tony. *The Story of a Disaster*. London: Hutchinson, 1967.

Barron, Paul, and Anna Leask. "Visitor Engagement at Museums: Generation Y and 'Lates' Events at the National Museum of Scotland." *Museum Management and Curatorship* 32, no. 5 (2017): 473–90.

Beale, Catherine. *The Ironbridge Spirit: A History of the Ironbridge Gorge Museum Trust*. Ceredigion: Ironbridge Gorge Museum Trust, 2014.

Belford, Paul, Marilyn Palmer, and Roger White, ed. *Footprints of Industry: Papers from the 300th Anniversary Conference at Coalbrookdale*. Oxford: BAR British Series 523, 2010.

Black, Graham. *Transforming Museums in the Twenty-First Century*. Abingdon: Routledge, 2012.

Buchanon, Angus. "The Origins and Early Days of the AIA." *Industrial Archaeology News* 169 (2014): 2–4.

Clark, Catherine. *Ironbridge Gorge*. London: English Heritage and Batsford, 1993.

---

65 Helen C. Graham, "The 'Co' in Co-production: Museums, Community Participation and Science and Technology Studies," *Science Museum Group Journal* (Spring 2016): unpaginated.

Cossons, Neil. "Foreword." In *Footprints of Industry: Papers from the 300th Anniversary Conference at Coalbrookdale*, ed. Paul Belford, Marilyn Palmer, and Roger White, xiii–xiv. Oxford: BAR British Series 523, 2010.

Fahy, Anne, ed. *Collections Management*. London: Routledge, 1995.

Geoghegan, Hilary. "Emotional Geographies of Enthusiasm: Belonging to the Telecommunications Heritage Group." *Area* 45, no. 1 (2013): 40–46.

——. "'If You Can Walk down the Street and Recognise the Difference between Cast Iron and Wrought Iron, the World is Altogether a Better Place': Being Enthusiastic about Industrial Archaeology." *M/C Journal: A Journal of Media and Culture* 12, no. 2 (2009): unpaginated.

Geoghegan, Hilary, and Alison Hess. "Object-Love at the Science Museum: Cultural Geographies of Museum Storerooms." *Cultural Geographies* 22, no. 3 (2015): 445–65.

Graham, Helen C. "The 'Co' in Co-production: Museums, Community Participation and Science and Technology Studies." *Science Museum Group Journal* (Spring 2016): unpaginated.

Granovetter, Mark S. "The Strength of Weak Ties." *American Journal of Sociology* 78, no. 6 (May 1973): 1360–80.

Hudson, Kenneth. *World Industrial Archaeology*. Cambridge: Cambridge University Press, 1979.

Kelleher, Shane. "From 'The Most Extraordinary District in the World' to 'Not All the World but a Very Poor Bit of the Fag End of It': Archaeology at the Ironbridge Gorge World Heritage Site." *Museum Archaeologist*, forthcoming.

——. "Industrial Archaeology at the IGMT: Past, Present and Future." *Broseley Local History Society Journal* 32 (2013): 18–32.

La Porte, Angela M., ed. *Community Connections: Intergenerational Links in Art Education*. Reston: National Art Education Association, 2004.

Marstine, Janet. *Critical Practice: Artists, Museums, Ethics*. Abingdon: Routledge, 2017.

Marstine, Janet, Jocelyn Dodd, and Ceri Jones. "Twenty-First Century Museum Ethics: A View from the Field." In *International Handbook of Museum Studies: Volume 4: Museum Practice, Critical Debates in the Museum Sector*, edited by Conal McCarthy, series editors Sharon Macdonald and Helen Rees Leahy, 69–96. Chichester: Wiley, 2015.

Mckenzie-Cook, Scott. "Lates at the Science Museum." *CultureHive* 2 (2013): 2. www.culturehive.co.uk/wp-content/uploads/2013/11/Lates-at-the-Science-Museum.pdf [accessed July 6, 2018].

McKie, Robin. "Can Slag Heaps Help Save the Planet?" *The Guardian*, April 23, 2017. www.theguardian.com/science/2017/apr/23/can-slag-heaps-help-save-the-planet-carbon-dioxide-capture-climate-change [accessed July 9, 2018].

Meyer, Morgan. "Caring for Weak Ties: The Natural History Museum as a Place of Encounter between Amateur and Professional Science." *Sociological Research Online* 15, no. 2 (2010): unpaginated.

——. "On the Boundaries and Partial Connections between Amateurs and Professionals." *Museum and Society* 6, no. 1 (2008): 38–53.

Mol, Annemarie. *The Logic of Care: Health and the Problem of Patient Choice*. London: Routledge, 2008.

Monti, Francesca, and Suzanne Keene. *Museums and Silent Objects: Designing Effective Exhibitions*. Abingdon: Routledge, 2016.

Muensterberger, Werner. *Collecting: An Unruly Passion, Psychological Perspectives*. Princeton: Princeton University Press, 2014.

Museums Association. *Department for Innovation, Universities and Skills: Informal Adult Learning—Shaping the Way Ahead.* June 2008. www.museumsassociation.org/policy/01062008-informal-adult-learning-shaping-the-way-ahead [accessed July 17, 2018].

Palmer, Marilyn. "Industrial Archaeology: A Thematic or Period Discipline." *Antiquity* 64, no. 243 (1990): 275–82.

Palmer, Marilyn, and Peter Neaverson. *Industrial Archaeology: Principles and Practice.* London: Routledge, 1998.

Pretes, Michael. "Touring Mines and Mining Tourists." *Annals of Tourism Research* 29, no. 2 (2002): 439–56.

Swade, Doron. "Founding and Early History of the CCS." *Computer Resurrection: The Bulletin of the Computer Conservation Society* 68 (Winter 2014/15): unpaginated.

Tronto, Joan C. *Caring Democracy: Markets, Equality and Justice.* New York: New York University Press, 2013.

——. "Interview with the Critical Ethics of Care Foundation," October 16, 2009. https://ethicsofcare.org/joan-tronto/ [accessed July 9, 2018].

——. *Who Cares? How to Reshape a Democratic Politics.* Ithaca: Cornell University Press, 2015.

Vieira, Sacha, and Liliana Sousa. "Intergenerational Practice: Contributing to a Conceptual Framework." *International Journal of Lifelong Education* 35, no. 4 (2016): 396–412.

Acknowledgements

The authors would like to thank the members of the HMS, the leaders and members of the IYAC, and the anonymous poets from the Science Museum "Late" held on Wednesday, September 30, 2015.

SECTION TWO

"UNLOVED" COLLECTIONS

Chapter 4

"STOREHOUSES OF UNIMAGINED TREASURES": DELIGHTFUL RUMMAGING AND ARTISTS' RESPONSES TO "UNLOVED" COLLECTIONS

ALEXANDRA WOODALL*

Introduction

> If you are squeamish
> do not poke among the beach rubble.[1]

This fragment of poetry by Sappho begins DeSilvey's paper, "Observed Decay: Telling Stories with Mutable Things," in which the author talks about decay as "a process that can be *generative of a different kind of knowledge*."[2] Here, using the same poem to frame the chapter, I explore another "different kind of knowledge," generated not through the literal decay of objects but through what happens when artists and others are invited in to "poke among the beach rubble." This may include actually accessing the hidden depths of museum storage and their often-forgotten collections, getting up close and personal with the stuff of the storerooms through touch, or imagining and making new things in response. All of this, I argue, is about an encounter with objects that is primarily an emotional or affective one,[3] one without "prerequisite of information"[4] yet where sensory

---

1 See additional translation in Anne Carson, *If Not, Winter: Fragments of Sappho* (London: Virago, 2002), 293, and her note, 379.

2 Caitlin DeSilvey, "Observed Decay: Telling Stories with Mutable Things," *Journal of Material Culture* 11, no. 3 (2006): 318–38 (323) (author's original italics).

3 Margaret Wetherell, Laurajane Smith, and Gary Campbell discuss interpretations of emotion and affect in the Introduction to their edited book: Laurajane Smith, Margaret Wetherell, and Gary Campbell, ed., *Emotion, Affective Practices and the Past in the Present* (Abingdon: Routledge, 2018), in particular noting that they are "flowing, dynamic, recursive and profoundly contextual, challenging static and neat formulations." See page 1 of this reference.

4 Sandra Dudley, "Museum Materialities: Objects, Sense and Feeling," in *Museum Materialities: Objects, Engagements, Interpretations*, ed. Sandra Dudley (Oxford: Routledge, 2010), 8.

---

* Alexandra Woodall is a Lecturer in Arts Management at the University of Sheffield, UK. She has a PhD from the School of Museum Studies at the University of Leicester, UK, entitled "Sensory Engagements with Objects in Art Galleries: Material Interpretation and Theological Metaphor." She was supervised by Professor Sandra Dudley and, together with an international team, they have undertaken object-based research in India. She has undertaken museum consultancy, and was Head of Learning at the Sainsbury Centre for Visual Arts at the University of East Anglia, UK, until 2018. Prior to this she held several positions, including at the Royal Armouries in Leeds, Manchester Art Gallery, Museums Sheffield, and at Kettle's Yard in Cambridge. She has an MPhil in Mystical Theology and a PGCE from the University of Cambridge. She is a mentor and professional reviewer for the Museums Association.

encounter, particularly touch, can elicit an immediate and visceral response. Touch directly links audiences and/or artists with the objects' histories and contexts, their original makers or owners, and their material embodiment, not least through a connection of hands revealed by fingerprints, patina, or marks of wear and tear.[5] In addition, building on work exploring artists' interventions in museums[6] and on activist projects such as that of artist Fred Wilson in his *Mining the Museum* exhibition,[7] this chapter examines such artistic interventions and engagements particularly in relation to stored or hidden collections rather than displayed ones. These interventions provide important sources of interpreting collections, and thus they generate "a different kind of knowledge" that prioritizes an initial emotional "gut response." This, I argue, has the potential to shape museum methods and practices both behind the scenes and within exhibitions.[8]

A small but growing body of work is focused on museum storage areas as sites for museological research. Geoghegan and Hess note that "despite their invisibility to the public, stored objects and their stubborn physicality are at the heart of what defines a museum."[9] Brusius and Singh ask in their edited volume: "why is it that, when most museum objects lie in storage, it is the gallery and the exhibition that have come to take such an important place in both the self-representation of museums and the public's perception of these institutions?"[10] In this chapter, I explore museum storage areas through three artistic projects and ask what happens when hidden objects in storage are actually made accessible for these creative imaginings to take place. Rather than just enabling intangible access, here the projects all involve hands-on touch and the physical need to rummage through and work with stored collections as a form of knowledge that is primarily an emotional material engagement rather than being based purely on empirical data, scientific experiment, or historical contextual information, for example.[11]

---

5 Stephen Greenblatt, "Resonance and Wonder," in *Exhibiting Cultures: The Poetics and Politics of Museum Display*, ed. Ivan Karp and Steven D. Lavine (Washington, DC: Smithsonian Institution Press, 1991), 42–56 at 45; Constance Classen and David Howes, "The Museum as Sensescape: Western Sensibilities and Indigenous Artifacts," in *Sensible Objects: Colonialism, Museums and Material Culture*, ed. Elizabeth Edwards, Chris Gosden, and Ruth Phillips (Oxford: Berg, 2006), 199–222 (202).

6 See, for example, Danny Birchall, *Institution and Intervention: Artists' Projects in Object-Based Museums*, unpublished MA dissertation, University of London, 2012; Chris Dorsett, "Making Meaning beyond Display," in *Museum Materialities: Objects, Engagements, Interpretations*, ed. Sandra Dudley (Oxford: Routledge, 2010), 241–59.

7 Fred Wilson and Howard Halle, "Mining the Museum," *Grand Street* 44 (1993): 151–72.

8 For a discussion on the politics of stored collections, see the Introduction in Mirjam Brusius and Kavita Singh, ed., *Museum Storage and Meaning: Tales from the Crypt* (Oxford: Routledge, 2018).

9 Hilary Geoghegan and Alison Hess, "Object-Love at the Science Museum: Cultural Geographies of Museum Storerooms," *Cultural Geographies* 22, no. 3 (2015): 445–46 (461).

10 Mirjam Brusius and Kavita Singh, "Introduction," in Mirjam Brusius and Kavita Singh, ed. *Museum Storage and Meaning: Tales from the Crypt* (Oxford: Routledge, 2018), 3.

11 See Alexandra Woodall, "Rummaging as a Strategy for Creative Thinking and Imaginative Engagement in Higher Education," in *Engaging the Senses: Object-Based Learning in Higher Education*, ed. Helen Chatterjee and Leonie Hannan (Surrey: Ashgate, 2015), 133–55; Dydia DeLyser, "Collecting, Kitsch and the Intimate Geographies of Social Memory: A Story of Archival Autoethnography," *Transactions of the Institute of British Geographers* 40 (2014): 209–22.

We know that visitors like to explore places that are not usually open to the public. Yet what is it about the voyage behind the scenes that so resonates with visitors and, in this case, with artists, and how might this impact upon museum practices? The title of this chapter is a quotation taken from a short story by Saki (the pen-name of Hector Hugh Munro, 1870–1916), *The Lumber Room* (meaning an attic-like space). Artist Mark Hearld also used it to name his exhibition held at York Art Gallery on its reopening following a capital development and transformation project, which was open to the public between August 2015 and May 2017—*The Lumber Room: Unimagined Treasures*.[12] Intrigued by the title and contents of this exhibition, I sought out the original Saki story. The "lumber room" is discovered one day by the protagonist of the tale, a young boy named Nicholas. Somewhat akin to the public perception of a museum storeroom, the room is a place out of bounds in his aunt's large house. Yet bold Nicholas ventures in. Artist Mark Hearld used Saki's narrative as a basis for his curation of objects from across the diverse collections in York, which were displayed alongside works on paper, ceramics, and paintings that he had created in response.[13]

Following a brief summary of Saki's tale drawing out its relevant themes, this chapter focuses on what might happen when visitors or, in this case, particularly when artists are encouraged to venture into those hidden spaces and explore the "unloved" collections of museums.[14] Focusing in particular on artists' interventions with neglected collections, this chapter argues that rather than museum storage areas being places of unimagined treasures, they might instead become places for imagining (and reimagining) treasures through a sensory, unmediated, and emotional encounter. There are (usually) no labels or interpretation, and the drawers and boxes lend themselves to being explored in a way that perhaps contrasts with the formality of the museum gallery setting. Indeed, they might be places for questioning the notion of what is "treasure" or is of value within a museum, and they might be spaces through which museum processes (for example, curating, documenting, conserving, and interpreting) can be laid bare. Looking at ways in which artists have brought forlorn collections to life, not least through the act of touching, this chapter focuses on three examples.

The case study methodology includes a bricolage approach of (participant) observation, analysis of exhibition interpretation and artists' writings, and individual interviews with artists and museum staff to explore how creative experiences in stored collections challenge the very notion of the "unloved" collection. After outlining each case study, the chapter makes comparisons and draws contrasts between them, developing the idea of "material interpretation" and rummaging as methodology. This chapter concludes by suggesting that through these sorts of hands-on encounters and artistic interventions, notions of the values of things, of institutional attitudes towards collections care, and of the processes carried out in museum storage areas are at once both developed and

---

12 "The Lumber Room: Unimagined Treasures" was curated by Mark Hearld: www.yorkartgallery. org.uk/exhibition/the-lumber-room-unimagined-treasures/ [accessed July 2, 2019].

13 This is a familiar but nevertheless dynamic trope in museum practice, often enabling museums to be self-critical about their practices. For a brief and useful historical overview tracing artists' interventions in museums, see Birchall, *Institution and Intervention*.

14 But arguably in a series of practices which could be extended to other audiences.

challenged. Further, this chapter argues that the creativity and enthusiasm shown by artists visiting these stored collections might be something that museums can develop for all audiences by way of a new emotionally engaged approach to public programming that explores what constitutes knowledge in the museum.

"The Lumber Room"

Champion of the satirical short story, Saki wittily mocked Edwardian culture, and his stories often recognize the clever cunning of children, played out against the rigid stupidity of the adult authority figures. In Saki's tale *The Lumber Room* (1914) ("lumber" here meaning "miscellaneous stored objects"), the main character is Nicholas, a young boy who, due to an incident in which he found a frog in his bread and milk earlier in the day, is not allowed to go to the seaside with his cousins. Instead, his aunt keeps him at home, where he is under strict instructions not to go into the gooseberry garden. It soon becomes apparent that Nicholas has no intention whatsoever of visiting the gooseberry garden. Yet he does have another motive:

> By standing on a chair in the library one could reach a shelf on which reposed a fat, important-looking key. The key was as important as it looked; it was the instrument which kept the mysteries of the lumber-room secure from unauthorised intrusion, which opened a way only for aunts and such-like privileged persons. Nicholas had not had much experience of the art of fitting keys into keyholes and turning locks, but for some days past he had practised with the key of the schoolroom door; he did not believe in trusting too much to luck and accident. The key turned stiffly in the lock, but it turned. The door opened, and Nicholas was in an unknown land, compared with which the gooseberry garden was a stale delight ...[15]

Once in the lumber room, Nicholas peers around. It lives up to his expectations. Large and dimly lit, the "storehouse of unimagined treasures" contains "wonderful things for the eyes to feast on." In this room, his aunt, as someone who thought that "things spoil by use," had consigned numerous items "to dust and damp by way of preserving them." But for Nicholas, "it was a living, breathing story; he sat down on a roll of Indian hangings, glowing in wonderful colours beneath a layer of dust, and took in all the details of the tapestry picture."[16]

The story continues, describing Nicholas's experience of the other objects of delight in the lumber room—from snake-like candlesticks to a duck-shaped teapot, a sandalwood box filled with brass creatures to a book illustrated with coloured birds—and each time the thing is described more vividly to include his imaginings of the life histories behind the object. Eventually he is rudely interrupted by the shouts of his aunt coming from the garden, where she is engaged in energetic and rather hopeless searching for him among the artichokes and raspberry canes. Saki wryly writes, "It was probably the first time for twenty years that anyone had smiled in that lumber-room."[17]

---

15 Saki, *Tobermory and Other Stories*, selected by Martin Stephen (London: Phoenix, 1998), 121–22.

16 Saki, *Tobermory and Other Stories*, 122.

17 Saki, *Tobermory and Other Stories*, 123.

There are several features in this tale that can be drawn out as pertinent to museum practices, particularly in relation to "unloved" collections. Firstly, just like the museum storeroom, here, the room under lock and key is only for "privileged persons" to access. It needs to be kept secure from "unauthorised intrusion," which immediately gives the space some sort of sense of mystery for anyone who is not allowed in, and there is something deeply exciting (but also unsettling) about the prospect of going into an "unknown land." By virtue of there being a key, there is a power hierarchy at play. Somebody owns and has access to this key, meaning that somebody else does not. So it is with museums, not least in the language of curators as "keepers."

Secondly, the tale enters into one of the deepest paradoxes of the use of objects in museums: that "catch-22" that museums have to enable access to objects while at the same time needing to preserve those objects.[18] Here, in the lumber room, just as in many museums, the aunt thinks that "things spoil by use" and to lock them away, out of sight, is the best way of preserving them, in this case even where dust and damp may do far more damage. We might even ask whether the non-use of objects is more damaging, since the object torn (sometimes violently) from its original context by being in a museum[19] is no longer the object it once was and can never again be such; some element of its original object-ness is destroyed just as the object is saved.

Finally, the story is explicit in its descriptions of the emotional and visceral responses Nicholas has to this object-filled space. The sheer joy of being in this unloved room full of stuff is revealed not least through his secret smile. Nicholas's emotional response to material things is expressed through sight and touch ("peeping" at and turning the pages of a book) but without language. He simply sits "for many golden minutes revolving the possibilities" and he smiles.[20] All these themes, central to debates around museum materialities and emotional encounters, will emerge further through the case studies that follow.

The three case studies include projects at Manchester Art Gallery, York Museums Trust, and Museums Sheffield, all regional organizations in the north of England. Each case study demonstrates the complex and nuanced role that artists might play in bringing forlorn collections to life, through rediscovery, imagination, use, reuse, and to inspire new making and thinking practices. Each case study also explores ways in which rummaging offers alternative ways to conceptualize what constitutes knowledge in a museum. Building on work about museum materialities, particularly that of

---

18 See the conference proceedings from UCL's "Catch-22" event on this topic, held in 2009: "What's the Damage?," www.ucl.ac.uk/conservation-c-22/conference [accessed January 4, 2018].

19 See Susan Vogel, "Always True to the Object, in Our Fashion," in *Grasping the World: The Idea of the Museum*, ed. Donald Preziosi and Claire Farago (Hampshire: Ashgate, 2003), 653–62 (653); Classen and Howes, "The Museum as Sensescape," 200; Sven Ouzman, "The Beauty of Letting Go: Fragmentary Museums and Archaeologies of Archive," in *Sensible Objects: Colonialism, Museums and Material Culture*, ed. Elizabeth Edwards, Chris Gosden, and Ruth Phillips (Oxford: Berg, 2006), 269–301 (274).

20 Saki, *Tobermory and Other Stories*, 123.

museum anthropologist Sandra Dudley,[21] the chapter's proposed method of "material interpretation" (discussed below) sees a delight in rummaging and actually being able to use neglected collections. This in turn can transform and make transparent museum practices and even lead to new methodologies for public programming. Perhaps above all, the case studies, like Nicholas's experiences in the lumber room, provoke and generate a different type of knowing about objects and collections in storage—a knowledge that is born out of affective encounter.

Mary Mary Quite Contrary

The first case study in which artists explored "unimagined treasures" in store is a project inspired by the Mary Greg Collection of Handicrafts of Bygone Times at Manchester Art Gallery (MAG), "Mary Mary Quite Contrary."[22] This collection consists of hundreds of domestic objects, ranging from old spoons and rusty keys to basketry, miniature children's books, and dolls' houses. Gathered together by Mary Greg (1850–1949), these things were mainly given by her to the gallery in the 1920s. Often handmade, often worn out, these objects had been largely in storage at the gallery since the 1950s. Until the first decade of the 2000s, the objects had not been displayed, had been considered for potential disposal, and had never had a dedicated curator. Yet through a series of hands-on, open-ended, and lovingly entitled "rummages," in which two artist-lecturers (Sharon Blakey and Hazel Jones from Manchester School of Art at Manchester Metropolitan University [MMU]) were invited behind the scenes, all sorts of creative outpourings began to emerge. It became apparent firstly that such engagements were giving rise to a type of sensory knowledge not often prioritized within museums (what is here referred to as a "material interpretation") and secondly that this type of immediate encounter was enabling an interesting collaborative critique of institutional practices.

The "rummages" started, in a manner similar to that of Nicholas's forays into the lumber room, in adventurous, possibly clandestine, and at the very least ad hoc ways.[23] Between 2007 and 2010, the remit of the Interpretation Development team at Manchester Art Gallery, of which I was part, was to devise creative projects to engage audiences with collections interpretation.[24] Contrasting with other interpretive posts in different organizations, whose remits were often to create and write interpretive text,

---

21 Sandra Dudley, ed., *Museum Materialities: Objects, Engagements, Interpretations* (Oxford: Routledge, 2010).

22 "Mary Mary Quite Contrary: Investigating the Mary Greg Collection," www.marymaryquite contrary.org.uk [accessed January 4, 2018].

23 See Woodall, "Rummaging as a Strategy for Creative Thinking and Imaginative Engagement in Higher Education."

24 Now defunct due to cuts following the demise of Renaissance in the Regions funding, members of the Interpretation Development team involved in this project were the author and Liz Mitchell, who has since written her PhD on Mary Greg as a maker of collections, at Manchester Metropolitan University, and whose research blog can be found at: https://untidycollector.wordpress.com/ [accessed January 4, 2018].

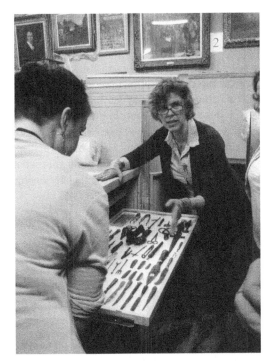

Figure 4.1. A rummage. Photograph by Alexandra Woodall.

our role was to encourage others (for example, young people, children, and artists) to interpret, often in a-textual ways. Because of the experimental nature of this role, we were fortunate to be able to develop new ideas that were often slightly "under the radar" and with few visitor targets or external "key performance indicators" to report, unlike our colleagues, for example, in the learning team. In short, we could take risks and play both with ideas and things, and we were able to experiment with working with different audiences. Exploring the Mary Greg Collection was one such project. Based on a previous collaboration in which the artists had explored the values of forgotten things in an exhibition entitled *Out of the Ordinary* (MMU Special Collections, 2006), Sharon Blakey and Hazel Jones were invited to come and "rummage" through the stored Mary Greg Collection (see figure 4.1) to see what would happen. Artist Hazel Jones describes her experiences thus:

> It was basically: "Here are all the cupboards open. I'm here watching you but *go forth and have a look and see what you can find!*" It was brilliant—it was just—because you could *open* a drawer. You could look for a couple of seconds and then—you know, think "this is amazing but it's not the sort of thing I'm excited by" and you could be quite quick, whereas if the curator was sort of fetching stuff out for you, it's a very slow process, isn't it? And we had a very quick editing process going on. You know, like you're scanning cupboards at one point, the first time we went. I think not even fetching much out, just scanning what was in the cupboards to start to get to feel for what sort of things [...] and

then we could pick and choose and explore more, and the fact that we could go back more than once, and we did, was even better because each time you went back, even drawers you'd looked in quite well before, you found *even more* in that drawer.[25]

There is, of course, a long-established practice of inviting artists into museums to intervene, and through the practice of institutional critique,[26] but inviting artists to explore the stored collections in this way had not been undertaken previously at Manchester Art Gallery. In his significant contribution to the field, *Art and Artifact: The Museum as Medium*, curator James Putnam states: "The activities taking place behind the scenes in museums have been *as important* as the modes of display in public areas. There is the interesting contrast between revealing and concealing, as illustrated in the common process of choosing to exhibit one object while keeping others in reserve storage."[27]

The Mary Greg project aimed to develop reflection on some of these important activities behind the scenes, both to reveal what was already there but also to develop new ways to reimagine the collection and the institution itself. And, above all, the process was a joyous and individual one.

> The rummages allow you to make your own pathway through things, to have the agency of a degree of discovery. And that might be discovery of just something at the back of the cupboard, or it might be the discovery that actually this thing that you've picked up has the most fantastic tiny grain of pins in it, or something like that—it could be discovery at a whole level, series of levels of intimacy—but it is *your* discovery, it's not something that an anonymous curator has discovered and then written up on a label and said "Oi, look at this!" It is absolutely yours, and nobody else's. And in that moment, it's a purely personal private thing. You might choose to share it and then it becomes a different kind of discovery, but in that moment, it belongs to you.[28]

In advocating the rummage as an "intrinsically creative and serious act, comparable to the maker's playful experimentation in the studio," Blakey and Mitchell have nevertheless described rummaging as "neither a word nor activity that museums and galleries generally encourage; it conjures up loss of control and wayward behaviour, undermining the museum's authoritative role as guardian of material culture."[29] Indeed, rummaging

---

25 Interview recorded on June 15, 2013 in Alexandra Woodall, *Sensory Engagements with Objects in Art Galleries: Material Interpretation and Theological Metaphor*, unpublished PhD thesis, University of Leicester, 2016, 133.

26 See James Putnam, *Art and Artifact: The Museum as Medium* (London: Thames & Hudson, 2001, reprint 2009); Kynaston McShine, *The Museum as Muse: Artists Reflect* (London: Thames & Hudson, 1999); Claire Robins, *Curious Lessons in the Museum: The Pedagogic Potential of Artists' Interventions* (Farnham: Ashgate, 2013).

27 Putnam, *Art and Artifact*, 16 (author's italics).

28 Interview recorded on June 9, 2013 in Woodall, *Sensory Engagements with Objects in Art Galleries*, 134.

29 Sharon Blakey and Liz Mitchell, "A Question of Value: Rethinking the Mary Greg Collection," in *Collaboration through Craft*, ed. Amanda Ravetz, Alice Kettle, and Helen Felcey (London: Bloomsbury, 2013), 170–85 (176).

may feel somewhat renegade.[30] It allows an equality of access and interpretation not often paralleled in usual curator-visitor relationships. Yet perhaps it is because of this, and its tactile nature, that it is such a valuable museum experiment. I now wish to illustrate the value (and challenges) of rummages as material interpretation by turning to an unlikely object: a headless zebra.

At some point during an early rummage in 2008, the project team came across a cupboard in which there were several cardboard solander-type boxes. On opening the first box, a menagerie began to appear. It seemed apparent that these boxes contained animals from at least one Noah's Ark (see figure 4.2). Bearing traces of lives lived—having been played with—many of the animals were in a state of disrepair, missing tails, hooves, and ears. In one of these, a box that became a subject for the photography of Ben Blackall, lay a pair of zebras. Two by two. Except one of them was headless. Blakey comments in a blog entry focusing on brokenness and use that she loves the headless zebra and, on finding this and accompanying letters from the archive that discussed the missing animals, she began working on a series to restore and remember these animals.[31]

The Noah's Ark animals were clearly fragile, and to position them upright "two by two" or "notate" them (to use de Waal's phrase), to make them present, as in the example image below, was not viable (they simply would have collapsed). Yet they could still be held, felt, smelt, and observed, in and out of their storage boxes.

Sometime later, during another playful rummage with the artists, a small white packet was found, upon which was written the mysterious "LOOSE PARTS." Opening this little parcel up revealed a wonderful horde: tails, hooves, legs, ears, and the missing zebra's head (see figure 4.3).

Yet, as already noted, one of the recognized values of this collection lay in its brokenness and in the narrative of things missing, the spaces and traces of former lives lived prior to the gallery. This narrative could only be told through the materiality of the collection. Imagine the surprise of the artists, then, some weeks later when revisiting the boxes, to discover that the headless zebra was no longer headless! The project team struggled to contain their disappointment on seeing a pair of gleaming, pristine zebras, reunited by meticulous (and anonymous) conservators, complete with heads. Had something been lost in the very process of bringing these two parts together to make a present "whole?"[32] Arguably, the emotional significance and value of this zebra actually lay in its prior incompleteness, in its traces of life and use, the patina and sense of connection with the children who had once played with it, the story of its brokenness. Yet all too often museums shy away from these powerful stories of the broken, preferring

---

30 Alexandra Woodall, Liz Mitchell, and Sharon Blakey, "Mary Mary Quite Contrary: The Mary Greg Collection at Manchester Art Gallery," *The Ruskin Review and Bulletin* 7, no. 1. (Spring 2011): 36–46 (43).

31 "Missing Objects," www.marymaryquitecontrary.org.uk/archives/1546 [accessed September 9, 2015].

32 This question has also been posed in an earlier paper by Alexandra Woodall, "Mary Greg's Bygones: A Misplaced Collection?," *Social History Curators' Group News* 66 (2010): 7–9, and in Blakey and Mitchell, "A Question of Value."

Figure 4.2. Tray of Noah's Ark animals, including a headless zebra, in the Mary Greg Collection. © Ben Blackall for Manchester City Galleries, licensed under CC BY-NC-SA 3.0.

Figure 4.3. Loose parts including the zebra's head. Photograph by Alexandra Woodall.

the neat, the conserved, and the complete. These stored "unloved" objects can reveal far more and have far more potential for emotional engagement than things on display. I now turn to another project whose aims were to ask exactly this sort of question about the values of things yet which perhaps in reality asked another sort of question, beyond the object itself.

Finding the Value

Finding the Value was an exhibition held in 2014 that took place at York St. Mary's, a deconsecrated church and site for contemporary art that forms part of York Museums Trust (YMT).[33] Five artists (Andrew Bracey, Alison Erika Forde, Yvette Hawkins, Susie MacMurray, and Simon Venus)[34] were invited to create new work responding to and actually using a collection of objects (including books, paintings, and ethnographic

---

33 "Finding the Value: Contemporary Artists Explore Aspects of the Madsen Collection," www.yorkstmarys.org.uk/exhibition/finding-the-value/ [accessed July 2, 2019].

34 Andrew Bracey (www.andrewbracey.co.uk); Alison Erika Forde (www.alisonerikaforde.com); Yvette Hawkins (http://yvettehawkins.co.uk); Susie MacMurray (www.susie-macmurray.co.uk); and Simon Venus (www.facebook.com/simonvenusauto mata) [all accessed February 29, 2016].

and decorative art) that had been bequeathed to YMT by a pair of siblings who, ironic-
ally, were entirely unknown to the Trust during their lifetimes, Peter Emil Madsen and
his sister Karen Madsen. The bequest also consisted of Peter Madsen's wide-ranging
collections of objects. Where these items resonated with YMT's acquisition policies,
some were immediately accessioned into the main collection. Some were sold at auction,
but the remaining objects were given to the commissioned artists to use in whatever
ways they saw fit, including through reconfiguring, reimagining, wrapping, and even by
allowing silkworms to build cocoons over them. This encounter by artists, another form
of "material interpretation," allowed for discussions about the values of objects to take
place in a public forum, as well as discussions about what it means to use, or even to use
up, an object.

   In her Introduction to the Madsen Commissions, then Chief Executive Officer (CEO)
of York Museums Trust and curator of the exhibition, Janet Barnes, speaks about the
origins of the project. She talks about the market value of aspects of the collection that
were accessioned and sold, but she also notes that the remaining items of lesser value
"may well have been objects of high value in terms of personal meaning or affection."[35]
But this will never be known. She asks, "How can the curator respond to these
human values as opposed to straightforward calculations of financial worth?"[36] The
project, also described as "a cultural entrepreneurial risk," arose as an attempt to answer
this question.

> We decided to take these works, both images and objects, as the raw material for new
> works. It is intended that the new works should respond to, investigate and develop
> the values and cultural meaning of the original works. It may even be the case that the
> financial value of the new works will greatly exceed the present value of the original
> material. It is hoped to be a creative questioning of, and experiment in, the inheritance
> and development of cultural values.[37]

Although there are similarities between this project and "Mary Mary Quite Contrary,"
there are significant differences. Firstly, unlike the Mary Greg project, the Madsen
project always had an outcome in mind: an exhibition of new work by artists who
specifically applied for an official commission. Although still a risk, the York project was
arguably less open-ended than the serendipitous one at Manchester Art Gallery. There
would be a display at the end of the process. The second significant distinction is that at
York St. Mary's, the project was initiated by the CEO. There was never anything "under
the radar" about it; the project and its challenging of institutional hierarchies, notions
of value, and attitudes towards access and emotional response were being promulgated
deliberately from the top.

   So, what emerged from this shift in hierarchy? How did these artists with distinct
practices respond? What aspects of the collection and ideas of its use and ownership

---

35 Janet Barnes, *Finding the Value: Contemporary Artists Explore Aspects of the Madsen Collection*
(York: York Museums Trust, 2014), 8.

36 Barnes, *Finding the Value*, 9.

37 Barnes, *Finding the Value*, 9.

were brought to the fore in the ensuing exhibition? Here, I will outline a few key aspects that highlight some of the similarities and differences in approach between the artists, a diverse group working in different media, at different stages in their careers and practices, and all responding in individual ways to the Madsen Collection. Perhaps one significant question is the extent to which any of the artists actually used the works themselves as raw materials for material interpretations, as Barnes set out in her aims for the project. Were some of the artists more concerned with the stories surrounding the objects or with their "museumification" than with the things in themselves?[38] Does this matter? In order to answer this, I focus on just three of the artists' responses.

Susie MacMurray is a British artist whose work includes drawing, sculpture, and architectural installations. A former classical musician, she retrained as an artist, graduating with an MA in Fine Art in 2001. She lives in Manchester, UK, and has an international exhibition profile, showing regularly in the USA and Europe as well as in the UK. In a catalogue essay for an earlier exhibition at Agnew's Gallery, *The Eyes of the Skin*, Kathleen Soriano states, "Whilst the sense of loss has nearly always been present in her [MacMurray's] work, it is also as much about the nature of memories and remnants of our existence."[39]

MacMurray's work for *Finding the Value* was entitled *Legacy* and was "centred on the idea of the gift and how that context transforms the perception of the object that has been given."[40] Through carefully wrapping objects in golden wire, they are transformed mysteriously and somehow elevated to a, perhaps, more precious status than the original object. Yet viewers will never know what the original item was. Rather than dwell on the materiality of the chosen objects, MacMurray uses the sensory act of wrapping as her form of material interpretation. But ultimately, the wrapped items go beyond this materiality. They extend into the realm of ideas and indeed of human relationships, where object is understood as gift.[41] The important thing here is not necessarily the object itself, but that it has been given. MacMurray's response is, above all, an emotional one. "My immediate response to the collection had been an intense sense of poignancy: these things, amassed through a lifetime, must have had personal significance and had many stories and private memories attached to them, none of which are now available to us. I was struck by what a loaded gesture the act of giving such a collection is. It touches all sorts of areas, from trust and responsibility to subjective perceptions of value and worth."[42]

---

38 Dudley speaks of the need to return to the object rather than use it to punctuate another narrative or where the object might just be part of the "object-information package," overridden by a label. Dudley, *Museum Materialities*, 3.

39 Kathleen Soriano, "Catalogue Essay for 'The Eyes of the Skin,'" Agnew's Gallery, November 9–December 2, 2011, www.susie-macmurray.co.uk/published-materials/eyes-of-the-skin [accessed July 2, 2019].

40 Barnes, *Finding the Value*, 16.

41 See Marcel Mauss, *The Gift: The Form and Reason for Exchange in Archaic Societies* (London: Routledge Classics, 1954, reprint 2002).

42 Barnes, *Finding the Value*, 16.

Likewise, artist Simon Venus was also drawn to the notion and story of the bequest itself rather than the individual items forming the gift. He states of his work *Passed On*: "I became fascinated by how such a generous gift was made by just two letters, without the parties ever meeting, and that there is almost no information about or image of either Karen or Peter."[43] His resulting work is site specific: The church location led him to the idea of triptych "as homage to absent donors, with figurative imagery acting as stand-ins for them."[44] His emergent cabinet of curiosity display is part mechanical surreal automaton, part memento mori, and part eulogy to the Madsens themselves. He states: "Intrigued by how little is known about the Madsens, I felt their collection took on a greater significance in bearing testimony to their existence, outliving them, given new life and meaning, they march on in time transformed from personal to public ownership and from private collection to contemporary art."[45] But his work also questions museum processes: what makes the Madsens' objects cross into the domain of contemporary art? In Venus's work, labels were included both to lead and to mislead the visitor and were "chosen to subvert traditional museum labelling whilst the artificial ageing gave them a level of authority and authenticity."[46]

The third artist discussed here, Yvette Hawkins, is a visual artist of British–South Korean origin working across installation and sculpture. Like Simon Venus, Hawkins's work also challenges institutional practices. In her words, her work "explores themes which encompass hybridity, tradition, migration and preservation which relate to 'the cultural other' and specifically about her mixed-race heritage and nomadic upbringing occupying forty-five homes across two nations. Craft also plays an important role in the making of work, often involving traditional skill centred techniques such as book-binding, embroidery and printmaking."[47]

Hawkins's response to the Madsen Collection was entitled *Casing In* and focused on the relationship between decay and preservation (see figure 4.4).[48] The artist states:

> I was particularly excited to find a small collection of Japanese hand-bound books in the Madsen Collection, and a collection of prints and paintings on Japanese rice paper. I was intrigued by markings and perforations through some of the book covers and pages that, on first inspection, were assumed to be intentionally made. These delicate marks are actually the trails left by insects—a beautiful tracery which coincidentally mirrors the landscape drawings found within the books. I worked with silkworms and their fascinating spinning techniques to mend and preserve books from the collection, which had been subject to both these insects and the decay of time.[49]

---

43 Simon Venus, "Finding the Value," unpublished essay, 2014.

44 Barnes, *Finding the Value*, 18.

45 Barnes, *Finding the Value*, 18.

46 Venus, "Finding the Value."

47 Yvette Hawkins, "Yvette Hawkins: About," https://yvettehawkins.co.uk/about/ [accessed July 2, 2019].

48 See DeSilvey, "Observed Decay."

49 Barnes, *Finding the Value*, 14.

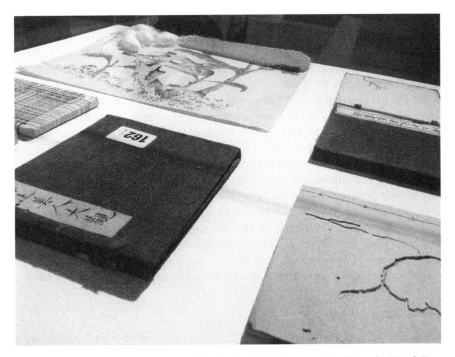

Figure 4.4. Detail from *Casing In*, York St. Mary's, 2014. Photograph by Alexandra Woodall.

Of all the artists involved in *Finding the Value*, arguably Hawkins's response to the brief was the one that found the value. It focused not on the gift or on the stories behind the gift's objects but on the objects themselves. Her process has resonance with Ingold's statement that making "is a process of correspondence: not the imposition of pre-conceived form on raw material substance, but the drawing out or bringing forth of potentials immanent in a world of becoming."[50] Her collaboration with and care for silkworms was a direct consequence of the insect trails found within the Madsens' Japanese books. Echoing the conservation of objects undertaken in museums, Hawkins's silkworms conserve, make, and remake the books. They transform them, laying bare institutional practices of conservation, restoration, and access; they destroy pages and rebuild them and reveal the objects in a new light for the viewer. Here, the artistic inter-vention is possible through a hands-on encounter with these otherwise forgotten, worn, and bookworm-eaten books.[51] The books are changed forever, used, and used up in this process of being shown.

---

50 Tim Ingold, *Making: Anthropology, Archaeology, Art and Architecture* (Abingdon: Routledge, 2013), 31.

51 These new works inspired by the Madsen Bequest developed an already strong tradition in York of dynamic, risk-taking, and imaginative working, both with artists and with objects. Under the visionary leadership of Janet Barnes CBE (Chief Executive from 2002 to 2015), York Museums

In her volume on the pedagogic role of artists' interventions in museums, Claire Robins suggests that "When artists have been commissioned to intervene in collections in order to disrupt visitors' expectations ... the host museum often intends to signal a shift in the way its collection and itself, as an institution, are understood."[52] This is certainly the case at York Museums Trust, which has successfully worked with contemporary artists in the way Robins suggests to reinterpret its collections for visitors. Indeed, the way in which this has been achieved as a form of material interpretation, especially by Hawkins, is, perhaps, the most successful answer to the initial project where Barnes sought to use the objects as raw material. Following Sandra Dudley's call for museums to refocus on the encounter with the very objects at their heart rather than to exist simply as places to find out factual information about things, elements of this project at York St. Mary's have actively explored "the magic of things themselves."[53] *Finding the Value* has managed to enable at least one of its artists to "return to the material reality of the material, to shift attention back to objects as objects, focusing again on aspects of those things' apparently trivial and obvious material qualities and the possibilities of directly, physically, emotionally engaging with them."[54] In this way, unvalued objects are given new lives. I now turn to the third case study, which also focuses on exposing museum processes.

What Can Be Seen

The third case study, *What Can Be Seen*,[55] is another collaborative project, an exhibition held at Museums Sheffield's Millennium Gallery in 2017. This saw artists Tim Etchells and Vlatka Horvat playfully reimagining the city's historic collections and, importantly, responding to their experiences of museum documentation and packaging in the storerooms. Particularly interested in collections of collections, the artists spent time delving behind the scenes and working with museum curators to create a display that juxtaposed objects in unusual ways, but they also explored their experiences behind the scenes through a series of new photographs. This exploration raised numerous questions for museum staff about what it means to lay bare museum processes to a questioning public. Like the previous projects discussed here, this too rethought the value of objects through what the artists called an "archaeology of the storage space." Tim Etchells is

---

Trust was arguably at the forefront in the UK of engaging with creative practitioners and developing the use of accessioned objects within artistic interventions. In 2009, for example, *Five Sisters*, a site-specific installation by painter Matthew Collings and mosaicist Emma Biggs, used real items from the accessioned stored archaeological collections to create a huge mosaic of pottery, which spanned the nave of York St. Mary's.

52 Robins, *Curious Lessons in the Museum*, 213. See also Putnam, *Art and Artifact*.

53 Sandra Dudley, ed., *Museum Objects: Experiencing the Properties of Things* (Abingdon: Routledge, 2012), 12. See also Dudley, *Museum Materialities*.

54 Dudley, *Museum Objects*, 11.

55 "Tim Etchells and Vlatka Horvat: What Can Be Seen," www.museums-sheffield.org.uk/museums/millennium-gallery/exhibitions/past/tim-etchells-and-vlatka-horvat-what-can-be-seen [accessed July 2, 2019].

an artist and a writer based in the UK. He has worked in a wide variety of contexts, notably as leader of the world-renowned performance group Forced Entertainment, and in collaboration with a range of visual artists, choreographers, and photographers. His work spans performance, video, photography, text projects, installation, and fiction. He is currently Professor of Performance and Writing at Lancaster University.[56] Vlatka Horvat, born in Čakovec, Croatia, also works across a wide range of forms: sculpture, installation, drawing, performance, and photography. Her work has been presented internationally in a variety of contexts—in museums and galleries, theatre and dance festivals, and in public spaces. After twenty years in the USA, she is currently based in London.[57]

Over a period of two years, these artist-partners were invited by the Head of Exhibitions and Display at Museums Sheffield, Kirstie Hamilton, to work collaboratively to engage with the collection in storage, because the institution was "very keen and interested in having a different set of eyes to look at both what they have and what they do."[58] Rather like the rummages used in the Mary Greg case study, the project started as an "open-ended expedition," with the artists spending a week in the storerooms and with different collections curators, describing it as feeling like "kids in the candy store," and with "a huge amount of openness and trust sort of extended on the part of the museum and the curators."[59]

These rummages slowly began to turn into an exhibition with a three-part structure, reflecting the artists' different experiences and interests in the storerooms. Both immediately fell in love with a particular set of objects: the Sorby Slides (see figure 4.5). This is a collection of scientific slides developed by Sheffield-born Henry Clifton Sorby (1826–1908). By cleaning and staining marine biology specimens and placing them onto glass lantern slides, Sorby developed a new technique for viewing sea creatures. Many of these slides are in Museums Sheffield's collections. Etchells and Horvat partly just wanted an excuse to display these objects, but they also began to develop additional motivations inspired by their time in the storerooms, which they categorized in three distinct ways.

Firstly, they noticed they were drawn to collections of collections: "the museum holds [items] which are somehow many versions of the same thing,"[60] such as, for example, the Sorby Slides, which are "endless iterations of these sorts of specimens preserved in a particular way," and also numerous drawings by the eminent Derbyshire archaeologist Thomas Bateman (1821–1861)[61] showing positions of bones found through archaeological digs. There is something about the repeat nature of these collections that the artists wanted to represent.

---

56 "About: Tim Etchells," http://timetchells.com/about/ [accessed January 4, 2018].

57 "CV: Vlatka Horvat," www.vlatkahorvat.com/cv/ [accessed January 4, 2018].

58 Vlatka Horvat, interview by Alexandra Woodall via Skype, September 15, 2017.

59 Vlatka Horvat, interview by Alexandra Woodall via Skype, September 15, 2017.

60 Tim Etchells, interview by Alexandra Woodall via Skype, September 15, 2017.

61 Interestingly, Thomas Bateman was also Mary Greg's great-grandfather. See "Thomas Bateman," www.marymaryquitecontrary.org.uk/archives/509 [accessed July 2, 2019].

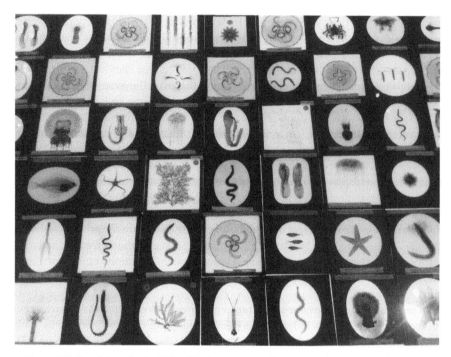

Figure 4.5. Detail from Sorby Slides, Museums Sheffield. Photograph by Alexandra Woodall.

Secondly, the artists showed interest in the particular ways in which objects in museums are categorized. In a large vitrine, they thus displayed objects "selected by and organized according to physical properties and irrespective of their place in the collection or their value"[62] rather than following any classical museum taxonomy. This playful approach arose as a direct result of the stored objects, which were "in a dormant state" and "waiting out of sight":[63] "We were very fascinated with, I think, the encounter that we had with the objects, the artefacts, the specimens in the storage because there they are somehow off the stage, out of the spotlight, off the podium. They're sort of returned in a way to a banality."[64] So, in the vitrine, a teddy bear lies alongside a puffer fish, bits of glass that had come from the bottom of a hearth in a glass workshop, shells, and Victorian domestic appliances (see figure 4.6).

Etchells and Horvat also began to notice a category of "unworthy" exhibits: things that had not yet been conserved or that needed something to be done to them before they could be displayed. Old oil painting frames, wrapped in polythene, fell into this category as items to which they were drawn aesthetically, and the exhibition title plays on the idea

---

62 Tim Etchells, interview by Alexandra Woodall via Skype, September 15, 2017.

63 Vlatka Horvat, interview by Alexandra Woodall via Skype, September 15, 2017.

64 Tim Etchells, interview by Alexandra Woodall via Skype, September 15, 2017.

Figure 4.6. "What Can Be Seen" detail, Museums Sheffield. Photograph by Alexandra Woodall.

that things are and are not seen, depending on who and where the viewer is situated, not least within the museum's institutional hierarchy. They describe this vitrine element of the exhibition as "demystifying the work that goes on in this invisible life of objects, away from public view and away from display mode."[65] The artists also expressed a desire to display objects exactly as they had been encountered behind the scenes, to replicate their own emotional encounter. So an entire drawer of Victorian clocks found its way into a case, in different stages of disassembly and still semi-wrapped in tissue. Mirroring the way in which Hazel Jones described the sensation of opening drawers full of Mary Greg's collections, here "We were interested in quite an unruly and cacophonous sort of selection of things that seemingly didn't really go together or have anything to do with each other. I think as that process went on, the curators got more and more drawn into that as well, and quite a few of them said to us, 'Oh, it made me actually look at things that I haven't looked at in a whole or in a different sort of way ...' "[66]

The third aspect that piqued the artists' interest was the notion of traces. In particular, the artists were drawn to textual traces in the storerooms, especially traces of the human hand, perhaps where a curator had labelled a box or had written a little note

---

65 Vlatka Horvat, interview by Alexandra Woodall via Skype, September 15, 2017.

66 Vlatka Horvat, interview by Alexandra Woodall via Skype, September 15, 2017.

to him- or herself. They refer to this as "archaeologizing the storage space," "gathering little narrative clues and hints of people's work which become these sorts of phrases and fragments of language that sort of activate imagination in different ways, and also speak to the processes of categorization and preserving and so on."[67] The artists found themselves drawn to traces in the card index where there were gaps or some sort of institutional failure, for example, where a label had been photographed, bluntly stating, "useless, destroyed."

> We were very drawn to things that were "unidentified object from an unknown country" or "no further context available" or [...] "items about which something is uncertain," and there was also quite a strand of things in the storage that the museum wasn't sure if they owned [...] and we learned then through research that all the museums have those kinds of objects. There's even a sort of classification, letter "x," which identifies that there's some sort of dubious status of the item [...] and that can happen when an object gets separated from its record, or the record goes missing and they cannot be matched, or something goes out on loan and comes back and doesn't get properly logged, so it enters into this kind of limbo state of uncertainty.[68]

Yet the artists were concerned with the ethics of their approach throughout. What would the curators think? They note that they would never have "disrespected the specimens in any way," and if an object had a problematic status in relation to culture or history in an exhibition that did not contextualize (such as theirs), it would not be right to show it. Likewise, they developed positive relationships with curatorial staff, who they believed may have been "puzzled" about what they were up to but who were "very supportive" and engaged in questions about making sure the work was contextualized (with a supporting film) to ensure that visitors understood the museum's current policies and procedures with regard to acquisitions and disposals and that visitors were aware that a lack of information about every single object in a museum's collection was far from unusual.

Perhaps more so than the other two case studies, Museums Sheffield's project is about laying bare those museum processes and being transparent towards, and thus significantly respecting, its audiences by sharing its (and every museum's) fallibility. The artists were particularly struck by the amount of trust they were shown by museum staff, and they noted of their experience with the curators that "you come away thinking these are not jobs, these are people's lives" and that it was "humbling" and "heartening."[69] "In a way that's something that steps the museum down off the sort of machinic, you know, rigorous, you know, entirely infallible system, system, system, and maybe it opens it at a more human level, and I think that's one of the things that I think works in that show, that people responded to it in that creative sort of way."[70] So here, perhaps above all other examples, those museum processes are exposed.

---

67 Tim Etchells, interview by Alexandra Woodall via Skype, September 15, 2017.
68 Vlatka Horvat, interview by Alexandra Woodall via Skype, September 15, 2017.
69 Vlatka Horvat, interview by Alexandra Woodall via Skype, September 15, 2017.
70 Tim Etchells, interview by Alexandra Woodall via Skype, September 15, 2017.

Concluding Remarks

In their paper "Object-Love at the Science Museum: Cultural Geographies of Museum Storerooms," Geoghegan and Hess refer to their work as marking "a departure from the preoccupation with the public spaces of museums to go behind the scenes."[71] They describe three related motivations for this work: to develop the field of museum geography, to link a focus on materiality of objects with the notion of "affect" and object-love, and to develop autoethnography as a method.[72] They argue that "the storeroom reveals a set of spatial relations involving intimacy and distance, connection and disconnection rarely experienced in the everyday world."[73] While their research is about curators and conservators responding to "their" collections, here, the research has opened up those collections to ownership beyond staff—to artists invited into those storerooms or to explore those less-treasured collections. Just as for Geoghegan and Hess's curators and conservators, "object-love, incorporating the personal and national need to care for objects and material heritage, underpins the form and function of the storeroom,"[74] so too does object-love underpin the response of the artists in this paper.

The important role of emotion in the object encounter as something that goes beyond traditional learning (or knowledge) is noted by Chatterjee: "the experiences elicited by touch ... go beyond, but do not exclude, learning and enjoyment, to include deep emotional responses stimulated by object handling."[75] Indeed, Pye also states, "objects can touch us as much as we can touch them."[76] It is these emotional responses that are particularly visceral and "alive" within the storerooms. Ingold speaks of material thus: "Materials are ineffable. They cannot be pinned down in terms of established concepts or categories. To describe any material is to pose a riddle, whose answer can be discovered only through observation and engagement with what is there. The riddle gives the material a voice and allows it to tell its own story: it is up to us, then, to listen, and from the clues it offers, to discover what is speaking."[77] Yet through opening up storerooms, this riddle is opened to a multiplicity of responses, not least its emotional resonance.

By way of some concluding remarks, I will focus on two benefits of enabling "delightful rummaging" that could go beyond the artist audience to a wider public. Firstly, material interpretation is a valid way of enabling emotional response as a different type of museum knowledge, one that allows for playfully imagining and reimagining collections. Secondly, deliberately opening up areas behind the scenes, making museum processes

---

71 Geoghegan and Hess, "Object-Love at the Science Museum," 445.

72 Geoghegan and Hess, "Object-Love at the Science Museum," 446.

73 Geoghegan and Hess, "Object-Love at the Science Museum," 451.

74 Geoghegan and Hess, "Object-Love at the Science Museum," 461.

75 Helen Chatterjee, ed., *Touch in Museums: Policy and Practice in Object Handling* (Oxford: Berg, 2008), 4.

76 Elizabeth Pye, "Understanding Objects: The Role of Touch in Conservation," in *The Power of Touch: Handling Objects in Museum and Heritage Contexts*, ed. Elizabeth Pye (Walnut Creek: Left Coast, 2007), 121–38 (134).

77 Ingold, *Making*, 31.

more transparent, enables critical rethinking of institutional practice. A willingness to engage in these sorts of practices of "letting go" of ownership and giving over authority on collections to artists is a direct political, democratizing, and arguably more ethical act by the institution.[78]

In her volume *Museum Objects: Experiencing the Properties of Things*, Sandra Dudley notes, "it is perhaps especially remarkable that more work has not focused on the physical and sensory attributes of objects and their implications for the uniqueness, actual and potential, of the museum experience."[79] The sorts of projects in this chapter are exactly those which aim to explore these materialities of objects, particularly through affective encounters with objects that were, at first, not on display. One strand linking all the case studies is their focus on material interpretation as affective and sensory: artists make new work in response to objects because they have been able to encounter them first-hand and with their hands. In some instances, they even used the objects up in their new creative endeavours in a process invested with emotion.

While rummaging and opening up the storerooms or neglected collections will not be appropriate in all museums and with all collections, there are elements of this approach that could be appropriated into museum strategy, not least in approaches to public programming. A focus on the materiality of objects, on engaging with makers in particular to provide new ways of interpreting objects through their materiality, might go some way towards meeting the recommendation made in the *Collections for People* report[80] that Collections Access Officers should be employed to engage the public with collections. Perhaps, indeed, it is time for some kind of "rummage facilitator" role across the sector. Responding to material is, after all, what makers do, having a "particular sensitivity to the way material bears traces."[81] Of course, many museums and galleries already have artists in residence,[82] but this call has a different emphasis. Artists might play a particular role in actually engaging the various visiting publics (and staff) with "unloved" objects in imaginative, creative, and new ways. Indeed, we might go one step further to reflect on

---

78 Robins, *Curious Lessons in the Museum*, 213.

79 Dudley, *Museum Objects*, 5.

80 Suzanne Keene with Alice Stevenson, and Francesca Monti, *Collections for the People* (London: UCL Institute for Archaeology, 2008), 71–72. Recent work at Derby Museums' Silk Mill: Re:Make, as a space for makers, is one such example of this type of approach. See "Re:Make," http://remakemuseum.tumblr.com [accessed September 20, 2015]. The Museums Association's Collections 2030, launched in March 2018 with its focus on the use of collections, will be significant for future developments in this area.

81 On discussing the response of one artist to a wooden spoon: "I had not particularly noticed the wear on that spoon and the fact that the wear on that spoon must have come from somebody doing that [stirring motion], lots and lots and lots and lots of times. And that's what she saw. She saw that act, that movement, that sort of describing of a movement in the wear and tear on that spoon." "H," interview by Alexandra Woodall, June 9, 2013, in *Sensory Engagements with Objects in Art Galleries*.

82 See Kirsten Wehner and Martha Sear, "Engaging the Material World: Object Knowledge and 'Australian Journeys'," in *Museum Materialities: Objects, Engagements, Interpretations*, ed. Sandra Dudley (London: Routledge, 2010), 143–61 and especially Robins, *Curious Lessons in the Museum*.

the role of the museum as enabler of access; using objects, even using up objects, might be seen as something positive, even as a restoration of life to things. Interviewees spoke of museum objects as being dead things, using a variety of metaphors to do so. Yet what if, through a process of making things present and accessible, we let them die a more natural death (and therefore truly live)? There are conservators using this line of argument, so the notion of "sacrificing" objects is less controversial than it might at first appear. "If a few objects disappeared, or were damaged, there would still be objects enough left to satisfy everybody in the future."[83] And, going even further, this could actually be an ethical imperative, since "using collections, even if we risk losing some items is not irresponsible, but it should be judiciously encouraged as it makes objects accessible."[84] Objects are not meant to exist forever. One interviewee has even suggested that being "sacrificed" from a collection is actually an act of regaining something of its original life:

> It is a difficult one because you don't want the objects to get damaged but [...] if they're just lying in a drawer gathering dust, they're not doing anybody any good. So you obviously need [...] sacrificial objects [...] Things that you've got multiples of, surely you can sacrifice one? [...] I mean, most of the objects are pretty sturdy, aren't they? I mean they've been battered around. They've been lying in the ground. They've been used. Actually, what's a few more scratches? Actually, a few more scratches is probably improving them and [...] it's actually probably going to be improved by being handled. It's going to give it life again, isn't it? See, you're not sacrificing it; you're giving it life. You're sacrificing it from the collection. Am I getting too poetic here? [...] Objects tell stories by the marks on them as well. So handling them is going to leave more stories, isn't it?[85]

Through material engagements and interpretation, activities such as the rummaging and handling described in this chapter will enable those objects to further develop their social and emotional lives, biographies, and agency.[86] In fact, delightful rummaging is to reunite these objects with their lost materiality, a materiality that is, above all, a materiality in relation to people, and these people are largely lacking when the objects are in storage.[87] Like Saki's lumber room, behind the scenes of museums there are also "storehouse[s] of unimagined treasures." It is our job to make the storerooms accessible

---

83 Jan Hjorth, "Travelling Exhibits: The Swedish Experience," in *Towards the Museum of the Future*, ed. Roger Miles and Lauro Zavala (London: Routledge, 1994), 99–115 (106), cited by Elizabeth Pye, "Collections Mobility Perspectives on Conservation: Emphasis on the Original Object," in *Encouraging Collections Mobility: A Way Forward for Museums in Europe*, ed. Susanna Pettersson, Monika Hagedorn-Saupe, Teijamari Jyrkkiö, and Astrid Weij (Berlin: Finnish National Gallery, Erfgoed Nederland, and Institut fur Museumsforschung, 2010), 136–49 (141).

84 Pye, "Collections Mobility Perspectives on Conservation," 145.

85 "J," interview by Alexandra Woodall, June 15, 2013, in "Sensory Engagements with Objects in Art Galleries."

86 See also arguments made by Cornelius Holtorf, "Averting Loss Aversion in Cultural Heritage," *International Journal of Heritage Studies* 21, no. 4 (2015): 405–21.

87 "The concept of materiality is required because it tries to consider and embrace subject-object relations going beyond the brute materiality of stones and considering why certain kinds of stone and their properties become important to people," Christopher Tilley, "Materiality in Materials," *Archaeological Dialogues* 14, no. 1 (2007): 16–20 (17).

and to unlock their doors, not least to artists, to imagine and reimagine not only their material treasures but also their processes, their people, and their relationships, to keep these objects alive and in use and to enable that emotional response of object-love and joy to emerge. In order to give hidden collections their full affective, emotionally charged potential to be "generative of a different kind of knowledge," a knowledge that is so often overlooked within traditional museum displays with their object-information packages,[88] it is imperative that we cast any squeamishness aside, "poke among the beach rubble," and delight in enabling new ways for people to encounter material objects.

Bibliography

Barnes, Janet. *Finding the Value: Contemporary Artists Explore Aspects of the Madsen Collection.* York: York Museums Trust, 2014.

Birchall, Danny. *Institution and Intervention: Artists' Projects in Object-Based Museums.* Unpublished MA dissertation, University of London, 2012.

Blakey, Sharon, and Liz Mitchell. "A Question of Value: Rethinking the Mary Greg Collection." In *Collaboration through Craft*, edited by Amanda Ravetz, Alice Kettle, and Helen Felcey, 170–85. London: Bloomsbury, 2013.

Brusius, Mirjam, and Kavita Singh, ed. *Museum Storage and Meaning: Tales from the Crypt.* Oxford: Routledge, 2018.

Carson, Anne. *If Not, Winter: Fragments of Sappho.* London: Virago, 2002.

Chatterjee, Helen, ed. *Touch in Museums: Policy and Practice in Object Handling.* Oxford: Berg, 2008.

Classen, Constance, and David Howes. "The Museum as Sensescape: Western Sensibilities and Indigenous Artifacts." In *Sensible Objects: Colonialism, Museums and Material Culture*, edited by Elizabeth Edwards, Chris Gosden, and Ruth Phillips, 199–222. Oxford: Berg, 2006.

DeLyser, Dydia. "Collecting, Kitsch and the Intimate Geographies of Social Memory: A Story of Archival Autoethnography." *Transactions of the Institute of British Geographers* 40 (2014): 209–22.

DeSilvey, Caitlin. "Observed Decay: Telling Stories with Mutable Things." *Journal of Material Culture* 11, no. 3 (2006): 318–38.

Dorsett, Chris. "Making Meanings Beyond Display." In *Museum Materialities: Objects, Engagements, Interpretations*, edited by Sandra Dudley, 241–59. Oxford: Routledge, 2010.

Dudley, Sandra, ed. *Museum Materialities: Objects, Engagements, Interpretations.* Oxford: Routledge, 2010.

———, ed. *Museum Objects: Experiencing the Properties of Things.* Abingdon: Routledge, 2012.

Geoghegan, Hilary, and Alison Hess. "Object-Love at the Science Museum: Cultural Geographies of Museum Storerooms." *Cultural Geographies* 22, no. 3 (2015): 445–46.

Greenblatt, Stephen. "Resonance and Wonder." In *Exhibiting Cultures: The Poetics and Politics of Museum Display*, edited by Ivan Karp and Steven D. Lavine, 42–56. Washington, DC: Smithsonian Institution, 1991.

Hjorth, Jan. "Travelling Exhibits: The Swedish Experience." In *Towards the Museum of the Future*, edited by Roger Miles and Lauro Zavala, 99–115. London: Routledge, 1994.

Holtorf, Cornelius. "Averting Loss Aversion in Cultural Heritage." *International Journal of Heritage Studies* 21, no. 4 (2015): 405–21.

---

88 Dudley, "Museum Materialities," 5.

Ingold, Tim. *Making: Anthropology, Archaeology, Art and Architecture*. Abingdon: Routledge, 2013.

Keene, Suzanne with Alice Stevenson, and Francesca Monti. *Collections for the People*. London: UCL Institute for Archaeology, 2008.

Mauss, Marcel. *The Gift: The Form and Reason for Exchange in Archaic Societies*. London: Routledge Classics, 1954. Reprint 2002.

McShine, Kynaston. *The Museum as Muse: Artists Reflect*. London: Thames & Hudson, 1999.

Ouzman, Sven. "The Beauty of Letting Go: Fragmentary Museums and Archaeologies of Archive." In *Sensible Objects: Colonialism, Museums and Material Culture*, edited by Elizabeth Edwards, Chris Gosden, and Ruth Phillips, 269–301. Oxford: Berg, 2006.

Putnam, James. *Art and Artifact: The Museum as Medium*. London: Thames & Hudson, 2001. Reprint 2009.

Pye, Elizabeth. "Collections Mobility Perspectives on Conservation: Emphasis on the Original Object." In *Encouraging Collections Mobility: A Way Forward for Museums in Europe*, edited by Susanna Pettersson, Monika Hagedorn-Saupe, Teijamari Jyrkkiö, and Astrid Weij, 136–49. Berlin: Finnish National Gallery, Erfgoed Nederland, and Institut fur Museumsforschung, 2010.

——. "Understanding Objects: The Role of Touch in Conservation." In *The Power of Touch: Handling Objects in Museum and Heritage Contexts*, edited by Elizabeth Pye, 121–38. Walnut Creek: Left Coast, 2007.

Robins, Claire. *Curious Lessons in the Museum: The Pedagogic Potential of Artists' Interventions*. Farnham: Ashgate, 2013.

Saki. *Tobermory and Other Stories*, selected by Martin Stephen. London: Phoenix, 1998.

Smith, Laurajane, Margaret Wetherell, and Gary Campbell, ed. *Emotion, Affective Practices and the Past in the Present*. Abingdon: Routledge, 2018.

Soriano, Kathleen. "Catalogue Essay for 'The Eyes of the Skin.'" Agnew's Gallery, November 9–December 2, 2011. www.susie-macmurray.co.uk/published-materials/eyes-of-the-skin [accessed July 2, 2019].

Tilley, Christopher. "Materiality in Materials." *Archaeological Dialogues* 14, no. 1 (2007): 16–20.

Venus, Simon. "Finding the Value." Unpublished essay, 2014.

Vogel, Susan. "Always True to the Object, in Our Fashion." In *Grasping the World: The Idea of the Museum*, edited by Donald Preziosi and Claire Farago, 653–62. Hampshire: Ashgate, 2003.

Wehner, Kirsten, and Martha Sear. "Engaging the Material World: Object Knowledge and 'Australian Journeys.'" In *Museum Materialities: Objects, Engagements, Interpretations*, edited by Sandra Dudley, 143–61. London: Routledge, 2010.

Wilson, Fred, and Howard Halle. "Mining the Museum." *Grand Street* 44 (1993): 151–72.

Woodall, Alexandra. "Mary Greg's Bygones: A Misplaced Collection?" *Social History Curators' Group News* 66 (2010): 7–9.

——. "Rummaging as a Strategy for Creative Thinking and Imaginative Engagement in Higher Education." In *Engaging the Senses: Object-Based Learning in Higher Education*, edited by Helen Chatterjee and Leonie Hannan, 133–55. Surrey: Ashgate, 2015.

——. *Sensory Engagements with Objects in Art Galleries: Material Interpretation and Theological Metaphor*. Unpublished PhD thesis, University of Leicester, 2016.

Woodall, Alexandra, Liz Mitchell, and Sharon Blakey, "Mary Mary Quite Contrary: The Mary Greg Collection at Manchester Art Gallery." *The Ruskin Review and Bulletin* 7, no. 1 (Spring 2011): 36–46.

Chapter 5

NO DATA, NO USE?
CHANGING USE AND VALUATION OF
NATURAL HISTORY COLLECTIONS

MARK CARNALL*

Introduction

EVEN THE SMALLEST natural history collection has objects that number in the tens or hundreds of thousands. However, unlike other kinds of museums, until relatively recently, the value systems for natural history specimens have been measured on a strictly scientific basis. Treasures in natural history collections will often be rare specimens of extinct species or those collected by a few widely celebrated biologists, such as Charles Darwin and Alfred Russel Wallace. Even specimens collected by this rare category of biologists, whose research—in this case evolutionary theory—expands beyond natural history into sociology and philosophy, are often organized taxonomically rather than kept together as a discrete collection. Although these specimens may be a highlight of behind-the-scenes tours, or star specimens, their day-to-day management is, as for other collections of biological specimens, insects, birds, and crustaceans, filed away in correct taxonomic order. This singular approach to natural history collections was highlighted in 2009 during the international Darwin 200 celebrations, celebrating the 200th anniversary of the birth of Charles Darwin, in the fact that museums still could not answer the question on an institutional, national, or international level: where are all the Charles Darwin specimens? This remains the case today, with Darwin specimens spread across a number of museums, universities, and private collections but with no centralized effort made to bring these specimens together in a resource like the Darwin Correspondence Project for museum collections.[1] This lack of connectivity and basic information about the natural history material associated with one of the most widely acknowledged and

---

I "Darwin Correspondence Project," www.darwinproject.ac.uk [accessed March 20, 2017].

* **Mark Carnall** is the curator of the 500,000 specimens held by the Oxford University Museum of Natural History. He has previously worked and volunteered at local authority, national, and other university natural history museums. He is currently the Collections Manager (Life Collections), with responsibility for the vertebrate and invertebrate (nonentomological collections) material. In addition to managing collections, he lectures on biology, palaeobiology, and museological topics. His research interests are digitization in museums, public engagement and natural history, and sector-wide advocacy for collections, models, casts, and replicas, as well as the implications of 3D printing on museum collections. In addition to collections management, Mark contributes to public engagement through a range of activities, ranging from stand-up comedy about natural history museums to lectures, informal talks, and workshops for all age groups.

celebrated thinkers ever known speaks volumes about some of the challenges in natural history collections, let alone the management of "lesser" collections.

Underneath this top category are specimens that are perceived to be of more value than others by taxonomists: the name-bearing type specimens. Name-bearing type specimens, or "type specimens" for short, are the specimens on which original descriptions of new nominal species-groups are based. As such, they represent the gold reference standard, and the specimens or descriptions should be referred to in taxonomic work. Today, the designation and description of type specimens are tightly controlled by the relevant code publishing body: either the International Association for Plant Taxonomy for algae, fungi, and plants or the International Commission on Zoological Nomenclature for animals (Shenzhen Code, ICZN).[2] The number of type specimens in a natural history collection still remains the dominant metric that natural history museums, especially larger ones, use to measure and compare their value. The high value of these types of specimens among natural history museums emphasizes that value is still measured in strictly esoteric terms, primarily the potential use of these collections for biological researchers undertaking descriptive work. As with the Darwin specimens mentioned above, there is no one central resource that lists by institution where all known type specimens reside and, in many cases, it falls to researchers themselves to do the leg work that museums should be undertaking on the collections they supposedly value the most. Although the concept of type specimens is one that sits at the heart of biological taxonomy, there exist many problematic elements to managing even this high tier of "valuable" collections.

Until the nomenclatural codes were formalized, descriptions of type specimens could be vague. Some are no longer than a line, and there was no requirement for formal deposition in a scientific repository. Although type specimens and series are perceived to be the gold standard specimens when it comes to alpha taxonomy, in many cases trying to locate and reanalyze the original specimens to fit in with modern taxonomic frameworks is an exercise in frustration that more often than not emphasizes issues with the whole process. The recent example of scientists at the Museum of New Zealand trying to find the first described specimen of the wandering albatross is a typical tale of riddles and dead ends that doesn't paint museums or previous standards for taxonomic name publishing in a positive light.[3] If anything, global specimen hunts, such as these, to resolve taxonomic quibbles hinder rather than help modern taxonomy, which is often only a part of modern biological research, the indexing work that all other biological information can be organized around. Resolving taxonomic issues for technical systematic sections of formal publications can be time-consuming work when it is actually the applied biology, conservation, or ecology that is the prime concern of a fixed-period research project, for example.

---

2 Shenzhen Code, www.iapt-taxon.org/nomen/main.php; International Commission on Zoological Nomenclature (ICZN), www.iczn.org [accessed February 17, 2020].

3 Alan Tennyson, "The Global Hunt for the Original Wandering Albatross," Museum of New Zealand, 2007, http://blog.tepapa.govt.nz/2017/03/10/the-global-hunt-for-the-original-wandering-albatross/ [accessed March 29, 2017].

Taxonomy itself, the branch of science that deals with classification and systematics looking at the fundamental relationships between organisms, has been in a state of crisis for a while, and this crisis in the assumed prime users of natural history collections has caused an identity crisis in natural history museums themselves, as the following section will examine.

A Brief History of Natural History

Many natural history museums were founded in the nineteenth century by scientists who, by today's standards, straddled both science and public engagement. Certainly, in the nineteenth century, natural history museums were developing in line with other museums. In the UK, leading biologists of the time, like Richard Owen, E. Ray Lankester, and Robert Grant, were defining natural history museums, publishing academic papers on fundamental aspects of biology, corresponding with like-minded leaders around the world, securing new museum specimens, pioneering object-focused teaching, and pushing the role of museums in public education by day. In the evenings, they were formulating natural history as an academic discipline, popularizing science through the mainstream media, lobbying high society and the government to build new institutions to science, securing philanthropy, and founding many of the great learned scientific societies.

This period is often considered romantically as a "golden age" for natural history museums, but the window into the natural world at the time was much narrower than it is today. Richard Owen and his contemporaries could never have imagined the complexity of life at a subcellular, molecular, and atomic level. Exploration of the oceans, the atmosphere, and remote parts of the world has revealed previously unknown groups of plants and animals. Statistical analysis, complex system modelling, and even the basic tools of visualization, observation, and recording have opened up entire fields of enquiry since then.

Decline

It is widely considered that the 1950s mark the beginning of a general decline in whole organismal biology, as zoology and botany departments and degrees gave way to biological sciences departments and degrees.[4] Herbaria and vertebrate research collection numbers slowed in growth to an eventual stop. The number of PhDs in natural history declined, as did natural history related courses and the number of introductory biology texts devoted to natural history.[5] The original professorships in zoology and botany gave way to cell biology, genetics, ecology, and evolution. Natural history, particularly the nature-study approaches, with field trips to the "living laboratory," became

---

4 Joshua J. Tewksbury, John G. T. Anderson, Jonathan D. Bakker, Timothy J. Billo, Peter W. Dunwiddie, Martha J. Groom, Stephanie E. Hampton, et al., "Natural History's Place in Science and Society," *Bioscience* 64, no. 4 (2014): 300–310.

5 Tewksbury et al., "Natural History's Place in Science and Society."

unfashionable, and the term "naturalist" condescendingly derogatory,[6] in contrast to developing statistical and experimental approaches to the life sciences.

These divisions between the natural historian and the modern biologist are still causing debate today. Natural history museums are teeming with undiscovered species,[7] but collections suffer from not having trained biologists who can describe them, or they suffer from neglect, damage, and loss.[8] Instead of new molecular techniques, modelling power, and tools like DNA barcoding being additions to biologists' toolkits, these specialist techniques have become disciplines in their own right but not without attracting the criticism that a narrow, focused approach to biology is intellectually impoverished[9] or that modern science values information over knowledge.[10] As the trends in academic biology changed, so did the structure of courses, fieldwork, and practical sessions, leading biologist and author E. O. Wilson to make career-spanning pleas for the plight of taxonomy and the need for "more boots on the ground" if we were to understand biodiversity.[11] Using museum specimens fell out of fashion, and many universities shrank their technician teams and shut down (or threw away) their teaching museums and collections. Likewise, in regional museums, expert curators became surplus to requirements, and many formal functions of these smaller museums, such as keeping biological records, maintaining amateur and professional society collections, and undertaking surveys, were abandoned or once-active centres mothballed. The closure of many of these museums and teaching collections was poorly documented, but a crowdsourcing project by the Natural Sciences Collections Association (NatSCA) is attempting to map all of these closed collections, as well as current collections identified as being at risk.[12]

In the UK, larger museums and a handful of university departments became refugia for biologists who still went into the field, could identify plants and animals, and collected specimens. Museum directorships and curatorships were no longer the high-status

6 Michael Robert Pyle, "The Rise and Fall of Natural History," *Orion: People and Nature* 20, no. 4 (2001): 16–23.

7 Ed Yong, "Natural History Museums Are Teeming with Undiscovered Species," *The Atlantic*, 2016, www.theatlantic.com/science/archive/2016/02/the-unexplored-marvels-locked-away-in-our-natural-history-museums/459306/ [accessed October 31, 2017].

8 Christopher Kemp, "Museums: The Endangered Dead," *Nature News*, 2015, www.nature.com/news/museums-the-endangered-dead-1.16942 [accessed October 31, 2017].

9 Quentin D. Wheeler, "Taxonomic Triage and the Poverty of Phylogeny," *Philosophical Transactions of the Royal Society of London B* 359 (2004): 571–83.

10 Malte C. Ebach and Craig Holdrege, "DNA Barcoding is No Substitute for Taxonomy," *Nature* 434 (2005): 697.

11 Edward O. Wilson, "The Plight of Taxonomy," *Ecology* 52, no. 5 (1971): 1; Edward O. Wilson, "The Coming Pluralisation of Biology and the Stewardship of Systematics," *BioScience* 39, no. 4 (1989): 242–45; Edward O. Wilson, "Taxonomy as a Fundamental Discipline," *Philosophical Transactions of the Royal Society London B* 359, no. 1444 (2004): 739; Edward O. Wilson, "Biodiversity Research Requires More Boots on the Ground," *Nature Ecology & Evolution* 1 (2017): 1590–91.

12 Natural History Near You, *Natural Sciences Collections Association*, n.d. www.natsca.org/NHNearYou [accessed October 31, 2017].

and sought-after positions in biological research; these shifted to heads of university departments and research laboratories. In stark contrast to previous generations, biology graduates were being prepared for broader, transferable skill sets across the range of scientific techniques and computing, but as the old joke amongst zoologists went, biological sciences graduates couldn't tell the difference between a chimp and a dog or a "snake and an earthworm."[13]

This decline in a specific kind of organismal expertise is still being felt today, as experts in museums and a handful of universities age and retire without being replaced. This has led to a so-called crisis in systematics and taxonomy in the UK and further afield. In the UK, three parliamentary inquiries on systematic taxonomic expertise report that this kind of expertise is in decline or extinct in specific cases like mycology[14] at a time when it is needed more than ever, as "[s]ystematic biology is at the heart of understanding the natural world."[15]

However, the emphasis on the scientific value of natural history collections as the core justification for their existence sits at odds with the cultural role of these museums and the largely historical collections that are found within them. Outside of the problematic celebrated collectors and type specimen collections described above, the rest of natural history collections, the other 99 percent, don't naturally lend themselves to the perceived prime use of specimens in systematics, where that systematic expertise still exists. With less formal biological teaching, use, and new modes of display, once highly sought-after material is now confined to museum storerooms, "unloved" by even the community of specialists who look after them.

Vast Collections

Much of the bulk of natural history collections includes amalgamated amateur collections, particularly when it comes to insect, plant, mollusc, and bird egg collections, which number in the hundreds of thousands or millions. The scientific value of these varies almost with each collector. Many include specimens that lack the basic quality and type of information that would be considered useful when it comes to systematics or ecological studies. To be of most use, precise localities, habitats, date of collection, and details of preparation method are needed. Although accurate record keeping and labelling of specimens for entomological, botanical, and zoological collections, unlike other kinds that shall be examined later, has fortunately been a staple of this pastime, in the nineteenth century, locality was only recorded at the county level, which is of some value but not as useful as more precise information.

---

13 Ken Bowler, "Zoology Is the Latest Victim of Audit Culture," *Times Higher Education*, 2007, www.timeshighereducation.com/news/zoology-is-the-latest-victim-of-audit-culture/208193. article#survey-answer [accessed March 29, 2017].

14 House of Lords Science and Technology Committee, *Systematics and Taxonomy: Follow-Up* (London: Stationery Office, 2008), 17–26.

15 House of Lords Science and Technology Committee, *Systematics and Taxonomy*, 17–26.

Large Specimens, Smaller Collections

Unlike the large collections mentioned above, which tended to be collected in bulk by a single collector, collections of fluid-preserved, osteology, and vertebrate palaeontology specimens were collected more sporadically due to their size, weight (including entire whale skeletons), and need for preparation. Typically, even less care was taken to record the who, how, what, where, and why of specimen collection and preservation. Thanks to the nineteenth-century mode of descriptive zoology, information like collection locality and preparation method was seen as less important than the information that could be gleaned and published by comparative anatomists once specimens were prepared for study and publication in the museum. Many vertebrate specimens will only have a country- or continent-level provenance, and it is impossible to discern if this information is the descriptive distribution of the species known at the time or an accurate but vague collection locality. For morphometric analysis and genetic extraction, the exact method of preservation used to skeletonize, freeze, or preserve a specimen in fluid needs to be known in advance to infer whether DNA will be degraded or if the size and shape of anatomical features hasn't been statistically significantly affected by taphonomy. For example, freezing and using different fixatives and preservatives significantly affects the morphology in squid, masking true characteristics or anatomy used in identification and classification.[16] In bat specimens, bone lengths shrink in dry bone preparations and skins and are altered by the fixation and preservation in fluid preparations and even according to the position in which the specimen was initially prepared.[17] Even with the modern analytical techniques available, it can be time-consuming, expensive, and in many cases impossible to deduce the wide range of preservation methods, which were often bespoke, without primary documentation of methods, limiting their use in quantitative science.

Second-Class Collections

Lastly, there are the collections that traditionally—although this is still the case in some institutions—were considered ephemeral or as second-class collections. These are the specimens, which may have originally been acquired for use in displays and teaching and which include taxidermy, articulated skeletons, models, casts, and illustrations.

Taxidermy specimens are probably the category of specimens which most readily come to mind when thinking about the public face of natural history museums, even though they make up a comparatively small percentage of natural history collections and are considered of extremely limited scientific value, as not much of the "useful" part of the animal is preserved; normally just the skin, skull, and extremities. As artefacts, they

---

16 José Milton Andriguetoo-Gilho and Manuel Haimovici, "Effects of Fixation and Preservation Methods on the Morphology of a Loliginid Squid (*Cephalopoda: Myopsida*)," *American Malacological Bulletin* 6, no. 2 (1988): 213–17.

17 R. Olaf, P. Bininda-Emonds, and Anthony P. Russell, "Minimization of Potential Problems Associated with the Morphometry of Spirit-Preserved Bat Wings," *Collection Forum* 8, no. 1 (1992): 9–14.

are highly subjective representations of the organism they are supposed to represent, famously unreliable in the case of the Horniman Museum and Gardens' "overstuffed" walrus.[18] Perennially, taxidermy comes into popularity outside of formal natural history, yet much is still unknown or unrecorded when it comes to the historical study of taxidermy and taxidermists. Much of this value and the historical study of taxidermy is driven by individuals outside of museums and increasingly in the history of science and the art history field of animal studies. The seminal work on the history of taxidermy, among a still-slim scholarly field, remains *A History of Taxidermy: Art, Science and Bad Taste*.[19]

Much like taxidermy, articulated skeletons are of limited scientific use and were almost exclusively acquired and prepared for public display to communicate what whole organisms looked like. These specimens are of limited scientific use, as many are as subjectively constructed as taxidermy specimens. Many articulated skeletons do not account for the precise position and space occupied in life with connective tissue. Furthermore, bones glued, wired, and screwed together prohibit the access that osteological measuring and analysis requires in scientific research. In addition, many mounted skeletons and taxidermy specimens would have been sourced from zoos or wildlife parks and gardens, and most modern scientific research will seek to exclude captive-bred specimens, as a captive environment can unnaturally and starkly affect the physiology and pathology of organisms.

Models, casts, and other forms of replicas are traditionally the least valued of all natural history collections. Lacking any kind of biological material, these would normally have been acquired explicitly for teaching and display and treated as ephemera and not formally part of the collections at all. In fact, many natural history museums still do not consider these categories to be part of the museum collections, and they are not recognized as "museum material" or planned for formal incorporation into collections. Where these types of specimens have survived in storage after being removed from displays due to obsolescence and changing ideas in biological sciences, increasingly they are being recognized as valuable objects in their own right, but this is often driven by individual scholars. A notable example in this category are Blaschka glass models. The Dublin Blaschka Congress in 2006 marked the first scholarly meeting on the life and works of the Blaschka family, who made and supplied exquisite glass models of microorganisms, plants, and marine organisms to many museums in the nineteenth century. The conference firmly put Blaschka glass models on the map as important scientific and artistic objects in their own right.[20] Other recent work has achieved the same for Ziegler studio embryological wax models[21] and anatomical

---

18 Horniman Museum and Gardens, "Horniman Highlights Tour," www.horniman.ac.uk/collections/stories/horniman-highlights-tour [accessed March 29, 2017].

19 Patrick A. Morris, *A History of Taxidermy: Art, Science and Bad Taste* (Ascot: MPM, 2011).

20 "Special Issue: Proceedings of the Dublin Blaschka Congress," *Historical Biology: An International Journal of Palaeobiology* 20, no. 1 (2008).

21 Nick Hopwood, *Embryos in Wax: Models from the Ziegler Studio* (Cambridge: Cambridge University Press, 2002).

waxes.[22] However, there still remain many other casts and wax and plaster model collections that remain ephemeral and uncatalogued in natural history museums. These collections were valued so little that key primary evidence such as catalogues, sale books, invoices, and even archives associated with studios that produced models, casts, and replicas have not been widely preserved.

It is more by luck than by judgement that these collections still remain in natural history museums to be the focus of renewed work in the history of science, museums, and scientific display. There have been many brutal periods of disposal from natural history museums in accordance with strictly scientific value systems at the time, including the wholesale destruction or disposal of collections. Unfortunately, such little perceived value was placed on these collections and museums that in some instances it proves difficult to verify that they existed in the first place, and it isn't just the scientifically judged ephemeral collections that have suffered this fate either. Some of the most important historical natural history collections have failed to survive the value filter of modern science. For example, the collection of the Dutch zoologist, pharmacist, and collector Albertus Seba (1665–1736), whose personal collection was described as the greatest natural history cabinet at the time, contained many specimens that were originally described, and therefore are type specimens of many common animals, in Carl Linnaeus's formative works on biological classification. This collection was sold at auction in Amsterdam in 1752. Many specimens that didn't end up at major institutions or that aren't recognized as such today are presumed to be permanently lost.[23] The Musaeum Tradescantianum collections, assembled by father and son John Tradescant the Elder and John Tradescant the Younger, considered to be one of the first museums to be open to the public in England and eventually one of the founding collections of the museums at Oxford University, where the collection was transferred in the 1670s, has also suffered similar losses. Treated as just other natural history material, many specimens were presumed lost or destroyed due to teaching and demonstration, and it is only through attempts at reconstructing the collection that this historically important material is known. Only valued for its historical importance some 300 years later, fewer than 100 natural history specimens of the original collection been identified and isolated as part of a discrete sub-collection in the Oxford University Museum of Natural History.[24]

At universities, where perhaps cutting-edge scientific research and teaching use has been the strongest filter for value, natural history collections have suffered the most. At the height of the "crisis in university museums,"[25] the natural history collections

---

22 Monika V. Düring and Marta Poggesi, *Encyclopaedia Anatomica* (Cologne: Taschen, 1999).

23 Piotr Daszkiewicz and Aaron M. Bauer, "Specimens from the Second Collection of Albertus Seba in Poland: The Natural History Cabinet of Anna Jablonowska (1728–1800)," *Bibliotheca Herpetologica* 6, no. 2 (2006): 16–20.

24 Arthur MacGregor, "Tradescant's Rarities: Essays on the Foundation of the Ashmolean Museum 1683 with a Catalogue of the Surviving Early Collections," unpublished MA dissertation, Durham University, 1983.

25 Kate Arnold-Forster, " 'A Developing Sense of Crisis': A New Look at University Collections in the United Kingdom," *Museum International No. 207*, 52 no. 3 (2003): 10–14.

were disposed of in full or in part from Imperial College London, King's College London, Queen Mary's College London, Reading University, Bristol University, and most recently Birkbeck University.[26] Alienation from teaching and research, inadequate ethical and professional standards, and lack of identity, management, and structure have been cited for these declines.[27]

The downward spiral of decline and disposal of natural history collections, particularly at universities, is often complex. However, two examples of historical disposals from Oxford University Museum of Natural History emphasize that it is the case for perceived value and use, in addition to large collection size, that has been the motivation for disposal and also the reason why these disposal events were improperly recorded. For example, a note in a 1960s report on extant human remains at Oxford University draws attention to the disposal of anthropological material in 1935 then held by the Department of Zoology, which was part of the museum at the time. These remains were examined by Dr. Dudley Buxton and Miss Blackwood and "the useful specimens were removed to the Human Anatomy dept. and the remainder were destroyed." An account from a former museum assistant who worked at the museum at the time was given in 1960 to further note that the unwanted material was thrown into the foundations of the Physical Chemistry building and no note was made as to which specimens were disposed of.[28]

A separate, but potentially related, undated document at the Oxford University Museum of Natural History, titled "List of Specimens in the Loft Exclusive of Human Remains Which Have Been Dug up," is a list of zoological material, mostly mammalian osteology, the majority of which does not have clear provenance information such as collection locality, date, or age. At a later date, after the list was written, the specimens were assessed for worth, line by line. Most of them were assessed as not being useful and were crossed out with the annotations "no use," "keep for present," "sale list," and "thrown away." Many postcranial skeletons were thrown away, although the skulls were kept, and many are specimens that are uncollectible today but highly sought after by modern researchers, including elephant, lion, rhinoceros, and primate material. Of particular note is the "young imperfect skeleton and skull"—the thylacine—which had been annotated as "no use" and "thrown away" (see figure 5.1). Thylacines went extinct in 1936 and we now know that only 756 specimens exist in museums; just over 100 skeletons are known and subadult specimens, in particular, are comparatively rare.[29] Far from this specimen being useless, by today's value, it would have been extremely

26 Gill Sales, personal communication, March 22, 2017; Marta C. Lourenço, "Between Two Worlds: The Distinct Nature and Contemporary Significance of University Museums and Collections in Europe," unpublished PhD thesis, Conservatoire National des Arts et Métiers, 2005, 16; Jack Ashby, *Kingdom in a Cabinet* (London: Grant Museum of Zoology, 2006).

27 Lourenço, "Between Two Worlds."

28 J. Hull, *Cranial Catalogue: Human Skulls—Supplementary Note on Disposal of Human Crania (Folio vii)*, unpublished report, Grant Museum of Zoology, 1960.

29 Steven Sleightholme, "The International Thylacine Database," www.naturalworlds.org/thylacine/mrp/itsd/itsd_1.htm [accessed March 29, 2017].

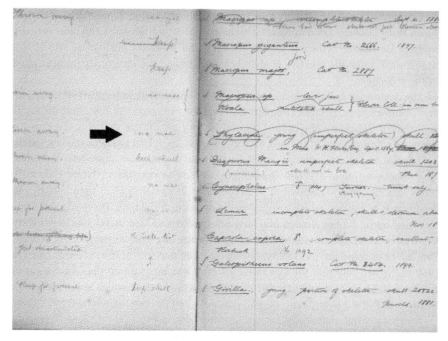

Figure 5.1. Scan from document "List of Specimens in the Loft Exclusive of Human Remains Which Have Been Dug up" from Oxford University Museum of Natural History. The arrow indicates the entry for a thylacine specimen noted as "no use" and "thrown away." © Oxford University Museum of Natural History. Used with permission.

important on scientific grounds alone. It is events like these, the superficial evaluation of natural history specimens' potential use based on the quality of the specimen and, most importantly, the associated data, that epitomize the selection criteria "no data—no use."

Of course, it is easy to take to task previous generations' perceived failings when compared to the modern professional and ethical museum standards that didn't exist at the time. But, sadly, incidents like these still occur. In March 2017, administrators at the University of Louisiana gave staff at the Louisiana Museum of Natural History just forty-eight hours to come up with a storage solution on campus for over six million fish specimens and a sizeable herbaria, or find institutions to donate the vast collection to, or the material would be destroyed at the end of July 2017.[30] A statement by the University administration cited no internal use in research and limited use in teaching as a justification for threatening to destroy one of the largest fish collections in the world.[31] Following

30 Rhett Jones, "University Threatens Destruction of Millions of Specimens if Museum of Natural History Collection not Relocated," *Gizmodo*, 2017, http://gizmodo.com/university-threatens-destruction-of-millions-of-specime-1793745389 [accessed March 29, 2017].

31 Jones, "University Threatens Destruction of Millions of Specimens if Museum of Natural History Collection not Relocated."

backlash on social media and a call to the scientific community, a number of university departments and collections agreed to take on the material.[32] Interestingly, museums were not listed among the receiving institutions.

The narrow valuing of collections according to scientific value alone has had a huge impact on the part played by natural history museums within the museum sector and in broader culture. It is also problematic for publicly funded natural history museums to place such value on just one set of stakeholders' interests, in this case scientific research users. These attitudes are still pervasive in old and new ways in the modern natural history museum. For example, natural history museums, such as the Natural History Museum in London,[33] are planning to comprehensively digitize their collections, the rationale being that online collections are available to "everybody, all the time." However, the rather rote way in which many are planning to make their collections available digitally makes little or no concession to accessibility beyond the trained researcher. Even headline-making collaborations, such as the partnership between the Natural History Museum London and the Google Cultural Institute,[34] actually offer very little to virtual visitors not already knowledgeable in natural history.[35] Although narrated and animated content does fulfil this goal, such as the eleven "exhibits,"[36] the hundreds of thousands of digital objects alongside the standard natural history "tombstone data"—scientific name, accession number, taxon author—fail to be engaging in their own right without interpretation.[37]

Cultural Capital

Natural history museums also have much harder work to do in explaining some of the fundamentals of a natural history museum's working. The sculpture, paintings, and archaeological material that visitors are likely to encounter in museum displays are all far easier to understand in principal as basic objects in terms of their aesthetic expression.

---

32 Bonnie Bolden, "Safe: ULM Natural History Collections Go to Universities from Mississippi to Texas," *USA Today*, 2017, www.usatoday.com/story/news/education/2017/06/28/safe-ulm-natural-history-collections-go-universities-mississippi-texas/436901001/ [accessed October 30, 2017].

33 Natural History Museum, "Digital Museum," *Natural History Museum blog*, n.d. www.nhm. ac.uk/our-science/our-work/digital-museum.html [accessed October 30, 2017].

34 Google Cultural Institute, now rebranded as Google Arts & Culture, is a Google webpage hosting images, maps, and curated stories from large cultural organizations around the world. Aside from the stories told through images, animation, and video, much of the content appears to be existing digital resources and metadata hosted on Google Arts & Culture.

35 Google Arts & Culture, "The Natural History Museum," n.d. www.google.com/culturalinstitute/beta/partner/natural-history-museum accessed March 29, 2017].

36 Google Arts & Culture, "The Natural History Museum '11 exhibits'," n.d. www.google.com/culturalinstitute/beta/search/exhibit?p=natural-history-museum [accessed March 29, 2017].

37 Google Arts & Culture. "The Natural History Museum '*Symphurus sayademalhensis*'," www.google.com/culturalinstitute/beta/asset/symphurus-sayademalhensis-chabanaud-1955/OQEXKjL8ljA4ow [accessed March 29, 2017].

How they were made and why is, to some extent, universally appreciable.[38] Museum visitors can empathize much more easily with artefacts than they perhaps can with taxidermy, fluid-preserved specimens, or scanning electron microscope images.[39]

Objects that are explicitly artificed are also given a much higher cultural capital than the esoteric and often complex value of natural history specimens. Some of these cultural value differences between art museums and natural history museums were explored in the 2014 Art and Science of Curation project, part of "Curating Cambridge: Our City, Our Stories, Our Stuff."[40] Art theft and forgery is international headline news and is a well-established genre of art history and popular art history. Arguably, the recent spate of thefts from natural history museums of financially valuable rhinoceros horn failed to make the same waves in the mainstream media. Similarly, natural history museum professionals refuse to ascribe a value to their collections, so that each specimen is both at the same time valuable as a unique genetic resource or data point but valueless in that there is resistance to financially valuing natural history objects. There are complaints from the sector when auction houses do.[41] A good example of this attitude is presented by Simon Timberlake in discussion with an unnamed Keeper of Natural History who "was quite unable to accept the concept of a geological collection having any major value other than to science itself."[42] Perhaps as a consequence of skewed value systems within natural history museums themselves and a primary focus on science, natural history museums do not have the same cultural capital as art and archaeology museums. Interestingly, in the UK context, this is a reverse of the perceived value of the sciences compared to the humanities in contemporary universities in the so called "war on the humanities."[43]

Cultural Value

It is understandable why natural history collections do, perhaps, have less cultural capital or value across the museum sector and wider, when the professionals tasked

---

38 Tristram Besterman, "Foreword," in *The Value and Valuation of Natural Science Collections*, ed. John R. Nudds and Charles W. Pettitt (Bath: Geological Society of London, 1997), xi.

39 See Scott Billings, "Is It Real? Taxidermy," *More Than a Dodo Blog*, 2017, https://morethanadodo. com/2017/07/04/is-it-real-taxidermy/ [accessed July 23, 2018].

40 Mark Carnall, "When Two Tribes Go to War: Art and Science 'Curatorship,'" *The Art and Science of Curation*, n.d. www.artandscienceofcuration.org.uk/when-two-tribes-go-to-war-art-science-curatorship/ [accessed March 29, 2017].

41 Mark Carnall, "Natural History under the Hammer," *UCL Museums and Collections Blog*, 2013, http://blogs.ucl.ac.uk/museums/2013/12/04/natural-history-under-the-hammer/ [accessed March 20, 2017].

42 Simon Timberlake, "A Scientific/Historical/Educational Heritage for Whom: The Value of Geological Collections in a Small Museum," in *The Value and Valuation of Natural Science Collections*, ed. John R. Nudds and Charles W. Pettitt (Bath: Geological Society of London),127–35.

43 Alex Preston, "The War against Humanities at Britain's Universities," *The Observer*, 2015, www. theguardian.com/education/2015/mar/29/war-against-humanities-at-britains-universities [accessed September 20, 2017].

with managing the collections are unable or unwilling to value them in more than one dimension. The broader epistemology of value is covered elsewhere in this volume, but it is only relatively recently that the cultural value of natural history collections has been considered. The First International Conference on the Value and Valuation of Natural Science Collections in 1995 marked a turning point in a holistic approach to unpicking value and natural history museums and the perception of undervalue that continues today.[44]

The professionalization of museums has been transformational for many natural history museums. In the UK, the development of professional codes and standards, from the Museums Association's *Code of Ethics for Museums* (2015)[45] to the Collections Trust's SPECTRUM standard (2017)[46] and Arts Council England's museum accreditation scheme (n.d.),[47] has pushed many natural history museums to move away from chaotic collections to more rational, reasoned, and accountable institutions. Subject specialist networks that grew out of grass roots networks of frustrated museum professionals, such as the Natural Sciences Collections Association, the Geological Curators' Group, and the University Museums Group, now provide support for development as well as national and international direction and leadership. There's a healthy amount of new professional input into the sector from museum studies courses, with groundings in museum history, governance, and theory (although few courses have much natural history–specific taught content).

Through these networks and training programmes, newer generations of natural history museum professionals, including staff who have broader museum training and don't come from a purely scientific research background, are increasingly driving a trend towards the holistic management and use of collections across society. Instead of focusing solely on the scientific use of scientifically important material, the whole collection, including the unloved and useless specimens, can be mobilized to use with a diverse range of audiences, from artists and school children to Twitter followers and humanities students. An ethical framework is also key in steering the conversation beyond the wording of policies and procedures, particularly for providing grounding in a wider schema of ethics. One of ten key points in the 2008 Museums Association *Code of Ethics for Museums* nicely enshrines the problems that a singular value system can create and emphasizes where responsibility for valuing collections should lie: "Society can expect museums to safeguard the long-term public interest in the collections."[48] Sadly, this wording, but not the spirit of it, is lost in the most recent version of the *Code of Ethics*

---

44 John R. Nudds and Charles W. Pettitt, ed., *The Value and Valuation of Natural Science Collections* (Bath: Geological Society of London, 1997).

45 Museums Association, "Code of Ethics for Museums," 2015, www.museumsassociation.org/download?id=1155827 [accessed September 16, 2017].

46 Collections Trust, "Spectrum 5.0," 2017, http://collectionstrust.org.uk/spectrum/spectrum-5-0/ [accessed September 19, 2017].

47 Arts Council England, "Accreditation Scheme," www.artscouncil.org.uk/supporting-museums/accreditation-scheme-0 [accessed September 19, 2017].

48 Museums Association, *Code of Ethics for Museums* (London: Museums Association, 2008).

for Museums[49], but the placement of the responsibility on museums to safeguard public interest rather than on the public to be interested in what museums present perfectly encapsulates why a broader sense of value is needed in museums, particularly natural history museums. With this emphasis in mind, if specimens are "useless," it is because they are not being used by the museum. If collections are of no value, it is because they are not being valued by the museum.

This paradigm shift of value has also been reinforced with the recent developments in education, public engagement, and the science communication movement. Education and learning was at the core of the establishment of many museums and, in a natural history context, the learning purposes of the museums could not have been pried apart from the "behind the scenes" science. Although, as we have seen, this central mission waned in museums, and in particular natural history museums, in the early 1990s, only half of museums had any formal education offer and only one in five had education specialists.[50] It is easy to take for granted today's attitudes that public engagement through collections from outreach to community work, events, activities, and exhibition design is at the heart of the modern museum. The influential report *A Common Wealth*, published in 1997, paved the road for the modern role and purpose of museums.[51] In science museums generally, this has been boosted by the science communication movement, now a professional field in its own right and, more recently still, in the UK, public engagement is a key part of research impact.[52] There is growing evidence that there is a need for natural history education to address a lack of fundamental natural history knowledge and familiarity in western societies.[53]

This enormously positive movement has not progressed in natural history museums without criticism, and the rise of investment in public engagement and science communication expertise has been seen in some quarters as directly responsible for the decline in "old school" curatorship. The recent campaign for good curatorship, among other admirable goals, does carry the undertone that collections expertise should act as the gatekeeper to "ensuring sustainable use of collections," as well as the knowledge and context around them.[54] However, it is a broad range of expertise that can facilitate creative use of collections beyond collections expertise and value systems. Others have criticized the shift of ever-limited museum resources away from research and towards

---

49 Museums Association, *Code of Ethics for Museums*.

50 Nicholas Serota, "Museums and Young People," in *Learning to Live: Museums, Young People and Education*, ed. Kate Bellamy and Carey Oppenheim (London: Institute for Public Policy Research and National Museum Directors' Conference, 2009), 21–29 (21).

51 David Anderson, *A Common Wealth: Museums in the Learning Age* (London: Department for Culture, Media and Sport, 1997).

52 Research Councils UK, "Pathways to Impact," www.rcuk.ac.uk/innovation/impacts/ [accessed March 28, 2017].

53 Heather King and Marianne Achiam, "The Case for Natural History," *Science and Education* (2017): 1–15.

54 Campaign for Good Curatorship, "Manifesto," n.d. http://campaignforgoodcuratorship.org.uk/manifesto/ [accessed March 28, 2017].

the "Disneyfication" of natural history museums to tell the "story of the sciences."[55] In the UK, the natural history museum sector has been openly discussing a number of concerns, particularly around expertise, use, value, and funding. Three conference sessions in particular saw UK natural history museums engaging with the wider sector about these long-standing issues. A session titled "Elephant in the Room" at the 2012 Museums Association conference explored the perceived disproportionate cuts to natural history museum specialist staff and the lower cultural capital of natural history collections.[56] A year later, the session at the 2013 Museums Association conference titled "Dead Zoos" focused on the potential for natural history museums to engage their local publics in contemporary science, especially increasingly pressing environmental issues.[57] Later that year, the Oxford University Museum of Natural History hosted a one-day symposium, provocatively titled "Crap in the Attic," which really got back to basics in terms of how natural history museums can be used across a range of audiences and from scientific use to public engagement.[58]

Both by recognizing that scientists are just one stakeholder group for public natural history museums and that the public is also a significant stakeholder in science, natural history museums have a unique role in bridging science, art, history, collections, and ideas with the public. With this wider audience in mind, there are more opportunities to creatively use different kinds of collections, from displays, exhibitions, handling sessions, community outreach, and social media to widening the definition of users to artists, historians, geographers, engineers, and designers, a purely scientific value is no longer relevant to engaging these audiences. The rest of this chapter will examine some recent examples, in the spirit of these developments, which put the scientifically useless 99 percent of natural history collections to work.

Subverting Value

The advent and eventual acceptance and widespread uptake of social media has provided many museums with new opportunities for engaging and experimenting with their content, which could be longer than object labels, shorter than formal scholarly articles and publications, published relatively quickly, and experiment with different content tones beyond the normal formal, authoritative, and authorless one adopted by many museums. In addition, blogging, image blogging, and microblogging come with unique content-linking tools that aren't very well adopted or even possible outside of social

---

55 Kemp, "Museums."

56 Graham Oliver and Darren Mann, "The Elephant in the Room," conference paper presented at the Museums Association Conference, 2012.

57 Steve Garland (Chair), Darren Mann, Claire Brown, and Henry McGhie (speakers), "Dead Zoos," panel presented at the Museums Association Conference, 2013.

58 Oxford University Museums Partnership, "Crap in the Attic? The Management and Use of Natural History Collections," *YouTube*, 2013, www.youtube.com/watch?v=zzbjHCyKeNc [accessed March 29, 2017].

media: tagging, hashtags, hyperlinking, categorizing, and building up a body of work linked and tied together in a way not previously possible through traditional media.

In 2011, the university museums at UCL launched the UCL Museums and Collections Blog: not the first and by no means the last museums to engage with blogging. In November 2012, alongside other regular content, the Grant Museum of Zoology at UCL launched the blog series "Underwhelming Fossil Fish of the Month."[59] The aim of the series was to make use of a typically unloved and unlovable collection, the titular underwhelming fossil fish. The Grant Museum of Zoology holds a large collection of fossil fish but, as with many fossil collections, most are not the easy-to-observe, complete, or well-known species that may occasionally find their way into displays. The fossil fish collection had some specimens that at one time in the past were of scientific interest; however, at best, the interest was highly esoteric and even then this was debatable. The idea behind "Underwhelming Fossil Fish" was to subvert the normal trope of celebrating the amazing, fantastic, and unique treasures normally found in museums and instead to celebrate, with tongue in cheek, the dull mundanity, mediocrity, and obscurity of the Grant Museum's Fossil Fish collection. The scientific content is included in the blog posts too: Each monthly fossil is assessed under the categories of preservation, scientific research, and societal impact, but throughout, the reader is warned of how deeply unexciting each entry will be. Given that most species of fossil fish have had no real societal impact, this section is normally given over to outlandish embellishments, links to topical events, or hyper-obscure trivia from Donald Trump's ridiculous oratory style,[60] through to the fossil fish that "inspired" *8 Mile*, the film starring Eminem about an aspiring rapper in Detroit.[61] The success of the series relies on the reader expecting or being familiar with typical science content and knowing when it is being flagrantly subverted.

Among other potentially surprising aspects, through the lens of "Underwhelming Fossil Fish" specimens, the series has explored aspects of popular culture, including the music of Justin Timberlake, the film *The Devil Wears Prada*, a critique of labelling in art museums, supposed fossil fish–inspired first drafts of Lewis Carroll's *Alice's Adventures in Wonderland*, fossil fish philately, the bleak prospect of the future of the world under a certain US president, and subsequently a subversion of the already-subverted series with the one-off "Most Amazing Fossil Fish Ever Discovered" (MAFFED). Other regular features include awful artistic reconstructions (by a younger-than-he-looks up-and-coming paleoartist), imaging from the disappointing but cheap USB microscope,

59 Mark Carnall, "Underwhelming Fossil Fish of the Month," *UCL Museums and Collections Blog*, n.d. http://blogs.ucl.ac.uk/museums/tag/underwhelming-fossil-fish-of-the-month/ [accessed March 28, 2017].

60 Mark Carnall, "The Most Amazing Fossil Fish Ever Discovered," *UCL Museums and Collections Blog*, 2017, https://blogs.ucl.ac.uk/museums/2017/01/31/the-most-amazing-fossil-fish-ever-discovered/ [accessed September 19, 2017].

61 Mark Carnall, "Underwhelming Fossil Fish of the Month: May 2016," *UCL Museums and Collections Blog*, 2016, https://blogs.ucl.ac.uk/museums/2016/05/31/underwhelming-fossil-fish-of-the-month-may-2016/ [accessed September 19, 2017].

"identify the fossil fish from the box alone," occasional find-the-fossil challenges, fossil fish–inspired poetry, and end-of-year fossil fish–themed Christmas carols.

Now running at over fifty entries in the series, "Underwhelming Fossil Fish" has been hugely successful in drawing attention to a collection that would not otherwise have had any cause to be used in exhibitions, displays, or even for scientific research. "Underwhelming Fossil Fish of the Month" has also been featured as the subject of a stand-up comedy public engagement event,[62] been spotlit in the Palaeontology Association newsletter,[63] featured as an example of best practice in museum practice,[64] and been promoted in the mainstream media on the Radio 4 programme *Inside Science*.[65]

This example demonstrates that collections that would have been deemed unusable, even scientifically, in the past have now become a highlight of the Grant Museum's collections and an example of making the most of unloved collections precisely because they are unloved. Of course, this gimmick would not work if every museum followed the same format, but, referring back to the salient point in the 2008 UK Museums Association's *Code of Ethics for Museums*, it is within the museum's power to maintain or create a public interest in its collections with some creative interpretation and to use the wide range of communication tools now at many museums' disposal. This has been made possible due to the changing attitudes of museum professionals to engaging with wider audiences creatively and to exploring different voices and modes of communication enabled by technology. Although the traditional authoritative "voice" of the museum can be found in permanent display interpretation, museums today are also likely to be using blogging, microblogging, videos, podcasts, interventions, co-curation, and "takeovers." These different modes of communication are allowing a wider range of perspectives and voices to be heard from within museums and from outside, as well as allowing museums to be more reactive to current events and to openly explore their own museologies, in many cases critically.

Behind the Velvet Rope

It's a well-worn cliché that most behind-the-scenes spaces in museums are more engaging than the public displays, at least according to feedback from visitors who take part in behind-the-scenes tours. Part of this is undoubtedly wrapped up in the sense of privilege that visitors feel on accessing parts of museums that aren't normally accessible,

---

62 Mark Carnall, "Museums Showoff: Celebrating the Mundane," *UCL Museums and Collections Blog*, 2013, http://blogs.ucl.ac.uk/museums/2013/10/18/museums-showoff-celebrating-the-mundane/ [accessed March 21, 2017].

63 Mark Carnall, "Underwhelming Fossil Fish of the Month, or How to Get Some Use out of Your Useless Fossils," *Palaeontological Association Newsletter* 89 (2015): 75–81.

64 Mark Carnall, "The Grant Museum of Zoology, London," *Museum Practice*, 2015, www.museumsassociation.org/museum-practice/social-media-trends/15042015-grant-museum [accessed March 17, 2017].

65 BBC Inside Science, "Zika, Penguins, Erratum, Fossil Fish," *BBC Radio 4*, www.bbc.co.uk/programmes/b06yfjdp [accessed March 19, 2017].

and a good behind-the-scenes tour will employ theatrics to ramp up the feeling of exclusivity, from dramatic unboxings of interesting specimens and creative storytelling to the actual use of velvet ropes and curtains, which don't really serve any other purpose. Nonetheless, the stark contrast between the ordered, deliberate, and sometimes sterile curated public displays and the usual chaotic, random, and historically quirky nature of most museums' behind-the-scenes spaces means that the latter can be more inspiring.

Few museums, especially natural history museums, explore the unusual nature of an institution that collects, stores, and makes available dead organisms or engage visitors directly with their own museology, despite the fact that many visitors will often ask museological questions rather than questions around the themes of exhibitions or displays. Questions such as "Is it real?" "Did you kill it?" and "How old is it?" are some of the most frequently asked questions. Visitors are also often surprised when they find out that, typically, natural history museums display less than 1 percent of their collections; the rest are stored research, teaching, or otherwise undisplayable collections. Natural history museums rarely address these questions through their static interpretation, instead focusing on fact-based tokenistic interpretation related to diet, distribution, habitat, or the species on show.

After relocating to new premises in 2011, the opportunity to reinterpret the Grant Museum of Zoology collections opened up new opportunities to explore some of these questions alongside the usual tokenistic zoological interpretation. In 2012, the Grant Museum programmed a temporary display with an associated evening talk called "It Came from the Stores," focusing on normally undisplayable natural history specimens, ranging from imperfect specimens, thousands of superficially identical "duplicate" specimens, experimentally prepared scanning electron microscope stubs, mouse skins mounted on lolly sticks, wax models, a box of fifty rabbit skeletons divided into body parts, student boxes of microscope slides, and plastic dinosaurs accessioned into the museum collections.[66] As well as examining this eclectic collection of misfits, each of them was also used to exemplify an ongoing area of museum work not normally on display, such as the challenges of conserving some of these specimens, the editorial process when designing displays, issues with documentation backlogs, and the changes in value of different techniques throughout the history of science.

Many of these specimens have now been incorporated into the permanent history of the Grant Museum displays or discrete displays themselves, including the novel Micrarium display opened in 2013 (see figure 5.2).[67] The aim of the Micrarium was to make the most of another problematic and unusable category of specimens: microscope and lantern slides. The display is simple, featuring over 2,300 microscope slides mounted in a room with three light box walls, with a mirrored ceiling to create the

---

66 Mark Carnall, "It Came from the Stores: The Live Show," *UCL Museums and Collections Blog*, 2012, http://blogs.ucl.ac.uk/museums/2012/07/26/it-came-from-the-stores-the-live-show/ [accessed March 20, 2017].

67 Jack Ashby, "The Micrarium—A Place for Tiny Things—Opens," *UCL Museums and Collections Blog*, 2013, http://blogs.ucl.ac.uk/museums/2013/02/11/the-micrarium-a-place-for-tiny-things-opens/ [accessed March 22, 2017].

Figure 5.2. The Micrarium at the Grant Museum of Zoology UCL. Occupying a former closet space, this installation showcases "unusable" microscope slide specimens en masse to show the diversity of tiny life. © UCL Grant Museum of Zoology/Matt Clayton. Used with permission.

impression that the display area extends above. The interpretation is minimal; none of the individual slides are interpreted. The single label describes how most of the animals featured make up the majority of diversity of animal life, yet due to their small size, they are rarely displayed in museums. Museologically, microscope slides are problematic. They are rarely used in contemporary research and are typically difficult to display, yet they are numerous in natural history museums. Almost a third of the Grant Museum collections are microscope slides and at one point the collection was earmarked for disposal. Until the Micrarium, only a few had ever been displayed.

This model has been successful and influential; thousands of images of the display taken by visitors can be found online, and many museum professionals from other museums have visited the Grant Museum to take inspiration from the display and to take selfies using the mirrored ceiling.[68] The display was highly commended in the Museums and Heritage Award category "Project on a Limited Budget" and was widely featured and reviewed in the mainstream media. The Grant Museum now sells Micrarium wrapping paper in the museum shop, and Micrarium-inspired displays have been created at the National Museum Wales; the Victoria Gallery and Museum, Liverpool; and the Manchester Museum.

Much like the previous example of underwhelming fossil fish, "It Came from the Stores" and the Micrarium demonstrate that, with a bit of creativity, boosted by social media, previously problematic or perceived-to-be-"useless" natural history collections can be used not only to attract museum visitors but to address some of the core themes at the heart of many natural history museums, in this case biodiversity, collections management, the history of science, and, on a meta level, the politics of display. It is important to note that it is only happenstance that these microscope and lantern slide specimens ended up in the museum in the first place: The original scientific use of these specimens places them firmly in the category of ephemeral teaching aids. Lacking provenance data and with preservation issues associated with slide mounting techniques, their future potential scientific use is limited. It was the creative intervention that transformed these otherwise quotidian and common specimens found in all natural history museums into unique or notable specimens, which have the potential to eclipse the traditional treasures, the taxonomically important or Darwin specimens, as previously described.

Model Organisms and Museum Mascots

The last series of examples I wish to introduce here focuses on models in natural history museums. Like taxidermy and articulated skeletons, most models in museums were created explicitly for public display, such as enlarged anatomical cross sections, embryological waxes, Blaschka glass models, and models of nature's giants—dinosaurs, whales, and giant squid. Model-making was a much more integral part of museum practice in the past. Many museums employed their own sculptors, preparators, and model-makers to create models of organisms that were difficult to preserve off display otherwise. Few museums today have this in-house expertise, although it still exists, but many museums still display models, particularly large ones that were created in the nineteenth century. Where once the production and acquisition of models for display was associated with prestige and cutting-edge science, today there is a presumption that the real thing is preferable or preferred by museum visitors.

Although gigantic animals such as whales, giant squid, and dinosaurs are some of the most impressive animals, displaying them presents a lot of problems for museums.

---

68 Jack Shoulder, "Micrarium Selfies at the Grant Museum," *Jack's Adventures in Museum Land,* 2017, https://jacksadventuresinmuseumland.wordpress.com/2017/01/19/micrarium-selfies-at-the-grant-museum/ [accessed March 23, 2017].

Whale skeletons themselves can be a technical challenge to mount, as the skeletons can weigh many tonnes. But skeletons alone do not accurately convey the filled-out mass of the largest creatures to live on earth. Giant and colossal squid are extremely rarely encountered in the wild and with no hard parts are nearly impossible to display. Likewise, specimens in giant tanks of preserving fluid don't quite convey the majesty of the living animal. Although dinosaur specimens are a staple of most natural history museum displays, rarely are they the real fossil because complete three-dimensional fossils are seldom discovered. Mounting fossil material also has the same challenges as mounting whale skeletons, except that the bones are made of solid rock and, therefore, weigh substantially more. It's for these reasons that creating models of these animals, or combining casts of original material and replicas of missing bones for dinosaur skeletons, is really the only way these organisms can be displayed. In the nineteenth and twentieth centuries, there were "arms races" amongst the larger museums to manufacture or secure the most accurate models of these giants at a time when animals like giant squid and the larger whales were rarely encountered as living organisms at all.[69] Despite the huge effort to produce these accurate giant models, changing museum displays and modes of interpretation resulted in many being removed from display. Due to the prohibitive sizes of storing these models or the fact that many of them were built into displays, so irremovable without destroying them, original models are extremely rare. For example, giant squid models that were once pride of place at the Museum of Comparative Zoology at Harvard University, the Smithsonian Institution National Museum of Natural History, and the Natural History Museum of London have been lost or destroyed.[70] Given that there's no biological material and some of the earlier models were inaccurate, models of all shapes and sizes in natural history museums were and are still treated as ephemeral specimens despite their value to the history of science and science education.

Recently, and again in part thanks to social media, natural history museums have been rethinking the value and use of their model collections in response to the public love of these iconic specimens. As discussed above, for many curators, large models can present significant challenges: They are logistically problematic to move around for refurbishment projects, difficult to protect from the enquiring hands of visitors, and require scaffolding and specialist lift equipment to take apart or clean. However, many of these models have captured the hearts of the visitors to museums and some, like the Natural History Museum of London's blue whale model, are icons for the museum. This model was immortalized in the 1967 song "Museum," by Donovan, which sings of meeting beneath the whale at the museum.

Seeking to take advantage of some of this public affection, in 2012, the Natural History Museum used its other iconic specimen—the composite cast/model of a *Diplodocus*— as a development opportunity, launching the "I Love Dippy" appeal campaign to raise

---

69 Ben Miller, "The Epistemological Challenge of Model Whales," *Extinct Monsters*, 2016, https:// extinctmonsters.net/2016/06/19/the-epistemological-challenge-of-model-whales/ [accessed March 15, 2017].

70 Richard Ellis, *The Search for the Giant Squid* (New York: Penguin, 1998).

£8.5 million to complete renovations to the central hall and to showcase more star specimens.[71] The *Diplodocus* composite model was rebranded as "Dippy," and visitors could pay to light up the specimen and "make Dippy roar." There was some surprise, then, in 2015, when Dippy, "the much-loved and iconic Diplodocus," who is a "memorable welcome to visitors as they enter the museum" and had been used to fund the redevelopment of the central gallery, was removed from the museum altogether—to embark on a UK-wide road trip from 2018 to 2020. Dippy was replaced in the gallery by the skeleton of a whale. Despite a petition spearheaded by UK newspaper the *Metro*,[72] the Natural History Museum launched a huge campaign bidding farewell to Dippy, in the run-up to the final weeks and days of the specimen's public display, by publishing a history of it.[73] Rather than slowly shuffling the much-loved specimen into the storerooms, the Natural History Museum capitalized on removing what would in the past have been considered "just another model" to raise awareness of the refurbishment. The tour to other UK venues was under the auspice of "Making iconic items accessible to as many people as possible," and through corporate sponsorship, Dippy would be free to view at the proposed tour venues.[74]

Other natural history museums have also used models in similar campaigns to raise awareness of iconic specimens and institutions. In 2015, as part of the Oxford University Museum of Natural History's nomination for the Art Fund Prize for Museum of the Year, the museum organized the Dodo Roadshow. The ambitious roadshow, consisting of a national tour of a dodo model, cast of the head, and extremely rare skeletal material, toured the full length of Britain, from Land's End in Cornwall to John O'Groats in Scotland, stopping off at museums and other institutions on the way (see figure 5.3). The journey was documented through social media, cartoons, and blog posts featuring Q&A sessions with other museums' iconic specimens and mascots such as the Plymouth City Museum and Art Gallery's tub gurnard,[75] the Black Country Living Museum's steam hammer,[76] and the Potteries Museum and Art Gallery's slipware owl. Although the Oxford University Museum of Natural History didn't win the Art Fund Museum of the Year award, it did

71 Natural History Museum, "I Love Dippy Appeal," *Natural History Museum Blog*, n.d. www.nhm. ac.uk/support-us/love-dippy/index.html [accessed March 20, 2017].

72 "Save Dippy," *Change.org*, n.d. www.change.org/p/natural-history-museum-save-dippy [accessed March 20, 2017].

73 Natural History Museum, "*Diplodocus*: This Is Your Life," *Natural History Museum Blog*, 2016, www.nhm.ac.uk/discover/diplodocus-this-is-your-life.html [accessed March 19, 2017].

74 Natural History Museum, "Dippy on Tour," *Natural History Museum Blog*, n.d. www.nhm.ac.uk/ about-us/national-impact/diplodocus-on-tour.html [accessed March 19, 2017].

75 Rachel Parle, "Dodo Roadshow: Plymouth City Museum," *More Than a Dodo Blog*, 2013, https:// morethanadodo.com/2015/06/09/dodo-roadshow-plymouth-city-museum/ [accessed March 21, 2017].

76 Scott Billings, "Dodo Roadshow: Black Country Living Museum," *More Than a Dodo Blog*, 2015, https://morethanadodo.com/2015/06/10/dodo-roadshow-black-country-living-museum/ [accessed March 20, 2017].

Figure 5.3. The Oxford University Museum of Natural History model dodo at Land's End embarking on the Dodo Roadshow to John O'Groats, stopping off at over twenty museums along the way. © Oxford University Museum of Natural History. Used with permission.

pick up two Museums and Heritage Awards: "Project on a Limited Budget" and the "Best of the Best" Award.

These examples, featuring traditionally ephemeral and scientifically unimportant museum specimens, demonstrate that natural history museums are embracing their role as cultural and scientific institutions. It is no coincidence that many of the approaches examined here have employed knowing irreverence, humour, and the unique tools of social media to raise awareness of natural history and to make the initial emotional connection between people and museums. When executed well, the serious scientific messages relating to biodiversity, extinction, conservation, and the public role of museums and science are still being delivered.

From boring fossil fish and mice skins on sticks to light-up dinosaurs with a silly name and dodos taking to the road, natural history museums are embracing their own staff's affection for their collections and the public's existing affection for specimens they have formed an attachment to. The scientific role and use of natural history museums continues in a slightly broader form than the period of strict taxonomic use, but the scientific value of collections now sits alongside the public and cultural value of collections, for which, as we've seen, with a bit of a creative push almost every museum specimen can possess. It's certainly less equivocal now to simply contend that a natural history specimen with no data has no use, and, as examples covered in this chapter show, there's a growing pool of examples of best practice for museum professionals to draw on before consigning "useless" material to the skip.

Bibliography

Anderson, David. *A Common Wealth: Museums in the Learning Age.* London: Department for Culture, Media and Sport, 1997.

Andriguetoo-Gilho, José Milton, and Manuel Haimovici. "Effects of Fixation and Preservation Methods on the Morphology of a Loliginid Squid (*Cephalopoda: Myopsida*)." *American Malacological Bulletin* 6, no. 2 (1988): 213–17.

Arnold-Forster, Kate. " 'A Developing Sense of Crisis': A New Look at University Collections in the United Kingdom." *Museum International No. 207,* 52, no. 3 (2003): 10–14.

Arts Council England. "Accreditation Scheme." www.artscouncil.org.uk/supporting-museums/accreditation-scheme-0 [accessed September 19, 2017].

Ashby, Jack. *Kingdom in a Cabinet.* London: Grant Museum of Zoology, 2006.

——. "The Micrarium—A Place for Tiny Things—Opens." *UCL Museums and Collections Blog,* 2013. http://blogs.ucl.ac.uk/museums/2013/02/11/the-micrarium-a-place-for-tiny-things-opens/ [accessed March 22, 2017].

BBC Inside Science. "Zika, Penguins, Erratum, Fossil Fish." *BBC Radio 4.* www.bbc.co.uk/programmes/b06yfjdp [accessed March 19, 2017].

Besterman, Tristram. "Foreword." In *The Value and Valuation of Natural Science Collections,* edited by John R. Nudds and Charles W. Pettitt, xi. Bath: Geological Society of London, 1997.

Billings, Scott. "Dodo Roadshow: Black Country Living Museum." *More Than a Dodo Blog,* 2015. https://morethanadodo.com/2015/06/10/dodo-roadshow-black-country-living-museum/ [accessed March 20, 2017].

——. "Is It Real? Taxidermy." *More Than a Dodo Blog,* 2017. https://morethanadodo.com/2017/07/04/is-it-real-taxidermy/ [accessed July 23, 2018].

Bolden, Bonnie. "Safe: ULM Natural History Collections Go to Universities from Mississippi to Texas." *USA Today,* 2017. www.usatoday.com/story/news/education/2017/06/28/safe-ulm-natural-history-collections-go-universities-mississippi-texas/436901001/ [accessed October 30, 2017].

Bowler, Ken. "Zoology Is the Latest Victim of Audit Culture." *Times Higher Education,* 2007. www.timeshighereducation.com/news/zoology-is-the-latest-victim-of-audit-culture/208193.article#survey-answer [accessed March 29, 2017].

Campaign for Good Curatorship. "Manifesto," n.d. http://campaignforgoodcuratorship.org.uk/manifesto/ [accessed March 28, 2017].

Carnall, Mark. "The Grant Museum of Zoology, London." *Museum Practice,* 2015. www.museumsassociation.org/museum-practice/social-media-trends/15042015-grant-museum [accessed March 17, 2017].

——. "It Came from the Stores: The Live Show." *UCL Museums and Collections Blog,* 2012. http://blogs.ucl.ac.uk/museums/2012/07/26/it-came-from-the-stores-the-live-show/ [accessed March 20, 2017].

——. "The Most Amazing Fossil Fish Ever Discovered." *UCL Museums and Collections Blog,* 2017. https://blogs.ucl.ac.uk/museums/2017/01/31/the-most-amazing-fossil-fish-ever-discovered/ [accessed September 19, 2017].

———. "Museums Showoff: Celebrating the Mundane." *UCL Museums and Collections Blog*, 2013. http://blogs.ucl.ac.uk/museums/2013/10/18/museums-showoff-celebrating-the-mundane/ [accessed March 21, 2017].

———. "Natural History under the Hammer." *UCL Museums and Collections Blog*, 2013. http://blogs.ucl.ac.uk/museums/2013/12/04/natural-history-under-the-hammer/ [accessed March 20, 2017].

———. "Underwhelming Fossil Fish of the Month." *UCL Museums and Collections Blog*, n.d. http://blogs.ucl.ac.uk/museums/tag/underwhelming-fossil-fish-of-the-month/ [accessed March 28, 2017].

———. "Underwhelming Fossil Fish of the Month, or How to Get Some Use out of Your Useless Fossils." *Palaeontological Association Newsletter* 89 (2015): 75–81.

———. "Underwhelming Fossil Fish of the Month: May 2016." *UCL Museums and Collections Blog*, 2016. https://blogs.ucl.ac.uk/museums/2016/05/31/underwhelming-fossil-fish-of-the-month-may-2016/ [accessed September 19, 2017].

———. "When Two Tribes Go to War: Art and Science 'Curatorship.'" *The Art and Science of Curation*, n.d. www.artandscienceofcuration.org.uk/when-two-tribes-go-to-war-art-science-curatorship/ [accessed March 29, 2017].

Collections Trust. "Spectrum 5.0," 2017. http://collectionstrust.org.uk/spectrum/spectrum-5-0/ [Accessed September 19, 2017].

Daszkiewicz, Piotr, and Aaron M. Bauer. "Specimens from the Second Collection of Albertus Seba in Poland: The Natural History Cabinet of Anna Jablonowska (1728–1800)." *Bibliotheca Herpetologica* 6, no. 2 (2006): 16–20.

Düring, Monika V., and Marta Poggesi. *Encyclopaedia Anatomica*. Cologne: Taschen, 1999.

Ebach, Malte C., and Craig Holdrege. "DNA Barcoding is No Substitute for Taxonomy." *Nature* 434 (2005): 697.

Ellis, Richard. *The Search for the Giant Squid*. New York: Penguin, 1998.

Google Arts & Culture. "The Natural History Museum," n.d. www.google.com/culturalinstitute/beta/partner/natural-history-museum [Accessed March 29, 2017].

———. "The Natural History Museum '11 exhibits'," n.d. www.google.com/culturalinstitute/beta/search/exhibit?p=natural-history-museum [accessed March 29, 2017].

———. "The Natural History Museum '*Symphurus sayademalhensis*'," n.d. www.google.com/culturalinstitute/beta/asset/symphurus-sayademalhensis-chabanaud-1955/OQEXKjL8ljA4ow [accessed March 29, 2017].

Hopwood, Nick. *Embryos in Wax: Models from the Ziegler Studio*. Cambridge: Cambridge University Press, 2002.

House of Lords Science and Technology Committee. *Systematics and Taxonomy: Follow-Up*. London: The Stationery Office, 2008.

Hull, J. *Cranial Catalogue: Human Skulls—Supplementary Note on Disposal of Human Crania (Folio vii)*. Unpublished report, Grant Museum of Zoology, 1960.

International Code of Zoological Nomenclature Online. "International Commission on Zoological Nomenclature," n.d. www.iczn.org/iczn/index.jsp [accessed March 28, 2017].

Jones, Rhett. "University Threatens Destruction of Millions of Specimens if Museum of Natural History Collection not Relocated." *Gizmodo*, 2017. http://gizmodo.com/university-threatens-destruction-of-millions-of-specime-1793745389 [accessed March 29, 2017].

Kemp, Christopher. "Museums: The Endangered Dead." *Nature News*, 2015. www.nature.com/news/museums-the-endangered-dead-1.16942 [accessed October 31, 2017].

King, Heather, and Marianne Achiam. "The Case for Natural History." *Science and Education* (2017): 1–15.

Lourenço, Marta C. "Between Two Worlds: The Distinct Nature and Contemporary Significance of University Museums and Collections in Europe." Unpublished PhD thesis, Conservatoire National des Arts et Métiers, 2005.

MacGregor, Arthur. "Tradescant's Rarities: Essays on the Foundation of the Ashmolean Museum 1683 with a Catalogue of the Surviving Early Collections." Unpublished MA dissertation, Durham University, 1983.

Miller, Ben. "The Epistemological Challenge of Model Whales." *Extinct Monsters*, 2016. https://extinctmonsters.net/2016/06/19/the-epistemological-challenge-of-model-whales/ [accessed March 15, 2017].

Morris, Patrick A. *A History of Taxidermy: Art, Science and Bad Taste*. Ascot: MPM, 2011.

Museums Association. *Code of Ethics for Museums*. London: Museums Association, 2008.

——. *Code of Ethics for Museums*. London: Museums Association, 2015. www.museums association.org/download?id=1155827 [accessed September 16, 2017].

Natural History Museum. "Digital Museum." *Natural History Museum Blog*, n.d. www.nhm. ac.uk/our-science/our-work/digital-museum.html [accessed October 30, 2017].

——. "*Diplodocus*: This Is Your Life." *Natural History Museum Blog*, 2016. www.nhm.ac.uk/discover/diplodocus-this-is-your-life.html [accessed March 19, 2017].

——. "Dippy on Tour." *Natural History Museum Blog*, n.d. www.nhm.ac.uk/about-us/national-impact/diplodocus-on-tour.html [accessed March 19, 2017].

——. "I Love Dippy Appeal." *Natural History Museum Blog*, n.d. www.nhm.ac.uk/support-us/love-dippy/index.html [accessed March 20, 2017].

Natural History Near You. *Natural Sciences Collections Association*, n.d. www.natsca.org/NHNearYou [accessed October 31, 2017].

Nudds, John R., and Charles W. Pettitt, ed. *The Value and Valuation of Natural Science Collections*. Bath: Geological Society of London, 1997.

Olaf, R., P. Bininda-Emonds, and Anthony P. Russell. "Minimization of Potential Problems Associated with the Morphometry of Spirit-Preserved Bat Wings." *Collection Forum* 8, no. 1 (1992): 9–14.

Oliver, Graham, and Darren Mann. "The Elephant in the Room." Conference paper presented at the Museums Association Conference, 2012.

Oxford University Museums Partnership. "Crap in the Attic? The Management and Use of Natural History Collections." *YouTube*, 2013. www.youtube.com/watch?v=zzbjHCyKeNc [accessed March 29, 2017].

Parle, Rachel. "Dodo Roadshow: Plymouth City Museum." *More Than a Dodo Blog*, 2013. https://morethanadodo.com/2015/06/09/dodo-roadshow-plymouth-city-museum/ [accessed March 21, 2017].

Preston, Alex. "The War against Humanities at Britain's Universities." *The Observer*, 2015. www.theguardian.com/education/2015/mar/29/war-against-humanities-at-britains-universities [accessed September 20, 2017].

Pyle, Michael Robert. "The Rise and Fall of Natural History." *Orion: People and Nature* 20, no. 4 (2001): 16–23.

Research Councils UK. "Pathways to Impact." www.rcuk.ac.uk/innovation/impacts/ [accessed March 28, 2017].

Serota, Nicholas. "Museums and Young People." In *Learning to Live: Museums, Young People and Education*, edited by Kate Bellamy and Carey Oppenheim, 21–29. London: Institute for Public Policy Research and National Museum Directors' Conference, 2009.

Shoulder, Jack. "Micrarium Selfies at the Grant Museum." *Jack's Adventures in Museum Land*, 2017. https://jacksadventuresinmuseumland.wordpress.com/2017/01/19/micrarium-selfies-at-the-grant-museum/ [accessed March 23, 2017].

Sleightholme, Steven. "The International Thylacine Database," n.d. www.naturalworlds.org/thylacine/mrp/itsd/itsd_1.htm [accessed March 29, 2017].

"Special Issue: Proceedings of the Dublin Blaschka Congress." *Historical Biology: An International Journal of Palaeobiology* 20, no. 1 (2008).

Tennyson, Alan. "The Global Hunt for the Original Wandering Albatross." *Museum of New Zealand*, 2007. http://blog.tepapa.govt.nz/2017/03/10/the-global-hunt-for-the-original-wandering-albatross/ [accessed March 29, 2017].

Tewksbury, Joshua J., John G. T. Anderson, Jonathan D. Bakker, Timothy J. Billo, Peter W. Dunwiddie, Martha J. Groom, Stephanie E. Hampton, et al. "Natural History's Place in Science and Society." *Bioscience* 64, no. 4 (2014): 300–310.

Timberlake, Simon. "A Scientific/Historical/Educational Heritage for Whom: The Value of Geological Collections in a Small Museum." In *The Value and Valuation of Natural Science Collections*, edited by John R. Nudds and Charles W. Pettitt, 127–35. Bath: Geological Society of London.

Wheeler, Quentin D. "Taxonomic Triage and the Poverty of Phylogeny." *Philosophical Transactions of the Royal Society of London B* 359 (2004): 571–83.

Wilson, Edward O. "Biodiversity Research Requires More Boots on the Ground." *Nature Ecology & Evolution* 1 (2017): 1590–91.

——. "The Coming Pluralisation of Biology and the Stewardship of Systematics." *BioScience* 39, no. 4 (1989): 242–45.

——. "The Plight of Taxonomy." *Ecology* 52, no. 5 (1971): 1.

——. "Taxonomy as a Fundamental Discipline." *Philosophical Transactions of the Royal Society of London B* 359, no. 1444 (2004): 739.

Yong, Ed. "Natural History Museums are Teeming with Undiscovered Species." *The Atlantic*, 2016. www.theatlantic.com/science/archive/2016/02/the-unexplored-marvels-locked-away-in-our-natural-history-museums/459306/ [accessed October 31, 2017].

Acknowledgements

I would like to thank the editors of this volume for approaching me to contribute to this book. I'd like to thank Janet Stott and Professor Samuel Oak for reading over the text. I'd also like to thank the staff of the Grant Museum of Zoology, UCL, and the Oxford University Museum of Natural History and the wider natural history museum community for the amazing work they continue to do and the opportunities I have been given to explore "unloved" museum collections.

Chapter 6

GETTING TO GRIPS WITH MEDICAL HANDLING COLLECTIONS: MEDICAL MEMORIES, SPECIALIST KNOWLEDGE, AND COMMUNITY ENGAGEMENT AROUND "UNLOVED" OBJECTS

MARK MACLEOD*

RESEARCH INTO MEDICAL collections demonstrates that numerous universities and hospitals collected in order to preserve the history of their profession and to train new generations.[1] Unlike some of the more esoteric subjects in this book, medical memories are shared by the majority of the population. For many, these memories tend to take a particular form associated with trauma and sickness. While positive associations towards medical collections will of course also be held by individuals, often the memories are more difficult. The emotive nature of many medical collections adds a unique layer of meaning to these objects, offering enhanced potential for them to be considered as "unloved." In this medical museum context, the term "unloved" is characterized by collections that not only have difficult associations but also lack aesthetic appeal and personalization. However, for professionals who worked with medical objects and medicalized bodies for decades, the emotional resonance may be very different.

My perspective on this subject is that of a museum practitioner who has observed many interactions between visitors and medical collections. I come to the issue of "care" for collections as someone interested in exploring the humanity within medical collections. This revaluing and re-evaluation of medical collections is becoming a common element of curatorial practice. Hence, over time, medical curation has become less about technically cataloguing specimens and soulless equipment and more about

1 Samuel J. M. M. Alberti, *Morbid Curiosities: Medical Museums in Nineteenth-Century Britain* (London: Oxford University Press, 2011).

* **Mark Macleod** is creating digital tours in Dunfermline, Scotland for residents and visitors to the area. He was Head of The Infirmary Museum for five years, before which he provided maternity cover at the University of St. Andrews Museums Collections Unit as Operations and Projects Curator. He worked as Membership Development Manager at Museums Galleries Scotland for four years, providing support to Scotland's museums and galleries and working with venues to engage with special events like the 2009 Kolkata Book Fair, the 2012 Olympic and Paralympic Games, and the 2014 Commonwealth Games. Before securing full-time work, Mark interned at the Peggy Guggenheim Collection, the Michael C. Carlos Museum, Atlanta, the Contemporary Art Museum St. Louis, the Pulitzer Foundation for the Arts, and the Missouri History Museum. These roles exposed him to varied collections and audiences. With an MA in Art History from St. Andrews, an MA in History with a concentration on Museum Studies, and an additional Graduate Certificate in Museum Studies from the University of Missouri, St. Louis, Mark continues to research how technology can improve the visitor experience irrespective of the object being viewed.

understanding how medical objects can become objects of universal enquiry and shared experience. Ultimately this helps us to understand what it means to be human. This subject follows wider shifts in the medical profession towards greater acknowledgement of emotions in medical work, both from the practitioner and patient perspectives, and it is a subject I will return to at the end of the discussion.[2]

This chapter focuses on the medical handling collection used at The Infirmary, Worcester, a collection comprised of seemingly "unloved" objects. Two specific themes will be drawn out in the discussions: the contribution that former medical and healthcare professionals, acting as "specialist volunteers," make to reviving and engaging others with medical collections and, second, the role of collaborative community-orientated projects as sites for the reinvigoration of these collections. In other chapters in this volume (see Smith, Hess, and Woodham and Kelleher), authors discuss how the skills and knowledge of retired professionals who are also collections enthusiasts might breathe life into stagnant objects. In this chapter, the "enthusiastic" collectors and carers (the volunteering team) offer a unique combination of technical knowledge of objects and specimens and experience of therapeutic or clinical care. By focusing both on this volunteer group and on the community projects themselves, this chapter demonstrates how a collection of largely utilitarian objects can successfully be repurposed to catalyze memory-making and emotional engagement beyond the medical profession.

An initial introduction to the history of medical museums will set the context for growing audiences visiting these specialist destinations.[3] By looking back into the history of medical collections we can see the importance of medical professionals as amateur collectors and curators. It is also possible to understand the changing mission and collection practices of medical museums and finally the legacies with which the modern medical curator must grapple. This discussion is followed by information on two venues in Worcester, UK, that form the focus of the chapter: The Infirmary and the George Marshall Medical Museum (GMMM). Case studies of projects conducted at The Infirmary in particular are used to illustrate how the wider use of "unloved" objects can stimulate a range of outputs. The chapter ends with lessons for wider museum practice around the benefits of working with handling collections.

The Development of Medical Collections in the UK

The most well-known family name associated with medical museums for over 200 years is Hunter. William Hunter (1718–1783) donated his museum and library from Great

---

2 See the Wellcome Trust–supported project "Surgery and Emotion," which looks at the place of emotion in practice, politics, and the representation of surgery from 1800 to the present day. www.surgeryandemotion.com [accessed July 3, 2019].

3 For example, The Infirmary grew its visitor numbers from zero to 8,000 in five years. And "rapid growth" in visitor figures is confirmed in the Wellcome Collection's Forward Plan 2018–2023, http://prev.wellcomecollection.org/sites/default/files/Wellcome%20Collection_Forward%20Plan_2018-23.pdf. Investment in other museums with medical collections also indicates a growth in interest, for example, the Thackray Medical Museum, Leeds, which is currently closed for a £4 million refurbishment programme.

Windmill Street, London, to his alma mater, the University of Glasgow. His instruction was for the collections to continue being used for thirty years by his nephew and colleague William Cruikshank. However, Cruikshank died within seventeen years of the bequest. The university took the opportunity to spend an £8,000 legacy left by Hunter to build a new museum in Glasgow and subsequently opened Scotland's first public museum in 1807, the Hunterian Museum.

The Royal College of Surgeons in London opened an anatomy collection in 1813, also called the Hunterian Museum. Formed from the collection of William's brother John Hunter (1728–1793), it had been purchased by the government for the nation and donated to the college. Anatomy collections were used to educate men interested in becoming surgeons, physicians, or apothecaries, fulfilling a role beyond books and lectures and delivering a corporeal experience. Predominantly housed in private anatomy schools and hospitals, the collections were updated and rotated depending on access to suitable specimens from donated or acquired bodies.[4] London's Hunterian Museum allowed limited access to members (who were all men) at certain times, days, and months. The Hunterian Museum, London, was the first example of a medical collection being exhibited in a location distant from hospitals or private anatomy schools in England.

In 1882, the Royal College of Surgeons permitted women restricted access to the museum. In time, the demand for visits grew, and opening hours became more accessible. In 2013, the collection was open to everyone, with visits in excess of 75,000 per year.[5] The purpose of these collections has evolved from offering a private educational opportunity to one of public education and curiosity, thus meeting the International Council of Museums' (ICOM) current definition of a museum that encompasses the role to conserve, preserve, and collect objects "for the purposes of education, study and enjoyment."[6]

The 17,000 specimens collected by surgeon John Hunter were amassed during his career and would have been a welcome resource for a growing number of surgeons and physicians taking up qualifications in the expanding world of medicine towards the end of the eighteenth century. John and his brother William had their collections located in their homes, which also acted as anatomy schools. Their collections were of a similar size: John's collection covered fifty-two feet by twenty-eight feet; William's was twenty feet by twenty-seven feet.[7]

---

4 Alberti, *Morbid Curiosities*, 80.

5 Samuel J. M. M. Alberti and Elizabeth Hallam, *Medical Museums: Past, Present, Future* (London: Royal College of Surgeons of England, 2013).

6 At the time of publishing, the ICOM definition of a museum is as follows: "A museum is a non-profit, permanent institution in the service of society and its development, open to the public, which acquires, conserves, researches, communicates and exhibits the tangible and intangible heritage of humanity and its environment for the purposes of education, study and enjoyment." ICOM, "Museum Definition," http://icom.museum/the-vision/museum-definition/ [accessed October 15, 2017].

7 Alberti, *Morbid Curiosities*, 42.

Medical practitioners have always been at the forefront of collecting—for example, the Hunter brothers and Sir Hans Soane, whose collection founded the British Museum—and today medical practitioners continue to collect specimens, books, and artefacts related to their profession for personal interest. About 100 miles west of London, two contemporary examples of medical museums exist, free and open to the public, thanks to the collector and former general practitioner Dr. George Marshall (1906–2001). The Infirmary and the GMMM opened in 2012 and 2002, respectively. A UK Medical Collections Group, including the GMMM, was established in 2005 and comprises an informal grouping of twenty-five London-based museums of health and medicine[8] alongside members from across the United Kingdom.[9] Displayed in universities, hospitals, former hospitals, asylum buildings, and the houses of innovators like Dr. Edward Jenner—pioneer of the smallpox vaccination in 1796—these collections fascinate and encourage curiosity about the history of medicine.

Physicians, surgeons, and anatomists were academic powerhouses of the nineteenth century. As industrialization increased wealth and leisure time, there were expanding opportunities to travel and, coupled with interests in attending new medical and philosophical societies, to share knowledge and conversation about the profession and its impact on the natural world. Subsequently, these educated men became interested in collecting. Their achievements in medicine and science can be celebrated today by viewing these collections and gaining an understanding of the values, ambitions, and challenges that this profession encountered. Medical collections became open to the public during the nineteenth century, at a time when science and peer-reviewed journals gradually changed minds on medical treatments based on tradition and folklore. The passing of the Anatomy Act of 1832 permitted legitimate access to unclaimed corpses, providing more opportunities for experienced and student medics alike to carry out hypothesis-based research and practise procedures. They could also expand anatomical examples and renew deteriorating "wet specimens" stored in alcohol in jars at existing hospitals and private museums.[10] Darwin's controversial *On the Origin of Species* (1859) provided an intellectual argument in support of further investigations to discover fundamental knowledge about the human body.

A desire to understand the human body is a strong starting point from which to work out what it means to be human and helps explain the interest of visitors in these displays over the last two centuries. Such a fascination and curiosity drives visits in the present century, as record numbers of visits are recorded at Britain's museums. Visit Britain reports indexed growth in audiences at museums and galleries in excess of 50 percent since

---

8 See the London Museums of Health and Medicine for further information, http://medicalmuseums. org/ [accessed October 15, 2017].

9 Including Bethlem Royal Hospital Archives and Museum, London; Metropolitan Archives; Hunterian Museum, Royal College of Surgeons; Pathology Museum, Queen Mary University; Queen Mary Hospital, Roehampton; Boots Archive; Royal College of Physicians; University London Hospitals Archives; Royal College of Nursing; Science Museum; the Robert Jones and Agnes Hunt Orthopedic Hospital; and the Thackray Medical Museum, Leeds.

10 Alberti, *Morbid Curiosities*, 80.

1989.[11] Being able to see what lies beneath the skin is taken for granted with today's access to the internet. Contemporary medical advances astound, and the ability to view microscopic particles provide insights into what 100 years ago was inconceivable. For example, a photograph from 1914 shows a nonpatient visiting the Worcester General Infirmary and paying a guinea to have their hand x-rayed just to see what was inside! Knowledge of DNA and the ability to assess susceptibility to illness fuels individuals' fascination with their bodies. Dr. Von Hagens's touring exhibition *Body Worlds*, comprising plastinated human specimens posed as if they are riding a horse or playing basketball, for example, takes two-dimensional anatomy textbooks to the next dimension. First displayed to the public in 1995, by 2008 it was reported that twenty-six million people had visited the exhibition worldwide.[12]

However, in a world where mainstream television broadcasts surgical procedures and a YouTube search for "human pathology" returns 382,000 results, can medical museums still be a place of enquiry for the visitor? What of medical instrument collections? What can they offer to a group of teenagers? How can the history of medicine be told through handling medical objects, and how can they generate creativity in a group of adults as they face retirement or are diagnosed with life-changing illnesses?

The Development of The Infirmary

The Infirmary exhibition, opened in 2012, is based at the University of Worcester (see figure 6.1). It displays and uses objects from GMMM, which is located at Worcestershire Royal Hospital. The handling collection that forms the main focus of this chapter was created from objects in GMMM's collection.

George Marshall was born in Leith, Edinburgh, and studied at Edinburgh Medical School before arriving at Worcester General Infirmary in 1931. He worked as a surgeon and general practitioner until 1970. Marshall became a consultant surgeon to the Worcester Royal Infirmary (WRI) at the introduction of the National Health Service in 1948 and treated the people of Worcestershire for many decades. It was joked by local residents that Marshall was someone who knew the population of Worcester "inside and out," and there are still visitors to the GMMM and The Infirmary who remember Marshall as their physician or colleague. As an enthusiastic collector of old medical equipment (he started collecting medical instruments while working at WRI), by the time of his retirement he had accumulated nearly 8,000 items, including ten death masks, believed to be of hung prisoners, discovered under the chapel at WRI. Today, at GMMM, these masks are a strong draw for people to visit the exhibition.

Marshall's collection was initially used for postgraduate teaching purposes at Ronkswood Hospital in Worcester. The idea of a public museum was proposed after a new "super hospital" was envisioned, which would amalgamate and replace regional

---

11 Visit England, *Visitor Attractions Trends in England*, 2016. Full report, www.visitbritain.org/sites/default/files/vb-corporate/Documents-Library/documents/England-documents/annual_attractions_trend_report_2016.pdf [accessed October 15, 2017].

12 Anonymous, "Doctor Defends Body Worlds Exhibition," *The Independent*, October 24, 2008.

Figure 6.1. The Infirmary entrance wall, The Infirmary Museum, Worcester.
© University of Worcester, Worcester.

facilities like WRI. With funding from the Heritage Lottery Fund,[13] GMMM opened in 2002 and displays a chronology of medical history, showing about 10 percent of the collection of 3,500 medical objects, with an additional 4,000 archival items, books, and photographs available for researchers to consult by appointment. The collection continues to expand through donations relevant to the collecting policy, and, as with many medical museums, engaging medical professionals in the process of contemporary collecting remains a key way of maintaining a dynamic and relevant collection.[14] A focus for the GMMM in particular is on acquiring objects with a Worcestershire provenance and that relate to modern medical techniques, subject to available storage space.

The Castle Street branch of WRI closed in 2002. This second infirmary site in Worcestershire had operated as a hospital for 231 years. The founding hospital, on Silver Street, ran out of room to grow within nineteen years of its opening in 1746. Due to lack of space and the poor design of the former domestic building, the site quickly became inadequate. Under the direction of Dr. John Wall, a purpose-designed building, "Worcester Infirmary," was commissioned in the 1760s from a local architect, Anthony Keck. His plans incorporated the latest in hospital design; it had high ceilings, enormous windows, and an on-site brewery.

Interestingly, in the second year of his role (secured at the age of eighteen), the young House Surgeon/Apothecary Charles Hastings introduced an anatomy museum to Worcester General Infirmary in 1813. Sadly, none of the contents have been discovered

---

13 Now known as the National Lottery Heritage Fund.

14 See Georgina Ferry, "The Art of Medicine: Collecting Modern Medicine," *The Lancet* 18 (2018): 278–79.

or are known to have been recorded. The floorplan of St. Thomas's Hospital, London, from 1848 also shows that it contained a museum, and St. Bartholomew's Hospital Museum is known to have existed by 1828.[15] Chaplin notes, "From the 1780s onward, anatomical teaching of all kinds became more firmly located within hospital settings."[16] From such activity, institutions accumulated specimen collections.

Ask any museum director or read a museum's mission statement and they will mention education, research, and entertainment along with preserving, conserving, and collecting as their principal roles. Alberti reports that 7,000 students and junior doctors attend training at the Wellcome Museum of Anatomy and Pathology each year.[17] Compared to the 75,000 public visitors, the proportion of visits from medical students and junior practitioners has drastically fallen from the 100 percent of visits to the Hunterian Museum in 1813. One could argue that this demonstrates that the purpose of the museums with medical and anatomical specimens has evolved from directly serving medical schools and their students to having a greater focus on educating, entertaining, and inspiring nonmedical visitors, and it is in this context that The Infirmary developed.

The Modern Remaking of The Infirmary, Its Handling Collection, and Volunteers

When WRI closed in 2002, the building lay empty until 2009, when the University of Worcester opened it as Worcester Business School and a city centre campus. In the course of planning the new campus, the historical importance of the WRI Boardroom convinced senior management to include a small exhibition about the building during its 231 years as a hospital. The first meeting of the Provincial Medical and Surgical Association was held in the Boardroom in July 1832 and within twenty-four years it had become the British Medical Association, led by local hero Dr. Charles Hastings. With support from the Heritage Lottery Fund, the Charles Hastings Education Centre, and the University of Worcester, the exhibition opened in 2012 and now has the mission to positively change the lives of visitors to the former WRI through telling the history of health and medicine there, using the building, objects, and oral histories. The exhibition and related events ask individuals to consider their own health and well-being in relation to the content of the exhibition. A character-led approach has been taken in the interpretation present in the exhibition, allowing the visitor to investigate what Dr. Wall and Bishop Isaac Maddox achieved by starting Worcester Infirmary in 1746 and later the purpose-built Infirmary.

There are 120 objects on display in The Infirmary's gallery (see figure 6.2), the majority on loan from GMMM. It is safe to say that many of the instruments were used in Worcestershire before Marshall added them to his collection of some 3,500 medical-related objects. The handling collection of over 100 objects is shared between The

---

15 Simon Chaplin, *John Hunter and the "Museum Oeconomy," 1750–1800*, unpublished PhD thesis, King's College London, 2009. Appendix 1, "John Abernethy" entry.

16 Chaplin, *John Hunter and the "Museum Oeconomy," 1750–1800*, 38.

17 Alberti and Hallam, *Medical Museums*, 29.

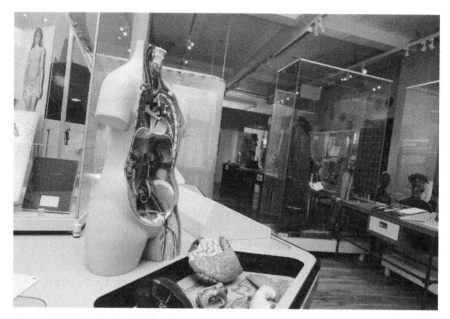

Figure 6.2. The Infirmary Museum exhibition, Worcester. ©University of Worcester, Worcester.
© University of Worcester, Worcester.

Infirmary and GMMM. Comprised of objects which are duplicates to the collection, they are also robust and replaceable should there be an accident and they get broken. Objects include brass-covered bleeding bowls, a range of designs for anaesthetic face masks from 1890 to 1960, various forceps, hip replacement joints, invalid cups, tongue depressors, and bedpans, to name a few. The objects in the handling collection date from the eighteenth century to the present day and provide participative engagement opportunities for people of all ages, backgrounds, and experiences.

As outlined in the introduction, a professional interest in the history of medicine is not unusual among medics. Some retired doctors and other healthcare professionals have collections and retain a strong interest in their former profession,[18] and they often pursue personal research projects in retirement, seeking publication through the British Society for the History of Medicine and similar specialist societies. Many of GMMM's and The Infirmary's regular volunteers are former healthcare professionals and offer their time and expertise in the support of cataloguing instruments, delivering tours, and giving public presentations on their areas of interest. Access to their specialist knowledge means that objects can be accurately identified quicker than a curator could do so. As the 2017 Mendoza Review[19] indicates, there is concern generally

---

18 The GMMM collections include subsequent objects donated by anaesthetists, sexual health experts, and GPs.

19 Neil Mendoza, *The Mendoza Review: An Independent Review of Museums in England* (London: DCMS, 2017).

in the museum sector around a decline in curatorial time and expertise. This, coupled with the draw that larger medical collections represented in National Museums provide for specialist museum staff, means that, generally speaking, smaller medical collections are managed by museum professionals who provide expertise across a range of areas, including care, interpretation, and education but not necessarily always in subject expertise. Passionate volunteers retired from the medical sector can therefore be invaluable colleagues to clear collection catalogue backlogs, identify gaps in collections, communicate with audiences, and research the significance of objects. The whole process enables the object to be available for exhibition, research, or education purposes in the future.

While this level of professional knowledge is valued by the museum, no doubt the greatest immediate benefit of specialist volunteers is to provide context to the objects with which they are familiar, as many have experience of using these objects or sometimes being treated using them! This allows for a mixture of factual interpretation (what the object is, what it was used for) and narratives, which grab audiences. Healthcare volunteers with The Infirmary and GMMM were trained from the 1960s, and their period of work covered the introduction of some significant treatments, i.e., heart transplant operations and hip-joint replacement surgery. These volunteers are able to provide their personal experiences, which allows storytelling to accompany a handling session. For example, this might include a handling session around the use of anaesthetic masks and hip-joint replacements. Details of the economic, political, and social situation, as experienced by the retired nurse or doctor at the time, certainly contribute to learning more about the technological changes the handling object represents. However, these facets also expand the narrative to allow more elements through which the audience can access the story and thereby understand the significance of this functional object.

The specialist volunteers at The Infirmary often have experience of being excellent communicators. Unlike some of the other volunteer groups discussed in this volume, the careers of the expert volunteers at The Infirmary were spent with people, and this can often be seen when they work with family audiences, teenagers, or members of the public.

The GMMM collection largely exists due to the artefacts' function and not their form. Therefore, the challenge of using the handling collection is in how they stimulate memories or as a catalyst for creativity. There is little or no "wow" factor on seeing the objects for the first time. In fact, as mentioned in the introduction, staff members and volunteers are aware of the potential negative associations a participant may have with the objects, for example, being reminded of a past procedure or treatment with an object, such as a 1950s feeding tube. Similarly, careful approaches are required when speaking with visitors, never seeking to dwell on contemporary treatments or medical scenarios in case they trigger an unpleasant memory. That said, if a former patient or staff member taking the tour wishes to share their story, they are supported to do so, and this will often lead to a discussion. In a similar way to the Tenement Museum in New York, where visitors are invited to stay for a cup of tea and a chat if they are particularly interested in or affected by any of the stories of immigration presented during their emotive tours, the

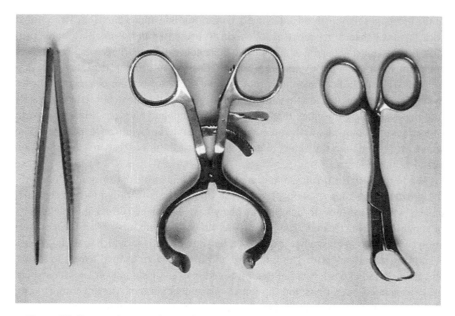

Figure 6.3. Tongue clamp, Molt mouth gag, and medical tweezers from handling collection, George Marshall Medical Museum, Worcester. © University of Worcester, Worcester.

specialist volunteers in Worcester offer first-hand experience and supportive comments for visitors affected by the objects' stories.

The Infirmary's education workshops' content encourages the audience to consider the smells and sounds of early patients' experiences in the building, e.g., the sound of the brass bleeding bowl being placed on the wooden table or imagining the echoing clang if it fell off the table onto the concrete slab floor! Feeling, seeing, and hearing original artefacts can stimulate visitors to imagine more features from the time period (see figure 6.3). They might be encouraged to imagine being examined by a surgeon in 1820 who did not know what bacteria was and failed to wash his hands between blood-letting different patients!

People Living with Dementia Creating Glassware

This section now moves on to consider some of the different nonspecialist communities that came into contact with the museum and its handling collection and the potential impact of their engagement with these "unloved" objects.

Museum objects need not be only interpreted for their historical value but can also be used for education, creative, and enlightening purposes; an individual can be inspired to use the object to stimulate their own interpretations of it. Supported by objects from the GMMM storerooms, one of three mini projects delivered between 2012 and 2013 helped to launch the new exhibition at The Infirmary, introduced above. Staff, volunteers, and an artist worked with local agencies and initiatives such as Dementia Cafes and Dementia Friends[20] with the aim of using the handling collection to stimulate creativity, reminiscence, and interest in the newly opened exhibition. This project is just one of a growing number of examples where museums have sought to bring people experiencing dementia into contact with objects in order to explore the therapeutic impact of this experience.[21] The project generated over seventy participant engagements over four weeks of workshops, and many more people were engaged during the outreach portion to recruit participants. The appointed artist worked in glass, and this provided an incentive to participants to return the following week to The Infirmary to collect their fired artwork.

In practical terms, concerns over safeguarding for participants who were living with dementia meant that the workshops that were part of this project included family members or carers. An important element was the tea break in the middle of workshops, with evaluations showing that this recharged energy and gave carers and family members a chance to chat to people in similar situations and gain some respite, as well as encouragement.

Principles governing the three mini projects were drafted in an Action Plan by external consultants and reflect elements of a collaborative and participatory design, where possible, so that participants gained knowledge and felt included and empowered.[22] The Action Plan was written in 2008, just as Nina Simon's blog "Museum 2.0" was having an impact on the United Kingdom museum sector in advance of her publication, *The Participatory Museum*, in 2010. In it she shares her experiences at Santa Cruz Museum of Art and History and case studies of participation models from museums all over the world. She asserts that participatory design is key to engaging audiences with an institution's mission and therefore leading to successes in engagement with communities and improving the organization's relevance.

Working with the dementia community gave the handling collection a new role, as it was used to recruit participants to the glassmaking part of the project. Attending five Dementia Cafes in the county, accompanied by the objects, was a method of introducing the mini project to those living with dementia and their carers, the majority of whom were family members. Playing "Guess the Object," using open questions, and passing

---

20 See the Alzheimer's Society on Dementia Cafes: www.alzheimers.org.uk/get-support/your-support-services/dementia-cafe and their separate initiative, Dementia Friends: www.dementia friends.org.uk

21 See, for example, Lois H. Silverman, "The Therapeutic Potential of Museums as Pathways to Inclusion," in *Museums, Society, Inequality*, ed. Richard Sandell (London: Routledge, 2002), 69–83; Libby Rhoads, "Museums, Meaning Making and Memories: The Need for Museum Programs for People with Dementia and Their Caregivers," *Curator, The Museum Journal* 52, no. 3 (July 2009): 229–40; Nuala Morse and Helen Chatterjee, "Museums, Health and Wellbeing Research: Co-developing a New Observational Method for People with Dementia in Hospital Contexts," *Perspectives in Public Health* 136, no. 3 (May 2018): 152–59.

22 Vicky Dawson and David Dawson, *Museum@WRI Activity Plan*, unpublished consultation report, 2010.

the objects around for everyone to hold and inspect closely enabled memories to be triggered and stories to be shared. Once recruited, participants were invited to attend the artist-led glass tile workshops at The Infirmary. Each participant could create something based on their interpretation of "what home meant to them."

The handling collection objects were available each week, should the participants wish to use them for inspiration, meaning that this collection of objects became a familiar sight for the participants. A final exhibition of the artworks created during the project was held for the public and family members to attend over the period of a month and proved very popular. Key learning points from the workshop included the observation that people living with dementia need encouragement to join a creative/new activity and to break with existing routines and that people living with dementia and their carers benefit from creative practice. The project also indicated that training for museum volunteers and staff in dementia awareness may support facilitation with the objects. For the participants and their carers, we also observed some tangible impacts; for example, several participants who came as individuals decided to join the local Dementia Cafe. Overall, it was clear to us that creative practice stimulated through engagement with "unloved" objects can lead to relaxation and contentment, both for people living with dementia and their carers.[23] Interestingly, some of the attendees at the Dementia Cafe included retired nurses who were quick to identify the twentieth-century objects with which they were familiar, showing just how relevant these so-called "unloved" collections can be.

Unfortunately, as is often the case with short-term funded projects, follow-up evaluation has not been able to successfully determine the long-term impact because the funding was time-limited.[24] This is a sector-wide issue, and longitudinal studies measuring impacts of cultural engagement are hard to locate. Of relevance here is the *Understanding the Value of Arts and Culture* report by the Arts and Humanities Research Council (AHRC), which illustrates strong examples of how engagement with art at a young age might influence the participants' involvement in civic duties, like voting, in later life.[25] Although not realized by the project manager at The Infirmary, Tony Butler, founder of the Happy Museum project, has subsequently articulated what was being attempted through this mini project much better: "Museums should realize their role as connector, viewing people not as audiences but as collaborators, not as beneficiaries

---

23 These findings are in keeping with those from similar studies with different kinds of collections. For example, Kate A. Hamblin, *Museums, Oral History, Reminiscence and Wellbeing: Establishing Collaboration and Outcomes* (Oxford: Oxford Institute of Population Ageing, 2016); Anna Hansen, ed., *Reminiscence in Open Air Museums: Results from the Erasmus+ Project Active Ageing and Heritage in Adult Learning* (Östersund: Jamtli, 2017).

24 The time-limited, project-orientated, and often "temporary" nature of collaborative work in museums is a common observation and potential limitation of this way of working. See Bernadette Lynch, *Whose Cake Is It Anyway? A Collaborative Investigation into Engagement and Participation in 12 Museums and Galleries in the UK* (London: Paul Hamlyn Foundation, 2011).

25 Crossick and Kaszynska, *Understanding the Value of Arts and Culture*, 60.

but citizens and stewards who nurture and pass on knowledge to their friends and neighbours."[26] This is something that The Infirmary continues to strive towards.

"Doors Open Day": Other Uses of the Handling Collection

At the time of writing, the handling collection continues to be used weekly for informal and formal education sessions and introduces all ages and experiences to the history of medicine and the important contributions that Worcester-based professionals—including Mr. Henry Carden, Sir Charles Hastings, and Matron Mary Herbert—made to medicine. Retired healthcare professionals, mentioned above, volunteer their time to take community groups and other visitors on walking tours of the building in which they trained. The tours include handling objects, providing additional opportunities for the audience to potentially access and further process their own memories of giving or receiving medical treatment or observing loved ones receiving treatments. The format also allows the audience to make new meaning with the building and from the personal narratives of the volunteer guides. For example, during "Doors Open Day," a former nurses' home—now administration offices—is opened to the public and tours given by volunteers. One room on the tour contains volunteers who were nurses, accompanied by some current student nurses. Present in the room are a number of twentieth-century handling objects, for example, forceps, previous nurses' uniforms, badges and buckles, and images from the past 150 years. The interaction between volunteers of different nursing generations prompted shared interactions facilitated by objects that for some could be perceived as boring or mundane "tools of the trade." This interaction is further stimulated by the inclusion of visitors from the public, many of whom were attracted to visit because they once lived and worked in or used the buildings at some point in the course of their lives.

These functional objects help to prod old memories to the surface, which are then shared and further enhanced by conversations with specialist volunteers and visitors to establish if they worked with any of the same people during their respective careers. Previous teaching regimes saw classes, or "sets," of nurses trained and living together; it doesn't take many questions to ascertain who knows who and then bring the conversation back to the present day to reminisce around these social ties. The WRI has been in existence for 231 years, and the nursing "family tree" depicting the relationships over generations is expansive and ever growing.

These events, which are shared experiences between healthcare professionals old and new and members of the public, help not only to generate new information for the museum about the social and experiential "biographies" of their collections but also to bring an immeasurable amount of emotion to participants, sparking interest for new and established museum volunteers. I argue that it is valuable for the museum and the participants of such projects to recognize that all of these experiences are derived from seeing, handling, and sharing an experience around an object as seemingly mundane as a tongue depressor.

---

26 Alison Bodley, *History to Health: Research into Changing Health Agendas for the UK Medical Collections Group* (Leeds: Thackray Medical Museum and Arts Council England, 2012), 12.

The Nature of Learning via Handling Objects

Objects designed for a specific purpose can be viewed through many different lenses. In the above projects and with ongoing work, medical instruments have been used to help people think about design, technology, materials, and chronology, among other things. With discussion they can be linked to topics that may be more relevant for the participant, for example, introducing a medical book group to Mary Shelley's classic novel *Frankenstein*; one of the pinnacle moments is the amalgamation of the monster using random body parts, what Alberti may call "fragments."[27] This scene can be envisaged through examining eighteenth-century operating instruments, which transport the person holding the instrument back in time to the context in which Shelley produced her inspiring and shocking work. Such flexibility allows the museum greater opportunities to engage with wider audience needs. For example, is the group composed of retired nurses? If so, they may be able to identify objects from the 1980s and share personal experiences and stories about their use. In contrast, for example, a group of Year 10 pupils (14–15-year-olds) can follow the graphic instructions on how to tie a sling from the First World War handling objects and compare them with how to tie a contemporary sling using a YouTube tutorial.

Each viewer has his or her own understanding of the world. Through the availability of functional medical objects in the handling collections, they can question design, locate and identify makers' marks, and then speculate about use. Visitors leave with new knowledge, the enjoyment of handling objects, and hopefully have an increased appreciation of present-day healthcare professionals using the latest technology. George Hein writes of a constructivist learning approach in museums,[28] and the handling medical collection is a good example of how this can be brought into practice. Rather than attaching to each object a label of up to fifty words, including name, purpose, date, manufacturer, medium, etc., as would be the case in the gallery, the handling collection has no such written interpretation. During handling sessions, individuals are asked open questions and encouraged to create their own questions to ascertain answers. What is it made from? Plastic? What is the oldest plastic object you have seen or own? When was plastic introduced? Does this help to date the object? When working with participants studying GCSE History of Medicine, this type of enquiry works well, as it encourages students to think beyond one period or topic in medicine; for example, the history of medicine Victorian surgery workshop, delivered by GMMM, links preanaesthetic practice to contemporary experiences through medical knives and saws that would not look out of place in a contemporary kitchen or toolbox. Participants could be presented with an up-to-date hip joint replacement and be challenged to come up with what it is for, when it was made, how common they think it is, etc. While this open and exploratory approach can be seen in handling sessions at other museums, it is worth remembering that it is a simple yet useful strategy for reinvigorating an "unloved" collection.

27 Alberti, *Morbid Curiosities*, 7.

28 George Hein, "Constructivist Learning Theory," *Exploratorium*, www.exploratorium.edu/education/ifi/constructivist-learning [accessed October 15, 2017].

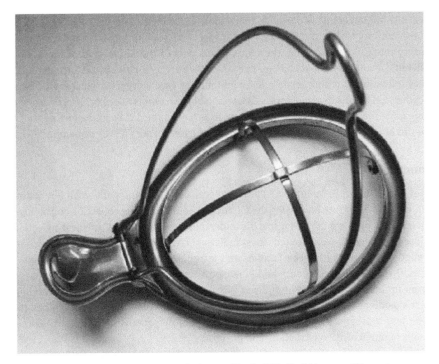

Figure 6.4. Schimmelbusch mask, George Marshall Medical Museum, Worcester.
© University of Worcester, Worcester.

Working with medical handling objects typifies the constructivist learning approach: Visitors can draw on their own knowledge and are enabled to have personal "aha" moments as they ask their questions. Everyone enters a museum with their own knowledge and experience, and this will govern how they view the objects on display or respond to the story being told. Learning is an active process, and asking the visitor to construct their own enquiry of the object helps with their learning and the retention of this learning. Hein also highlights the benefits of doing this socially, within an "authentic" context (like a former hospital building), with time to reflect and build on one's own existing knowledge.[29]

Over the years, thousands of people have handled this "unloved" collection at The Infirmary and leave with new knowledge about the objects. What is also exciting for museum professionals using this approach is that there is as much to learn from visitors and project participants too. For instance, the fundamental design of something like a Schimmelbusch mask (see figure 6.4) from 1890[30] reveals important features if the visitor is willing to delve beyond how it looks (a process which could be facilitated by a

---

29 Hein, "Constructivist Learning Theory."

30 Portable anaesthetic mask designed by Dr. Curt Schimmelbusch in c.1890 to deliver chloroform or ether fumes from liquid without it directly touching the patient's face.

specialist volunteer). It is portable, functional, and robust in nature, making it a very good handling object. It illustrates the bridge between nineteenth- and twentieth-century medical practice and, therefore, forms part of the foundation of innovations and rapid evolutions in medicine, like anaesthetic, an important advancement that every individual can appreciate and be grateful for. One volunteer remembered being anesthetized by this design of mask as a young boy for a minor surgical procedure, thus confirming the use of the mask in Worcester as late as the 1950s and allowing staff to add this story to presentations and enquire of older audiences if they remember its use.

Conclusion

What does it mean to be human? These projects, each working with small but distinct communities, illustrate how using the medical museum handling collection consisting of objects that could arguably fit a specific understanding of "unloved" medical collections to varying degrees contributed to stimulating creativity, building confidence, and strengthening bonds between families and introduced a new museum to its communities. Quacks in the eighteenth and nineteenth centuries used medical instruments to "drum up business,"[31] and The Infirmary is taking a similar approach to encouraging greater audience engagement and learning by utilizing the wider opportunities that these less aesthetically pleasing and "difficult" objects offer, which focuses on their design, manufacture, construction, and purpose.

In the seven years since its opening, it is estimated that 25 percent of the annual audience has held at least one of the objects in The Infirmary's handling collection, which is an impressive statistic! This chapter has highlighted projects that show why these functional and supposedly "uninteresting" objects are deployed. Ultimately, the objects offer flexibility in use whatever the event, be it education workshops, community engagement, or participant recruitment. The plain nature of their appearance makes them appropriate for all audiences aged six years and up,[32] allowing everyone with different levels of knowledge to interrogate them from a constructivist learning perspective.

Handling collections are a tool for most museums that can be deployed to engage audiences. Even medical artefacts have shown purpose in unexpected areas. Asking for support from existing or retired experts from the medical profession ensured that the interpretation and storytelling was factually correct. The projects discussed above also suggest that volunteers who are former medical and healthcare professionals offer a form of "professional enthusiasm" for these objects, which is influenced by their previous engagement with the objects as "tools of the trade." However, this does not mean that there is a lack of emotional engagement with the objects in this context; far from it, as many of these collections ultimately speak about human relationships despite at a

---

31 Roy Porter, *Quacks: Fakers and Charlatans in Medicine* (London: NPI Media, 2003), 138.

32 The Infirmary recommends visitors to be six years old or over to view the full exhibition because of the subject matter and level of content. When schools with children younger than six years old visit, a separate workshop with objects and storytelling is used to deliver knowledge about medical history.

surface level appearing to lack personalization. In the case of the specialist volunteers, the personally meaningful narratives are presented alongside more factual interpretations and are intertwined with them.

While the discussion above has emphasized the use of "unloved" collections in The Infirmary's handling collection and the interactions between these objects and the museum professionals and volunteers who care for them, the chapter offers wider lessons for any museum with a handling collection (whether this consists of a potentially "unloved" collection or not). For example, a key point for museums is to consider their existing collections with a view to working with local organizations so that it is possible to understand which audiences can be engaged by using their handling artefacts. Of course, projects that directly engage a community require adequate resources; however, the rewards for participants can be life-changing, as seen by an example from the Museums Association in Glasgow Museums' *Contact the Elderly*.[33] The Infirmary discovered that little specialist knowledge or experience with the objects was required. In fact, the participants required no medical background at all to successfully engage with the objects. Artefacts were approached using an inquisitive method and this has become the model for future events. Asking participants open questions about the objects to ascertain media, shape, feel, and potential date of use soon gets conversations started about related topics, such as "When did steel start to be used for manufacturing?" The objects act as catalysts for conversation and, similarly, the museum's staff and volunteers further that reaction and allow the conversation and experience to extend into areas suitable for the audience engaged. The mission is not to educate people on the method of use or diagnosis; it is to get people thinking about healthcare now versus in the past, considering questions such as: are we better off now than 200 years ago or five years ago? And should we do anything to consider our own health and lifestyle choices as a result of handling these objects? It is by connecting to today's world that these seemingly "unlovable" collections find their contemporary relevance.

Bibliography

Alberti, Samuel J. M. M. *Morbid Curiosities: Medical Museums in Nineteenth-Century Britain.* London: Oxford University Press, 2011.

——. "The Museum Affect: Visiting Collections of Anatomy and Natural History." In *Science in the Marketplace*, edited by Aileen Fyfe and Bernard Lightman, 371–403. Chicago: University of Chicago Press, 2007.

Alberti, Samuel J. M. M., and Elizabeth Hallam. *Medical Museums: Past, Present, Future.* London: Royal College of Surgeons of England, 2013.

Anonymous. "Doctor Defends Body Worlds Exhibition." *The Independent*, October 24, 2008.

Arts Council England. "Generic Social Outcomes," n.d. www.artscouncil.org.uk/measuring-outcomes/generic-social-outcomes [accessed October 15, 2017].

Bodley, Alison. *History to Health: Research into Changing Health Agendas for the UK Medical Collections Group.* Leeds: Thackray Medical Museum and Arts Council England, 2012.

---

33 Museums Association, "Museums Change Lives," n.d., 8, www.museumsassociation.org/download?id=1001738 [accessed October 15, 2017].

Chaplin, Simon. *John Hunter and the "Museum Oeconomy," 1750–1800*. Unpublished PhD thesis, King's College London, 2009.

Crossick, Geoffrey, and Patrycja Kaszynska. *Understanding the Value of Arts and Culture. The AHRC Cultural Value Project*. Swindon: AHRC, 2016.

Dawson, Vicky, and David Dawson. *Museum@WRI Activity Plan*. Unpublished consultation report, 2010.

Dodd, Jocelyn, Richard Sandell, Debbie Jolly, and Ceri Jones. *Rethinking Disability Representation in Museums and Galleries*. Leicester: Research Centre for Museums and Galleries, 2008.

Ferry, Georgina. "The Art of Medicine: Collecting Modern Medicine." *The Lancet* 18 (2018): 278–79.

Hamblin, Kate A. *Museums, Oral History, Reminiscence and Wellbeing: Establishing Collaboration and Outcomes*. Oxford: Oxford Institute of Population Ageing, 2016.

Hansen, Anna, ed. *Reminiscence in Open Air Museums: Results from the Erasmus+ Project Active Ageing and Heritage in Adult Learning*. Östersund: Jamtli, 2017.

Hein, George. "Constructivist Learning Theory." *Exploratorium*, n.d. www.exploratorium.edu/education/ifi/constructivist-learning [accessed October 15, 2017].

Lynch, Bernadette. *Whose Cake Is It Anyway? A Collaborative Investigation into Engagement and Participation in 12 Museums and Galleries in the UK*. London: Paul Hamlyn Foundation, 2011.

Macintyre, Iain. *Chamber of Curiosities: A Short History and Guide to Surgeon's Hall Museums*. Edinburgh: Someone and the Royal College of Surgeons of Edinburgh, 2015.

Mendoza, Neil. *The Mendoza Review: An Independent Review of Museums in England*. London: DCMS, 2017.

Morse, Nuala, and Helen Chatterjee. "Museums, Health and Wellbeing Research: Co-developing a New Observational Method for People with Dementia in Hospital Contexts." *Perspectives in Public Health* 138, no. 3 (May 2018): 152–59.

Museums Association. "Museums Change Lives," n.d. www.museumsassociation.org/download?id=1001738 [accessed October 15, 2017].

Porter, Roy. *Quacks: Fakers and Charlatans in Medicine*. London: NPI Media, 2003.

Rhoads, Libby. "Museums, Meaning Making and Memories: The Need for Museum Programs for People with Dementia and Their Caregivers." *Curator: The Museum Journal* 52, no. 3 (July 2009): 229–40.

Sandell, Richard, Annie Delin, Jocelyn Dodd, and Jackie Gay. "Beggars, Freaks and Heroes? Museum Collections and the Hidden History of Disability." *Journal of Museum Management and Curatorship* 20, no. 1 (2005): 5–19.

Silverman, Lois H. *The Social Work of Museums*. London: Routledge, 2010.

——. "The Therapeutic Potential of Museums as Pathways to Inclusion." In *Museums, Society, Inequality*, ed. Richard Sandell, 69–83. London: Routledge, 2002.

Simon, Nina. *The Participatory Museum*. Santa Cruz: Museum 2.0, 2010.

Thomas, Linda J., and Helen J. Chatterjee. *UCL Museum Wellbeing Measures Toolkit*, n.d. www.ucl.ac.uk/culture/sites/culture/files/ucl_museum_wellbeing_measures_toolkit_sept2013.pdf [accessed July 23, 2018].

Visit England. *Visitor Attractions Trends in England, 2016*. www.visitbritain.org/sites/default/files/vb-corporate/Documents-Library/documents/England-documents/annual_attractions_trend_report_2016.pdf [accessed October 15, 2017].

SECTION THREE

EMOTIONAL RESEARCH

Chapter 7

EMOTIONS AND LOST OBJECTS

SHEILA WATSON*

MUSEUM OBJECTS, THEIR collection, conservation, preservation, and display, are products, in part, of the Enlightenment concept of the mastery of "man" over creation through his rationality.[1] Museum objects were meant to be seen in order to facilitate knowledge and understanding and thus museum exhibitions offer typologies as way of exposition—so many types of flints, butterflies, or minerals in serried ranks. Alternatively, they are presented with factual information about make, type, accession details, and, occasionally, they are placed in some kind of context so their history and use can be inferred from their juxtaposition to other things. Rarely, however, do they convey information about their emotional significance to the people who owned and collected them. Indeed, museum professionals would omit such information from their files or just not think it important enough to ask the relevant questions from donors, because theirs was a scientific calling, which depended on dispassionate knowledge.

All this is important because it helps to explain why some objects and collections are just so dull. I know as a former museum professional and practitioner that I should not say this, but, to be frank, those of us who work in museums know that there are boxes of collections, items in drawers, things in corners that we are just not interested in. If we are not interested in them, why should the public be? Part of the reason, I suggest, is because they have become stripped of their emotional connotations. Susan Pearce wrote recently that "[F]or humans, one of the principle ways in which objects acquire special powers is the strength of feeling, which has been poured into them."[2] Pearce offered three categories by which emotional connections to objects could be understood. A personal, individual reminder of something, which is more than just a factual event—this she calls *souvenirs*. When objects

---

1 Margaret Archer, *Being Human: The Problem of Agency* (Cambridge: Cambridge University Press, 2008), 18.

2 Susan Pearce, "Foreword," in *Museum Materialities: Objects, Engagements, Interpretations*, ed. Sandra Dudley (London: Routledge, 2013), xvi.

---

* **Sheila Watson** is an Associate Professor at the School of Museum Studies, University of Leicester, where she helped design the innovative MA Heritage and Interpretation programme. Sheila joined the School of Museum Studies in 2003, following a career in museums and secondary schools. Her research to date has been focused on five main strands: the nature of history and archaeology in the museum and outside it; the relationships between museums, heritage, and different communities; emotions in the museum; the contribution of museums and material culture to a sense of place and identity; and the political role of national museums around the world. Sheila was formerly co-investigator in the international research project "European National Museums and the European Citizen" (EuNaMus). She was a trustee for Museums Sheffield (2010–2018) and has acted as consultant on several redisplay projects including the Norwich Castle project in Norwich, where she led aspects of the public consultation process and contributed to the development of interpretation strategy and display concepts.

have emotional meanings for more than one person then they become *heirlooms*, and when they are emotionally important for communities of any kind, they become *icons* or *relics*. However, these words compress within them a range of emotional meanings that can be concealed by this nomenclature. Is a souvenir a reminder of something happy or sad or both? Do all individuals in a community feel the same way about objects that are heirlooms for some? For one family member an object may be regarded with pleasure at the remembrance of things past; for another it may be associated with distress and unhappiness. For example, what emotions does the relic the Stone of Scone arouse in the Scots? A symbol of sovereignty and once taken by the English after a battle, the Stone is now exhibited in Edinburgh Castle. For some it may arouse feelings of intense patriotism; for others it may be an embarrassment, a symbol of dangerous exclusive nationalism.

Seeing objects in museums can be understood to be part of a ritual.[3] Much attention has been paid to the role museums play in regulating and managing society[4] and expressing the idea of progress in history and in science through the arrangement of material in exhibitions.[5] Collecting is also understood as a means of understanding the object, and those who control the ways in which collections are ordered and classified are those with power and authority.[6] Neither Bennett nor Hooper-Greenhill discusses the role of emotions in museum practice to the extent that the words, emotion, feelings, and affect are all absent from their surveys of the history of museums, both being more interested in Foucauldian power relations. Bennett's interests lie in museums as "passionless reformers," and to that extent this phrase appears in the index.[7] As such, these giants of museum theory were reflecting the academic interests of their time, just as I am with my interest in emotions in museums and the role of the object in engendering these. Here, I am one of a growing field of academics interested in emotion and affect in museums and heritage,[8] recognizing the power that emotions have over our understanding of the world around us.

Of course, there are some exceptions that prove the rule. Art has been regarded as a culturally acceptable way of expressing emotion, which is governed by rules that ensure both the artist and the viewer direct their emotional responses in certain acceptable ways. Thus we rarely see visitors to the great national galleries of the world weeping

---

3 Douglas Marshall, "Behavior, Belonging, and Belief: A Theory of Ritual Practice," *Sociological Theory* 20, no. 3 (2002): 360–80.

4 Tony Bennett, *The Birth of the Museum: History, Theory, Politics* (London: Routledge, 2002).

5 Bennett, *The Birth of the Museum*, 77.

6 Eilean Hooper-Greenhill, *Museums and the Shaping of Knowledge* (London: Routledge, 2003), 6–7.

7 Bennett, *The Birth of the Museum*, 275.

8 See Andrea Witcomb, "Beyond Sentimentality and Glorification: Using a History of Emotions to Deal with the Horrors of War," in *Memory, Place and Identity: Commemoration and Remembrance of War and Conflict*, ed. Danielle Drozdzewski, Sarah De Nardi, and Emma Waterton (London: Routledge, 2016), 205–20; Divya P. Tolia-Kelly, Emma Waterton, and Steve Watson, *Heritage, Affect and Emotion: Politics, Practices and Infrastructures* (London: Routledge, 2017); Laurajane Smith and Gary Campbell, "The Elephant in the Room: Heritage, Affect, and Emotion," in *A Companion to Heritage Studies*, ed. William Logan, Máiréad Nic Craith, and Ullrich Kockel (Chichester: Wiley-Blackwell, 2015), 446–60.

or dancing for joy in front of paintings and sculptures that express the most extreme examples of human suffering and endeavour. The emotions they elicit may be profound but they are managed. The ambience and context here inhibits overt expressions of feeling. Recently, in Romania, I witnessed a woman kneel in front of a painting of the Madonna and child. She was like any other young woman in Europe, fashionable, smart, pretty. As she knelt, she cried, sobbing quietly for several minutes. Her boyfriend stood by, watching. When she recovered herself, she stood up and they left the church, his arm protectively around her. Did you place her in your imaginations in an art gallery? Was such behaviour acceptable in such a location? Individuals may respond to the sacred in a gallery in unexpected ways, but the cultural expectation that the museum is a secular space inhibits religious responses.[9] While some museums facilitate visitors' religious engagement with objects, others see their collections and exhibitions as essentially secular and discourage any sign of religious response.[10] Yet many of the great religious works of art in the world were created to evoke emotional responses based on an engagement with the divine. Within an art gallery or in a museum storeroom they have become aestheticized and safe. Similarly, objects which we find beautiful we often categorize as art, as they are aesthetically pleasing. To these we are attracted and they give us pleasure, something well known to marketing experts and designers.[11]

Why Should We Care about Emotions and Objects?

"Emotion is an overriding influence in our daily lives. [...] It constitutes our experiences and colors our realities. Emotion dominates decision making, commands attention and enhances some memories while minimizing others."[12] We give objects personalities which satisfy the emotional needs of their users. Why, for example, do we name ships and trains and sometimes planes? Each name reflects an emotional state—whether it is pride, aspiration, or, in the case of some of the planes named and flown in the Second World War, cheeky defiance. "Because of people's natural tendency to perceive personality in things they also tend to form relationships with those things based in part on the personalities they perceive."[13]

However, this is not the only reason why we should care about emotions and their relation to objects. Emotions are integral to the way we understand the world and learn about it. Our preexisting feelings, along with the context in which we find ourselves,

---

9 See Steph Berns, *Sacred Entanglements: Studying Interactions between Visitors, Objects and Religion in the Museum*, unpublished PhD thesis, University of Kent, 2015; and Joan Branham, "Sacrality and Aura in the Museum: Mute Objects and Articulate Space," *The Journal of the Walters Art Gallery* 52/53 (1994/1995): 33–47.

10 Steph Berns, "Devotional Baggage," in *Religion in Museums: Global and Multidisciplinary Perspectives*, ed. Gretchen Buggeln, Crispin Paine, and S. Brent Plate (London: Bloomsbury Academic, 2017), 83–92.

11 Trevor van Gorp and Edie Adams, *Design for Emotion* (Waltham: Morgan Kaufmann, 2012), 3.

12 Byron Reeves and Clifford Nass, *The Media Equation: How People Treat Computers, Television and New Media Like Real People and Places* (Cambridge: Cambridge University Press, 1998), cited in Trevor van Gorp and Edie Adams, *Design for Emotion* (Waltham: Morgan Kaufmann, 2012), 4.

13 van Gorp and Adams, *Design for Emotion*, 5.

the impact of the object, and the narrative or design of an exhibition, all affect the way we respond emotionally.[14] We use emotions to help us decide to what we should pay attention. We could easily become overwhelmed by the numbers of objects and people, the amount of text and information we come across every day. Our brains appear to be making conscious decisions about what we should filter out and what we should pay attention to, but in most cases emotion drives this decision-making process and, in turn, this decides what we notice, how we respond to it, and what we learn from it.[15]

Our emotional response also governs the values we place on things. "Everything we experience is either good or bad,"[16] not because we judge this rationally but because we feel it to be so. This applies not just to objects but also to sounds, colours, smells, tastes, spaces, and light. An object in a storeroom will elicit such emotional responses whether we think we are examining it dispassionately or not. Research into the "cultural geography on the agency of museum objects"[17] demonstrates how storerooms are spaces that elicit sensory experiences engendered by the space itself. Not everyone will respond emotionally in the same way. For one person the musty smell of lavender on clothes may remind them of a beloved relative. For another it may arouse negative feelings associated with lack of cleanliness. Similarly, objects placed within narratives in exhibitions may provide emotional responses that challenge or confuse individuals when they are associated with the "wrong" emotion. Take, for example, an exhibition on Victorian washing systems. An adult who as a child participated at a museum in a much-enjoyed practical exercise in washing the Victorian way with dolly tub, wringer, and blue bag may feel very positive towards a system that was back-breaking, difficult work, much hated by most women and farmed out to washerwomen or servants whenever possible. Similarly, a stored object, for example, a wringer, may elicit similar positive meanings, completely at odds with those activities originally seen as unpleasant, hard, and undervalued by those who wore the clean clothes. The original object may appear to be "authentic" in the eyes of the beholder as it is old and original, but emotional responses to this item may be experienced through the emotional lens of an individual's experiences and ideals that bear little relationship to the feelings this material culture originally elicited.

Affect

I am going to offer two ways forward: one recognizes the power of imagination, memory, and personal association—the affect of the object upon us; the other examines the historical context of the object and attempts to identify the emotional responses to the object in the lifetime of its original owner(s). Affect is thus understood to be something separate from emotion and feelings and is conceptualized as "a phenomenological aspect of an

---

14 van Gorp and Adams, *Design for Emotion*, 23.

15 Jaak Panksepp and Lucy Biven, *The Archaeology of Mind: Neuroevolutionary Origins of Human Emotions* (New York: Norton, 2012).

16 van Gorp and Adams, *Design for Emotion*, 32.

17 Hilary Geoghegan and Alison Hess, "Object-Love at the Science Museum: Cultural Geographies of Museum Storerooms," *Cultural Geographies* 22, no. 3 (2015): 445–65 (450).

emotion."[18] Affects are private. However, they are capable of eliciting emotions, and with these come emotions and all their associated impact on individuals outlined above. Here, I am merely following in the footsteps of those who have already paved the way. Sandra Dudley's 2013 seminal work in *Museum Materialities* ensured that the affective role of the object would never again be overlooked. Meanwhile, many museum practitioners, designers, and academics have prioritized the notion of affect over emotion in a materialist manner, focusing on the ways in which the object's position in a museum, the impact of sound, lighting, space, text, and visuals all contribute to the visitor's experience and understanding of the message. However, Miller's (2008) work on *The Comfort of Things* offered us new understandings of the way possessions have importance for individuals, a means by which they have chosen to express themselves,[19] in the ways in which they are displayed, worn, or refashioned, reused, or preserved away from the sight of others. Indeed, it is often not so much the object itself that is important but its relationship with other items. Thus the positioning of a vase, an ornament, a picture, or the particular circumstances in which an item of clothing is worn and how it might always be paired with something else of significance may all have particular emotional meaning for an individual, a meaning that others are not normally invited to share.

I shall use some of my own objects as an example of this. I have an old desk of my grandmother's and on it are two spent cases from artillery shells in the Second World War, now used as pen holders. Between them is a letter holder of the old-fashioned kind with a fox at the front. I do not support fox hunting; I am not interested in military objects; the desk is now used as a place to display photographs of my family. Writing this, I realized that it is exactly positioned in my house as my grandmother had it in her dining room. Her photographs have been replaced with mine, but the objects on the desk, the shells used by my grandfather in the Home Guard in the Second World War, her letter holder where she kept postcards sent to her regularly by me and my cousins are the same. It was at that desk that she would write to us all once a week. These objects, in this order, are some of those "companions of our emotional lives"[20] whose meanings enable us to think about those we love, and thus "we love the objects we think with."[21] Any one of those items—the desk, the letter holder, the shells used as pen holders— would have its emotional significance diminished should they be separated. The affect is in the arrangement of the objects, their juxtaposition, rather than in the individual objects themselves. If any of these objects were to find their way to a museum collection, their use in the world, a reminder of a loved relative, would be superseded by their practical functions and their historical context. Their emotional significance would probably be lost in a museum documentation system and storeroom, where the objects would be separated according to typology and function. Many of the lost objects in storerooms

---

18 Perri 6, Susannah Radstone, Corrine Squire, and Amal Treacher, ed., "Introduction," in *Public Emotions*, ed. Perri 6, Susannah Radstone, Corrine Squire, and Amal Treacher (Basingstoke: Palgrave Macmillan, 2007), 6.

19 Daniel Miller, *The Comfort of Things* (Cambridge: Polity, 2008), 2.

20 Sherry Turkle, ed., *Evocative Objects: Things We Think with* (London: MIT), 5.

21 Sherry Turkle, *Evocative Objects*, 5.

will no longer be contextualized in the way of the example above. However, whenever we accept objects into collections, I suggest we should enquire into the ways in which such things were used and kept, and with which other pieces they were associated, in order to understand their affective properties in their original settings.

History and Emotions

Insights into the significance of emotional associations with objects in museums come from anthropologists such as Dudley and Miller. Dudley asks, "What would it be like for visitors more often than not to be able not only to read a text panel that explains a historical story associated with an object, but also to experience an embodied engagement with that object and thus form their own ideas and/or physical connection with those who made and used it in the past?"[22] I would go further and ask how we can experience the emotional significance of objects within the context of their original use and ownership. If this is impossible, for we rarely know much about the many hands through which an object has passed before it ends up in our storerooms, how can we understand the emotional significance of such objects as they were originally used?

More attention has been paid recently to the challenge of understanding past feelings for things, even when they lack any context of ownership or use, such as the trousers used as an example below. Some scholars have attempted to develop theoretical approaches to enable us to trace the emotional journeys of such objects on their serendipitous path from past to present, as well as to understand objects' emotional significance to contemporary users, viewers, and owners.[23] These ideas have been around for some time but are only now attracting the attention they deserve. They can be found within many disciplines, for example, in the fields of psychology,[24] archaeology,[25] philosophy,[26] anthropology,[27] history,[28] and art history,[29] among others.

---

22 Sandra Dudley, "Museum Materialities: Objects, Sense and Feeling," in *Museum Materialities: Objects, Engagements, Interpretations*, ed. Sandra Dudley (Florence: Taylor and Francis, 2010), 4.

23 Stephanie Downes, Sally Holloway, and Sarah Randles, "Introduction," in *Feeling Things: Objects and Emotions through History*, ed. Stephanie Downes, Sally Holloway, and Sarah Randles (Oxford: Oxford University Press, 2018), 1–23.

24 Mihaly Csikszentmihalyi and Eugene Rochberg-Halton, *The Meaning of Things: Domestic Symbols and the Self* (Cambridge: Cambridge University Press, 1981), 20–54; cited in Downes, Holloway, and Randles, "Introduction," 16.

25 Oliver Harris and Tim Flohr Sørensen, "Rethinking Emotion and Material Culture," *Archaeological Dialogues* 17, no. 2 (2010): 145–63.

26 Miller, *The Comfort of Things.*

27 Dudley, "Museum Materialities."

28 William M. Reddy, *The Navigation of Feeling: A Framework for the History of Emotions* (Cambridge: Cambridge University Press, 2001); Jan Plamper, *The History of Emotions: An Introduction* (Oxford: Oxford University Press, 2015); Barbara H. Rosenwein, *Emotional Communities in the Early Middle Ages* (Ithaca: Cornell University Press, 2007).

29 Jules David Prown, "The Truth of Material Culture," in *American Artefacts: Essays in Material Culture*, ed. Jules David Prown and Kenneth Haltman (East Lansing: Michigan State University Press, 2000), 1–19.

As a historian, I too am interested in the emotion associated with objects in the past. While "[T]he history of emotions has emerged in the past decade as an important research topic,"[30] it is only now developing as a serious topic of study in museums.[31] As it does so, it presents those of us working with objects with serious challenges. Most objects have mislaid or lost their original emotional connotations. They may well be documented with histories of donor, date of donation, description of object, and the context in which the object was originally used or collected, but the resonances of emotional use, display, and ownership are rarely made explicit. If we adopt Bevir's view, "as a nominalist, that all historical meanings are hermeneutic meanings, that is, the particular (conscious, subconscious, and unconscious) beliefs expressed or held by particular individuals at particular times,"[32] then we cannot understand these objects without the relevant historical information about those individual people for whom they had meaning. Such meanings are lost to us. Or are they?

Perhaps we can turn to ideas about emotional histories. In this I adopt a stance rooted in the philosophical ideas of historicism, where specific meanings are attached to particular periods, places, and cultures.[33] If we study how people behaved in the past and how they felt, just as we catalogue and display objects referring to events and contexts associated with them, so we can begin to think about understanding objects as signifiers of emotions typical of the societies in which the objects were originally located rather than general historical illustrations for narratives the museum wishes to expound to the visitor in displays.[34]

At the same time, we can adopt some of the methods expounded by Greenblatt,[35] who applied the concepts of "resonance" and "wonder" to works of art and who sought to understand the historical circumstances in which works of art were created so that we could "situate the work in relation to other representational practices operative in the culture at a given moment in both its history and our own."[36] However, Greenblatt appears interested in the exhibitionary performance of such objects and their contextual resonance. Thus he describes how a Jewish State Museum in Prague has objects once made and owned by Jews who died in the Holocaust. For Greenblatt, these objects, once we understand their historical context, have a resonance of "felt intensity of names, and behind the names, as the very term *resonance* suggests, of voices: The voices of those

---

30 June Purvis, "What Are You Reading? Review of Love and Romance in Britain, 1918–1970," *Times Higher Educational Supplement* 2214 (July 30–August 5, 2015): 47.

31 Sheila Watson, "Emotions in the History Museum," in *The International Handbooks of Museum Studies, Volume 1: Museum Theory*, ed. Kylie Message and Andrea Witcomb, series ed. Sharon Macdonald and Helen Rees Leahy (Oxford: Wiley, 2015), 281–301.

32 Mark Bevir, "Post-Analytic Historicism," *Journal of the History of Ideas* 73, no. 4 (2012): 659.

33 Paul Hamilton, *Historicism* (London: Routledge, 2003).

34 Dudley, "Museum Materialities," 10; Gaynor Kavanagh, "Objects as Evidence or Not?," in *Museum Studies in Material Culture*, ed. Susan M. Pearce (London: Leicester University Press, 1989), 125–37.

35 Stephen Greenblatt, "Resonance and Wonder," in *Exhibiting Cultures: The Poetics and Politics of Museum Display*, ed. Ivan Karp and Steven D. Lavine (Washington, DC: Smithsonian Institution, 1991), 42–43.

36 Greenblatt, "Resonance and Wonder," 43.

who chanted, studied, muttered their prayers, wept and then were forever silenced."[37] Moreover, he points out that many of these objects were collected by the Nazis and exhibited in synagogues, having been catalogued and displayed by Jewish curators, to whom he attributes a range of emotional responses to their role, such as "selflessness, irony, helplessness and heroism,"[38] before telling us that they too died in the camps. Here, Greenblatt is less concerned with the feelings of the original owners than with ours as we look upon the remnants of material culture cared for by those who were murdered. Once we understand the context of ownership, we can never divorce our own feelings from the resonance of those vanished voices, although this may not help us understand the significance of these objects to their original individual makers and keepers. However, so-called "lost" items in museums, without such evidence of ownership, once contextualized through historicism, can provide us with more nuanced understandings of the emotional contexts attributed to them by those who originally used or encountered them in some way.

Historicism performs two useful functions in that it requires us to understand the past through the original text and the interpretive text. Thus, in the instance of the interpretive text, historical research into the objects and the feelings they elicited in the past can be contrasted and compared with current responses to these physical remains. This hermeneutical tool, which "retains the idea of relating the individual work to a larger purpose into whose pattern it meaningfully fits,"[39] provides us with an intellectual and relatively dispassionate approach to the analysis of feelings and emotions that by their very nature will be subjective. It thus counters, in part, the accusation of those trained in the science of the Enlightenment that unless we know something with certainty in the sense that it can be observed, tested, and "proved," we cannot introduce it into a museum setting. At the same time this approach comes with a health warning. We need to be aware, as Greenblatt[40] points out, that our understanding of the emotions of the original owners and other past users and possessors of objects, even when located within a framework of written historical and similar contextual evidence such as images, cannot be anything other than something we have imagined. We can never know if such emotions are ours and theirs, only ours. First, we need to understand that all objects, until the Industrial Revolution and the exponential rise of consumables, must have evoked some very different emotions in their original context from those evoked by most objects today. Objects were far rarer, more often handed down from individual to individual. A sixteenth-century will is nearly always a list of household objects, clothing, and other day to day consumables bequeathed to the family, something we may find rather amusing or intriguing now, but for many such recipients these were essential items, not necessarily keepsakes or mementos but significant means by which the household could function. Cooking implements, bedding, clothes—all these were the stuff of life or lives

---

37 Greenblatt, "Resonance and Wonder," 47 (italics in the original).

38 Greenblatt, "Resonance and Wonder," 48.

39 Hamilton, *Historicism*, 3.

40 Greenblatt, "Resonance and Wonder."

themselves. Yet we display these or illustrate them as though they are part of our world, which they are not. When we do have documentary evidence relating to such bequests, they can confuse rather than enlighten us. For example, we shall never know the significance of Shakespeare's second-best bed bequeathed to his wife but we do know that beds were valuable items passed on to heirs. Was this second-best one a joke, an insult, a sign of affection?[41] As his wife, she was already entitled to a third of his estate and to continue to live in his Stratford house until she died. Most wills made it clear that specific items bequeathed to named individuals were things to remember the dead by—tokens of love and remembrance.[42] What is it about the words "second-best" that make us question this? Did they mean the same then as they do today? Shakespeare was a wordsmith. We can be sure he chose those words carefully and they were full of meaning, but this is now lost to us because we do not have the emotional context in which they were first written and read out.

We also tend now to understand objects as being more valuable the older they are. However, this is not necessarily the attitude of those who lived in the past, when most things were used and reused until they fell apart. Objects were made over to look new or were refashioned. There was no pride in the antiquity of everyday things, and few positive emotions were associated with such objects, perhaps not even the satisfaction we now feel when we make things last a long time in an age of disposable material culture. For in the past everything was designed to last. Only the very wealthy could afford ephemeral objects that did not stand the test of time. Only the very wealthy could collect curious objects and arrange them for their delectation and interest. No, for most people, there was more pride and enthusiasm for the new. Thus when we consider the objects museums keep, if we are to comprehend the emotional values they held in the past, we must try to divest ourselves of our current passions for the old and the antique. Such feelings would be alien to many of our ancestors.

Moreover, we know that objects were gendered and that many had emotional significances for one gender or another. For example, most Early Modern European homes had some form of devotional item. Rich or poor, there would be crosses, images, and texts. Burke points out that a study in Rome found that women owned mainly devotional images while men "preferred more profane subjects."[43] Thus when we consider the significance of these objects for their original owners, we need to be aware that they may have different emotional meanings for different members of the same family in a way that is not obvious as other more specifically gendered objects are. If we look at the way in which objects such as crosses are displayed as typologies in the Museum of

---

41 Anonymous, "Analysis of William Shakespeare's Will and Testament," www.nosweatshakespeare. com/resources/shakespeare-will-overview/. [accessed June 2, 2018].

42 Peter Burke, "The Meaning of Things in the Early Modern World," in *Treasured Possessions from the Renaissance to the Enlightenment*, ed. Victoria Avery, Melissa Calaresu, and Mary Leven (Cambridge: Fitzwilliam Museum, 2015).

43 Sixten Ringbom, "Icon to Narrative: The Rise of the Dramatic Close-Up in Fifteenth-Century Devotional Painting," *Åbo akademi* 31 (1965). Cited by Burke, "The Meaning of Things in the Early Modern World," 5.

the Romanian Peasant, what do we see? Do we have any sense of how the people who owned these hand-carved items felt when they used them as part of a prayer ritual? Do we understand the gendered emotions these elicited? No, we do not. Nor can we begin to feel what the people of the countryside felt when they made ritual Christian symbols such as these to hang outside. Nor are these emotions necessarily forgotten. There is a tree of crosses in the museum, and it is here and at the foot of a stone cross that visitors still leave offerings, though there is no encouragement for them to do this and they are immediately removed by museum staff. Emotional responses elicited by religious feelings are thus erased.

An "Emotional History" in Practice

Let us look at another object—one of my favourites. This is a pair of patched trousers found up a chimney in Toft Monks in Norfolk, UK (see figure 7.1). They are early eighteenth century in date—in other words, they are nearly 300 years old. We know nothing about this object—its original owner, the person or people who did the neat patchwork, or the work done by the wearer except that it was hard manual labour and that both the wearer and the patch-maker were very poor. It is very rare—surviving by accident—not an item kept and treasured over the years but something that was, presumably, just too worn out in the end to salvage, thus discarded and forgotten.

My first emotion when I saw these trousers was one of pity and sadness; pity for the poor who were driven to such extremes and sadness for the owner and the needleman or -woman who kept the patches neat. How terrible I thought it must be to have had to mend such objects so often and to wear them in public. What humiliation! Living as we do in an age when people's status cannot necessarily be understood from the clothes they wear, how did the wearer feel every day putting on these tokens of poverty, advertising this to the whole world? I was encouraged in this emotional response by the text I found on the website of the museum that had these trousers in storage:[44] "Imagine the teenage labourer that wore them and the mother that lovingly mended them. They were found stuffed up a chimney, possibly to stop witches from flying into the house."[45]

I tried to imagine this but could not do so. I do not know if the wearer was a teenager or if his mother patched them or if they were in a chimney to stop witches flying into the house; nor does the museum. So how can we begin to understand this object? I would suggest we can only do this through a more nuanced understanding of the emotional connotations associated with the trousers at the time. In so doing, we should be careful to distinguish between emotions then and now. Clothes are particularly resonant with twenty-first-century emotional associations. Shoes in particular are often the subject of study and exhibited as potent emotional symbols of the dead, particularly when they

---

44 They are now (2019) on display along with a similarly patched jacket at Gressenhall Farm and Workhouse in Norfolk, UK.

45 Norfolk Museums, "Our Norfolk Museums," www.museums.norfolk.gov.uk/Visit_Us/index.htm

Figure 7.1. Patched trousers from Gressenhall Farm and Workhouse; Museum of Norfolk Life. Reproduced by kind permission of Norfolk Museums Service. Used with permission.

represent victims of atrocities such as the Holocaust.[46] Like shoes, these trousers have been shaped by the contours of the body that wore them and, like shoes, such items of clothing, with evidence of textiles worn thin by labour over time, "are potent carriers of emotionality."[47] Yet this is but "emotional imaginings"[48] and does not help us understand what the original wearer felt about his garb. These trousers provoke twenty-first-century feelings, not a sense of how the owner felt wearing them. Indeed, as Holloway points out, "[W]hile the emotional implications of material culture have repeatedly been touched upon by historians, they have rarely been explicitly addressed in depth and detail,"[49] although the turn towards emotions has begun to encourage more complex case studies. We cannot begin to understand the emotions the final wearer felt when he put on these trousers without understanding the historical context in which he lived. For me, the article aroused feelings of sympathy. I assumed that whoever wore this garment cannot have taken much pleasure in his appearance, for it marked him out as an unskilled and impoverished labourer. The trousers may have been handed on to him. He may never have owned a new item of clothing. Most clothes went through a recycling process whereby they were handed down from rich to middling prosperous to poor, being cut, sewn, and reshaped on the way. These trousers may have within them materials from a wide range of other garments, whose significance and emotional connotations are now lost. Thus we just do not know what emotions were elicited by this garment. What appears to be something rather humiliating to us—the patching of garments through necessity, not fashion—was not so at this time. My sympathy may be misplaced. To be really poor at this time was to be almost naked. We know of people dying of cold in the London streets in the eighteenth century without clothes because they had pawned or swapped them for food.[50] If you had patched trousers you at least had something to wear. We also know that for most poor labourers, patched garments were the norm. They indicated not destitution but respectability. If you could patch your clothes and keep yourself decent you were on a higher rung than the beggarly poor. Without decent clothes (in the sense that they provided coverings for parts of the body society deemed should be concealed), a poor person could not work. Labourers, male and female, required good shoes and robust clothing to protect them in their labours. Rag fairs were held regularly in London (and probably elsewhere), during which time the poorer members of society would buy or barter used clothes[51] and presumably

46 Jennifer Hansen-Glucklich, *Holocaust Memory Reframed: Museums and the Challenges of Representation* (New Brunswick: Rutgers University Press, 2014).

47 Hilary Davidson, "Holding the Sole: Shoes, Emotions and the Supernatural," in *In Feeling Things: Objects and Emotions through History*, ed. Stephanie Downes, Sally Holloway, and Sarah Randles, 72–93. (Oxford: Oxford University Press, 2018), 72.

48 Davidson, "Holding the Sole," 91.

49 Sally Holloway, "Materializing Maternal Emotions: Birth, Celebration, and Renunciation in England, c.1688–1830," in *In Feeling Things: Objects and Emotions through History*, ed. Stephanie Downes, Sally Holloway, and Sarah Randles (Oxford: Oxford University Press, 2018), 154–71.

50 Tim Hitchcock, *Down and Out in Eighteenth-Century London* (London: Continuum, 2007).

51 James Grant, "Rag Fair," in *Lights and Shadows of London Life*, Vol. 1 (London: Saunders and Otley, 1842), 121.

used some of this material for patching articles of clothing. Nothing was wasted. Even then, the idea of clothes being worn to rags was framed within an emotional setting, as Grant wrote in 1842: "There are ... articles of wearing apparel in Rag Fair which, could their language be understood, would recite tales of distress, produced, not by crime or extravagance, but by misfortune, which would soften the hardest heart, and extort tears from the eyes of persons quite unaccustomed to the melting mood."[52] In other words, clothes were sold to relieve destitution, and we should feel sorrow for the original owner of the garments rather than the purchaser.

All material was reused, as the trousers in question demonstrate. However, we also know that the very poorest of the poor, those who were in receipt of parish support, often received good quality clothing as part of the poor relief system. King writes: "[M]uch of the received wisdom on the clothing of the very poor suggests that it was often patched and second-hand. Yet, the enduring feature which emerges from the records of the overseer of the poor is the frequency of clothing replacement for people in receipt of relief and the frequency with which replacements were new."[53] He goes on to add, "If this is true, why do we still so readily associate poverty, dependence and raggedness? One answer may be that the poorest clothing was associated not with the poor who received communal relief, but with the marginal poor who struggled, often successfully, to avoid dependence but in doing so generated very low living (and clothing) standards indeed"[54] and were thus subject to pity. If this is the case, the emotions the owner himself felt towards this garment may, however, have involved some element of pride in independence; a feeling that he had avoided the humiliation of having to ask for clothes from the parish authorities. At the same time, the female members of the household were judged by the manner in which they attended to the clothes of their children and the men in the family. In art, "[R]ags, the hallmark of the picturesque, denoted poverty but could also imply that poverty was well deserved, the result of fecklessness and idleness. Neat clothing, by contrast, indicated that the poor were doing all they could to make the best of their situation."[55]

Here we stray into the realm of contemporary eighteenth-century emotional responses to clothes such as these. For the trousers would have engendered feelings and emotions not only in the wearer but in those around him, in particular those on a higher social scale. We can work out middle-class attitudes to such garments from paintings. George Morland's companion pieces, *The Comforts of Industry* and *The Miseries of Idleness*, denote that "the state of a person's clothes in the home was a barometer of their moral state; rags, in this context, were a sign not of poverty, but of idleness, fecklessness, drunkenness, sluttishness, and other socially and politically undesirable vices."[56] At the same time, as Payne points out, those who wore neatly patched clothes might indeed live in severely deprived circumstances, but they were considered to be less dissolute

---

52 Grant, *Lights and Shadows of London Life*, 121.

53 Steven King, "Reclothing the English Poor, 1750–1840," *Textile History* 33, no. 1 (2002): 43.

54 King, "Reclothing the English Poor," 47.

55 King, "Reclothing the English Poor," 49.

56 Christiana Payne, " 'Murillo-Like Rags or Clean Pinafores': Artistic and Social Preferences in the Representation of the Dress of the Rural Poor," *Textile History* 33, no. 1 (2002): 48.

than many of the urban poor. The rural labourer was romanticized as living a life of "rustic simplicity" where "fresh air and a degree of independence were seen as a counterbalance to rural poverty ... labourers were regarded as exemplars of virtue, proof of the survival of a paternalistic social structure in which contentment and deference, it was argued, continued to flourish."[57] When, relatively rarely, a subject is depicted with patched and mended clothes, as is Thomas Barker's *Old Man with Staff*, c.1790,[58] the subject is shown sympathetically, looking straight at the viewer in a calm, composed, and dignified manner. We are encouraged to admire, not pity, him.

Moreover, we also know that the poor often possessed working and "best" clothes.[59] The latter were for Sundays and holidays. This item of clothing may have been one of several pairs of trousers owned by an individual, used for manual labour and not intended to be for anything other than dirty and rough work. Thus these trousers may have been for nonformal usage, an item of wear that was both practical and advertised the wearer's poverty but also his respectability and independent status.

What about the woman or man who mended them? Were they proud of the way they managed to salvage them every time they developed another hole? We know again that for the least fortunate in London, one identifier was the state of their clothes—not patched and redeemed by sewing and careful husbandry, but in rags and tatters. The Church enjoined its congregations to feed and clothe the poor, and this was, in some cases, to cover their nakedness. Thus these trousers are mute. They tell us nothing of how they made people feel at the time, nor how they were regarded by those who saw them on the original wearer. Indeed, the voice of the poor in the eighteenth century is rarely heard.[60] We can only conjecture. However, these objects are imbued with a kind of emotional resonance—they tell a story of hard work, perseverance, dedication, survival, and dignity, and, just as mass-produced objects elsewhere in this volume, they represent something significant to those who made and used them that can only be understand by appreciation of the context in which such objects were first purchased, used, and ultimately discarded. If we felt pity for the wearer of the trousers, perhaps we should reflect that this individual or individuals might have been proud to have been able to wear clothes that were decent. If we marvelled at the skill of the person who sewed them, perhaps we should consider that this might well have been something which demonstrated his or her ingenuity or was, perhaps, a common skill that most so-called respectable poor achieved. If we feel that people should not have to wear such clothes, then perhaps we should remember that at that time, every item of clothing worn and the cloth they were made from was hand-made on looms and took hours of hard work. The first power loom was not designed until 1784 by Edmund Cartwright and first built in 1785. Cloth

---

57 Payne, "Murillo-Like Rags or Clean Pinafores," 48.

58 See Christiana Payne, *Toil and Plenty: Images of the Agricultural Landscape in England, 1780–1890* (Dexter: Thomson-Shore, 1993), Plate 1, opposite page 52.

59 Christiana Payne, *Toil and Plenty*.

60 Peter Jones, "Clothing the Poor in Early-Nineteenth-Century England," *Textile History* 37, no. 1 (2006): 17–37.

was very expensive. We do know that clothes were very important signifiers of status in the eighteenth century, and to pity the wearer of this garment is, perhaps, to misunderstand his status in a society that recycled clothes until they fell apart.

We might also remind ourselves of the complexity of human feelings, and such objects can simultaneously provoke feelings of pride and shame, affection and disgust. However, the point here is that we just do not know the emotions of the wearer or the maker. Whenever we imagine these emotions, we are treating objects as "fictions."[61] While a historical understanding of the context in which this object was made and worn helps us imagine the emotions of the individuals who owned and wore it, and imagination can be just as important as written text for our ability to sense the past and make sense of it, nevertheless it remains just that, imagination, not subject to historical proof.

The trousers only survived because they were concealed in a chimney. Recent research has begun to consider the ways in which objects have a role as agents, where they are understood to possess[62] certain powers that can influence the ways in which we interact with them.[63] We know that items of clothing, most often shoes, were hidden inside houses with such regularity that the act of concealment and the very location of the hiding place must have had some kind of emotional significance for the original owners. Chimneys were one of the entrances and exits to houses and, unlike doors and windows, were rarely barred. Supernatural beings were understood to favour entry through chimneys. It is assumed that items like the trousers performed a ritual function of guarding the house from harm. Here, if we consider the positioning of the trousers to bear witness to "the affective relationships of people to the material world,"[64] these objects were imbued with power of some kind and have been termed "emotional,"[65] but their meanings are not clear, nor are the emotions associated with their concealment. Was it fear that led to their deposit or was it superstition, a sort of guarantee against something not quite right entering the house at some unspecific time—a kind of insurance policy? Most items thus concealed were well used, so the question arises, were they imbued with something of the original wearer that made them potent? However, we do not even know if these items were ritually deposited or not. The emotional history of the object, tantalizing in its anonymity and puzzling in its final use in a chimney, ends (for the time being) in a museum, where it poses as an unsolved mystery, a hint of the world we have lost, a shared past that the poor inhabited, once associated with the feelings of the owner, now all gone. What remains are the signs of wear and the shape of the trousers that hint at the original wearer's physique and the labour he undertook, along

61 Prown, "The Truth of Material Culture," 6, cited in Downes, Holloway, and Randles, *Feeling Things*, 14.

62 Susan Broomhall, "Dirk Hartog's Sea Chest: An Affective Archaeology of VOC Objects in Australia," in *In Feeling Things: Objects and Emotions through History*, ed. Stephanie Downes, Sally Holloway, and Sarah Randles (Oxford: Oxford University Press, 2018), 175–91.

63 Jane Bennett, *Vibrant Matter: A Political Ecology of Everyday Things* (Durham: Duke University Press, 2010).

64 Downes, Holloway, and Randles, "Introduction," 2.

65 Davidson, "Holding the Sole," 89.

Figure 7.2. Porcelain cup and saucer, Fitzwilliam Museum, Cambridge.
© The Fitzwilliam Museum, Cambridge. Used with permission.

with the neat patch-working he or someone else did to keep the trousers functional and decent. Whatever emotions we imbue the trousers with, they are our own.

Now let us take another example of an object which we find in many general collections in regional museums and in some art and fine art national ones—a porcelain cup and saucer (see figure 7.2). I am well-schooled in thinking that objects such as this one—fine porcelain with decoration—are examples of middle- and upper-class taste and wealth. My feelings towards them are regulated by this knowledge. Unlike the trousers, they do not belong with the labouring poor. I feel less personal interest in this porcelain, then, as none of my ancestors (as far as I am aware) were middle class until the twentieth century. I merely admire the skill of the maker and move on. Recently, this cup and saucer were displayed in the *Treasured Possessions* exhibition at the Fitzwilliam Museum, Cambridge; a wonderful temporary display, sadly now dismantled, that sought to unravel some of the personal meanings such objects would have had for the people who owned them.

First, though, let us look at the accession entry available on the Fitzwilliam Museum's website:[66]

Category:
soft-paste porcelain
Name(s):
cup and saucer

---

66 www.fitzmuseum.cam.ac.uk/collections

cup
saucer
teaware; category
Other Name:
goblet ou tasse à quatre pans rond; factory name
Date:
circa 1749–circa 1752
> Old catalogue slip dates the cup c.1745–52. Neither piece has a suspension hole in its footring, which suggests that they were made before 1752.

School/Style:
Rococo
Period(s):
mid-18th Century; Louis XV
Description(s):
> Soft-paste porcelain cup and saucer of four-lobed form, painted in enamels with sprays of flowers and foliage, and gilded.

> Soft-paste porcelain painted overglaze in blue, green, yellow, dark pink, purple, grey and black enamels, and gilded. Both cup and saucer have a four-lobed oval outline with curving sides. The cup has a harp-shaped handle with a kick at the lower end. Both are decorated with sprays of polychrome flowers and foliage, some outlined in black. On the cup a long leaf has been painted at the lip to the right of the handle to conceal a defect in the glaze. There are gold bands round the footrings and rims of the cup and saucer, and down the back of the handle.

The exhibition catalogue, *Treasured Possessions*, made the point that such objects were aspirational and tea-drinking spread rapidly among the general population.[67] By the 1740s, between 30 and 50 percent of inventories in different parts of Britain recorded chinaware. Even early in the eighteenth century, Samuel Parrett, a poor tinplate-maker worth only about £11 10s (£11.50), had an average of more than four-teen pieces.[68] His yearly income would probably have been around £40–£50. By the end of the eighteenth century, these objects were to be found in the homes of the respectable poor as painted by William Bigg in 1793, in a painting which is in storage at the Victoria and Albert Museum, London (see figure 7.3). Both the tin-maker and the poor woman saw these items as part of their essential comforts.

Without this background and our understanding of the way lost objects formed part of an individual's emotional landscape, we cannot hope to do anything more than understand the object through our imaginations and our modernist post-Enlightenment thinking. Such items were less signs of exclusionary taste and wealth and more an indi-cation of the improved living conditions of the poorer classes in society. Once I knew this, I felt more interest in this object. Note the use of the word "felt," which was intentional.

---

67 Maxine Berg and Helen Clifford, "Global Objects," in *Treasured Possessions from the Renaissance to the Enlightenment*, ed. Victoria Avery, Melissa Calaresu, and Mary Leven (Cambridge: Fitzwilliam Museum, 2015), 104.

68 Berg and Clifford, "Global Objects," 104.

Figure 7.3. *A Cottage Interior: An Old Woman Preparing Tea*, William Bigg, 1793. © The Victoria and Albert Museum, London. Used with permission.

I found an emotional connection with it through my feelings for those of my family who lived before me.

This turn towards emotions and affect poses challenges for both practitioners and academics. It requires us to engage with the subjective, to recognize that documented factual information may not be enough when it comes to understanding and interpreting our collections. Moreover, as the examples above have illustrated, cultural background, ignorance, personal experiences, misunderstanding, and prejudiced views can all affect our engagement with objects through eliciting emotional responses that reflect on us rather than on the object and the times in which it was made and used. It is no wonder that documentation and labels so often adhere to fact, not feeling. We can, of course, ignore the emotional and affective impact of collections on individuals in the past and in the present because we will never be able to prove exactly what most people, particularly the working classes, who rarely had the opportunity to record such ideas, thought and felt about this material culture. However, we can, if we choose, go some way towards shedding light on these lost associations, as I have aimed to do in the above discussions. To do so we need to be prepared to abandon our twenty-first-century attitudes. For the purpose of research into emotion, we need to comprehend how our sensibilities have been moulded by our times. Thus if I am to understand the emotional contexts of lost objects, I need to acknowledge my own feelings towards them and question these, even towards objects that appear devoid of anything other than academic interest.

For example, take a piece of slag from a foundry in an industrial museum storeroom. I am not attracted to it. Indeed, I acknowledge that I feel distaste for it. Why? I understand that it is waste from smelting ore, so for me it has become synonymous with dirt and hard, sweaty labour. I see it as just a lump of rubbish to be disposed of. It does not help that the word has a sexual connotation. In British English it also means a woman who has had several sexual partners, and is used in a derogatory manner by some men and women as a form of verbal aggression. However, what did it mean to the (mainly) men who worked the smelting process or to those who lived around the foundry that made it? Slag was, apparently, much sought after as fertilizer in some areas, and workers would spread it on their gardens to help them grow vegetables. What did they feel about it? Its production indicates the successful separation of metals from minerals, which rose to the surface of the molten metal and formed slag. Am I right in assuming that it was positively regarded by those who worked the furnaces as evidence of successful smelting and even more so when it helped increase crop yield? My emotional response to this object is a prejudiced and ignorant one. Slag is not so much waste as a material also used in making concrete and supporting sea walls. It has its own National Slag Association,[69] which promotes the beneficial use of slag in its many forms and describes it as "the **ultimate** sustainable product."[70] Having conducted this research, I now feel somewhat ashamed of my lack of enthusiasm for slag. I will feel differently about it from now on, and that feeling may help me understand more fully its role in society in the past and now.[71]

Thus to return to our lost objects. This paper has attempted to illustrate just how important historical contexts are to our understanding of the emotional contexts in which people in the past used the objects that are now under our guardianship. At the same time, it has suggested that the affect of the object can only be fully understood within the positioning of these items within the environment from which they originally came. Thus a piece of porcelain may well have been a treasured everyday item, symbolic of respectability and comfort, while a pair of patched trousers may offer us insights into the lives of the working poor. At the same time, my examples illustrate how we need to recognize, challenge, and understand our emotional responses to objects in order to comprehend them more fully. While I have only been able to touch on other ideas for consideration, such as gender, I hope that this paper has at least helped to open up a debate about the ways such lost objects can be revived to have their nuanced and complex meanings over time acknowledged in the twenty-first century.

Bibliography

6, Perri, Susannah Radstone, Corrine Squire, and Amal Treacher. "Introduction." In *Public Emotions*, edited by Perri 6, Susannah Radstone, Corrine Squire, and Amal Treacher, 1–33. Basingstoke: Palgrave Macmillan, 2007.

69 See www.nationalslag.org/common-uses-slag, [accessed June 2, 2018].

70 NSA (National Slag Association), www.nationalslag.org/ [accessed June 30, 2019].

71 See also Woodham and Kelleher, this volume.

Anon. "Analysis of William Shakespeare's Will and Testament." www.nosweat shakespeare. com/resources/shakespeare-will-overview/ [accessed June 2, 2018].

Archer, Margaret. *Being Human: The Problem of Agency*. Cambridge: Cambridge University Press, 2008.

Bennett, Jane. *Vibrant Matter: A Political Ecology of Everyday Things*. Durham: Duke University Press, 2010.

Bennett, Tony. *The Birth of the Museum: History, Theory, Politics*. London: Routledge, 2002.

Berg, Maxine, and Helen Clifford. "Global Objects." In *Treasured Possessions from the Renaissance to the Enlightenment*, edited by Victoria Avery, Melissa Calaresu, and Mary Leven, 103–11. Cambridge: Fitzwilliam Museum, 2015.

Berns, Steph. "Devotional Baggage." In *Religion in Museums: Global and Multidisciplinary Perspectives*, edited by Gretchen Buggeln, Crispin Paine, and S. Brent Plate, 83–82. London: Bloomsbury Academic, 2017.

——. *Sacred Entanglements: Studying Interactions between Visitors, Objects and Religion in the Museum*. Unpublished PhD thesis, University of Kent, 2015.

Bevir, Mark. "Post-Analytic Historicism." *Journal of the History of Ideas* 73, no. 4 (2012): 657–65.

Branham, Joan. "Sacrality and Aura in the Museum: Mute Objects and Articulate Space." *The Journal of the Walters Art Gallery* 52/53 (1994/1995): 33–47.

Broomhall, Susan. "Dirk Hartog's Sea Chest: An Affective Archaeology of VOC Objects in Australia." In *In Feeling Things: Objects and Emotions through History*, edited by Stephanie Downes, Sally Holloway, and Sarah Randles, 175–91. Oxford: Oxford University Press, 2018.

Burke, Peter. "The Meaning of Things in the Early Modern World." In *Treasured Possessions from the Renaissance to the Enlightenment*, edited by Victoria Avery, Melissa Calaresu, and Mary Leven, 3–10. Cambridge: Fitzwilliam Museum, 2015.

Csikszentmihalyi, Mihaly, and Eugene Rochberg-Halton. *The Meaning of Things: Domestic Symbols and the Self*. Cambridge: Cambridge University Press, 1981.

Damasio, Antonio. *Descartes' Error: Emotion, Reason, and the Human Brain*. Florida: Grosset/ Puta, 1994.

Davidson, Hilary. "Holding the Sole: Shoes, Emotions and the Supernatural." In *In Feeling Things: Objects and Emotions through History*, edited by Stephanie Downes, Sally Holloway, and Sarah Randles, 72–93. Oxford: Oxford University Press, 2018.

Downes, Stephanie, Sally Holloway, and Sarah Randles. "Introduction." In *Feeling Things: Objects and Emotions through History*, edited by Stephanie Downes, Sally Holloway, and Sarah Randles, 1–23. Oxford: Oxford University Press, 2018.

Dudley, Sandra. "Museum Materialities: Objects, Sense and Feeling." In *Museum Materialities: Objects, Engagements, Interpretations*, edited by Sandra Dudley, 1–20. Florence: Taylor and Francis, 2010.

Geoghegan, Hilary, and Alison Hess. "Object-Love at the Science Museum: Cultural Geographies of Museum Storerooms." *Cultural Geographies* 22, no. 3 (2015): 445–65.

van Gorp, Trevor, and Edie Adams. *Design for Emotion*. Waltham: Morgan Kaufmann, 2012.

Grant, James. "Rag Fair." In *Lights and Shadows of London Life*, Vol. 1, no. 121. London: Saunders and Otley, 1842. www.victorianlondon.org/publications8/lightshadows-03.htm [accessed May 3, 2019].

Greenblatt, Stephen. "Resonance and Wonder." In *Exhibiting Cultures: The Poetics and Politics of Museum Display*, edited by Ivan Karp and Steven D. Lavine, 42–56. Washington, DC: Smithsonian Institution, 1991.

Hamilton, Paul. *Historicism*. London: Routledge, 2003.

Hansen-Glucklich, Jennifer. *Holocaust Memory Reframed: Museums and the Challenges of Representation*. New Brunswick: Rutgers University Press, 2014.

Harris, Oliver, and Tim Flohr Sørensen. "Rethinking Emotion and Material Culture." *Archaeological Dialogues* 17, no. 2 (2010): 145–63.

Hitchcock, Tim. *Down and Out in Eighteenth-Century London*. London: Continuum, 2007.

Holloway, Sally. "Materializing Maternal Emotions: Birth, Celebration, and Renunciation in England, c.1688–1830." In *In Feeling Things: Objects and Emotions through History*, edited by Stephanie Downes, Sally Holloway, and Sarah Randles, 154–71. Oxford: Oxford University Press, 2018.

Hooper-Greenhill, Eilean. *Museums and the Shaping of Knowledge*. London: Routledge, 2003.

Jones, Peter. "Clothing the Poor in Early-Nineteenth-Century England." *Textile History* 37, no. 1 (2006): 17–37.

Kavanagh, Gaynor. "Objects as Evidence or Not?" In *Museum Studies in Material Culture*, edited by Susan M. Pearce, 125–37. London: Leicester University Press, 1989.

King, Steven. "Reclothing the English Poor, 1750–1840." *Textile History* 33, no. 1 (2002): 37–47.

Marshall, Douglas. "Behavior, Belonging, and Belief: A Theory of Ritual Practice." *Sociological Theory* 20, no. 3 (2002): 360–80.

Miller, Daniel. *The Comfort of Things*. Cambridge: Polity, 2008.

Norfolk Museums. "Our Norfolk Museums," n.d. www.museums.norfolk.gov.uk/Visit_Us/index.htm. [accessed September 16, 2015].

NSA (National Slag Association). www.nationalslag.org/. [accessed September 11, 2017].

Panksepp, Jaak, and Lucy Biven. *The Archaeology of Mind: Neuroevolutionary Origins of Human Emotions*. New York: Norton, 2012.

Payne, Christiana. "'Murillo-Like Rags or Clean Pinafores': Artistic and Social Preferences in the Representation of the Dress of the Rural Poor." *Textile History* 33, no. 1 (2002): 48–62.

——. *Toil and Plenty: Images of the Agricultural Landscape in England, 1780–1890*. Dexter: Thomson-Shore, 1993.

Pearce, Susan. "Foreword." In *Museum Materialities: Objects, Engagements, Interpretations*, edited by Sandra Dudley, xiv–xix. London: Routledge, 2013.

Plamper, Jan. *The History of Emotions: An Introduction*. Oxford: Oxford University Press, 2015.

Prown, Jules David. "The Truth of Material Culture." In *American Artifacts: Essays in Material Culture*, edited by Jules David Prown and Kenneth Haltman, 1–19. East Lansing: Michigan State University Press, 2000.

Purvis, June. "What Are You Reading? Review of Love and Romance in Britain, 1918–1970." *Times Higher Educational Supplement* 2214 (July 30–August 5, 2015): 47.

Reddy, William M. *The Navigation of Feeling: A Framework for the History of Emotions*. Cambridge: Cambridge University Press, 2001.

Reeves, Byron, and Clifford Nass. *The Media Equation: How People Treat Computers, Television and New Media Like Real People and Places*. Cambridge: Cambridge University Press, 1998.

Ringbom, Sixten. "Icon to Narrative: The Rise of the Dramatic Close-Up in Fifteenth-Century Devotional Painting." *Åbo akademi* 31 (1965).

Rosenwein, Barbara H. *Emotional Communities in the Early Middle Ages*. Ithaca: Cornell University Press, 2007.

Smith, Laurajane, and Gary Campbell. "The Elephant in the Room: Heritage, Affect, and Emotion." In *A Companion to Heritage Studies*, edited by William Logan, Máiréad Nic Craith, and Ullrich Kockel, 446–60. Chichester: Wiley-Blackwell, 2015.

Tolia-Kelly, Divya P., Emma Waterton, and Steve Watson. "Heritage, Affect and Emotion." In *Heritage, Affect and Emotion: Politics, Practices and Infrastructures. Critical Studies in Heritage, Emotion and Affect*, edited by Divya P. Tolia-Kelly, Emma Waterton, and Steve Watson, 1–11. London: Routledge, 2017.

Turkle, Sherry. "Introduction: The Things That Matter." In *Evocative Objects: Things We Think with*, edited by Sherry Turkle, 3–10. London: MIT, 2011.

Watson, Sheila. "Emotions in the History Museum." In *The International Handbooks of Museums Studies, Volume 1: Museum Theory*, edited by Kylie Message and Andrea Witcomb. Series editors Sharon Macdonald and Helen Rees Leahy, 283–301. Oxford: Wiley, 2015.

Witcomb, Andrea. "Beyond Sentimentality and Glorification: Using a History of Emotions to Deal with the Horrors of War." In *Memory, Place and Identity: Commemoration and Remembrance of War and Conflict*, edited by Danielle Drozdzewski, Sarah De Nardi, and Emma Waterton, 205–20. London: Routledge, 2016.

Chapter 8

CARE-FULL ACADEMIC LABOUR: ENCOUNTERING CARE IN COLLECTIONS-BASED RESEARCH

FRANCESCA CHURCH*

Foreword by Rhianedd Smith

THIS BOOK BEGAN with an exploration of how we might undertake a kind of museo-logical research and practice where history, theory, and contemporary co-production intersect. A growing number of researchers are engaging in research which pushes across interdisciplinary boundaries and sees collections as more than repositories for facts. The rise of collaborative doctoral funding in the UK[1] has provided a space in which professional practice and academic research may come together to explore new questions through research based in an archive or museum. This chapter explores the emotional experiences of an early career researcher navigating the boundaries between collector, collections care, collections-based research, and communicating significance.

Church's research was funded by the University of Reading as part of an initiative to facilitate a series of ambitious interdisciplinary doctoral research projects with university collections which had been under-researched. In this case the research focused on the collections of the Council for the Preservation of Rural England (now the Campaign to Protect Rural England CPRE) (see below), which are held in the Archive of the Museum of English Rural Life (MERL). By bringing together human geography and history, Church explored wider questions about how enthusiasm is organized and communicated by enthusiasts. Within this book we have asked what enthusiast collecting looks like today, but this research also examines the accompanying archival practice of enthusiasts. Church's interdisciplinary research project brings together the history of rural politics and enthusiast theory to pro-vide an insight into the role of enthusiasm in the history of activist organizations.

My own chapter has already outlined some of the history of the MERL and its ongoing work to demonstrate the contemporary relevance of collections that were originally

1 Collaborative Doctoral Awards (CDA) in the UK provides funding for doctoral research that is a partnership between a university and a non–higher education establishment. CDAs are often funded by a Research Council, but funding can come from other sources, as is the case with Church's research.

* **Francesca Church** is a PhD researcher at the University of Reading, based in both the Department of History and the Department of Geography and Environmental Sciences. Her doctorate is an interdisciplinary collections-based project entitled "Cultures of Amenity: The Council for the Preservation of Rural England (1926–50)," focusing particularly on the CPRE's archival collection held at the Museum of English Rural Life, Reading.

formed with the purpose of facilitating research. I also explored the collection of an enthusiast organization kept in the museum's library in the form of the TATHS Library. Within the MERL's object, library, and archival collections there are numerous such holdings, which were created to provide an administrative and organizational memory for government, research, and activist or enthusiast organizations. This chapter explores the final category, the collections created by groups concerned with the preservation of aspects of English rural life. In this way the editors hope to highlight the potential of archival research to provide deep histories of activism and enthusiasm.

The CPRE is a pressure group with over 40,000 members and supporters today. It was founded in 1926 following the publication of "The Preservation of Rural England" by Sir Patrick Abercrombie.[2] It was, and is, largely concerned with the development of housing and infrastructure in rural regions. At the time of its inception it was concerned with a risk of urban sprawl and ribbon development in the regions around English towns and cities. CPRE's activist work has largely been concerned with preventing this intrusion through engagement with planning initiatives and protected status, such as National Parks and greenbelt designation. Their archive demonstrates the inner workings of the organization, the way they gathered and organized evidence, and their methods for communicating with their wider membership and policymakers.

As this is a voluntary organization, it relies on public enthusiasm not only *for* the countryside but *against* the countryside being "concreted over." The source of this enthusiasm differs between members, and this is not a community that represents only people who have lived and worked in the countryside. A number of their campaigns have focused on proposed construction sites that will have an impact on aesthetics and therefore enjoyment of the countryside. This reflects wider shifts in the way that the countryside has been promoted and protected, not only as a place to live and work but also as a recreational space to which every citizen has an equal right.

Many of the enthusiast groups mentioned in this volume have their own collections, but this is one of two chapters where we also discuss their associated archival holdings. Geoghegan argues that a geography of enthusiasm needs to explore the spaces and social networks through which these often-dispersed groups of individuals make space for their shared passions.[3] Histories of enthusiasm may also use the archival holdings of these organizations to explore their deeper histories. Research into the history of disciplines such as archaeology regularly makes use of archival materials such as newsletters to uncover the significance of amateur networks in two fields that were only fully professionalized in the later twentieth century.[4] The field of the history of collecting has

---

2 Patrick Abercrombie, *The Presevation of Rural England* (London: Hodder & Stoughton, 1926).

3 Hilary Geoghegan, "Emotional Geographies of Enthusiasm: Belonging to the Telecommunications Heritage Group," *Area V* 44, no. 1 (2013): 40–46; Hilary Geoghegan, " 'If You Can Walk down the Street and Recognise the Difference between Cast Iron and Wrought Iron, the World is Altogether a Better Place': Being Enthusiastic about Industrial Archaeology," *M/C Journal: A Journal of Media and Culture* 12, no. 2 (2009): unpaginated.

4 For example, Kate Hill, *Women and Museums 1850–1914: Modernity and the Gendering of Knowledge* (Manchester: Manchester University Press, 2016).

also utilized archival materials within museums themselves, such as early catalogues, to trace the course of collections.[5] These historical researchers also regularly engage with the extant versions of their subject organizations. However, these researchers have in the past been less likely to write about their engagement with contemporary stakeholders and their own emotional connections to their research, perhaps due to disciplinary writing styles and accepted methods of working. This seems to be changing.

In this chapter, Church has referenced numerous examples of historical researchers actively exploring their "working practices" in archives and the emotional labour of archival research. In the field of "enthusiasm" studies this kind of reflection is more common, as interdisciplinary researchers have embraced a range of participatory and reflexive methodologies and a necessarily more experimental writing. DeLyser and Greenstein[6] and Geoghegan and Hess[7] have written themselves into their own research, as many other authors have done in this volume. Yet in the field of "enthusiasm studies" (if we can talk about this as a clearly defined field), a deeper historical approach often takes a back seat and contemporary social research methodologies take centre stage. Church's work is interesting, as it combines deeper historical archival perspectives, contemporary engagement with members of the CPRE community, and the creation of new materials. In this way her research becomes a part of the living archive and contributes to ongoing history-making within this group. Her writing reflects this in combining elements of a reflexive, historical, and activist approach that some might find initially jarring.

The concept of "object-love"[8] has been cited by many contributors to this volume, and to this Church brings the corresponding ideas of "archive fever." She both talks about her own experiences and critiques the idea of archive fever as a rite of passage when taken into consideration alongside the emotional pressures put upon the novice researcher. Among academics, curators, and enthusiasts, spending time immersing oneself in a confusing maze of data to amass specialist knowledge is often seen as a badge of honour. However, this can be espoused by those who have access to contacts, resources, knowledge, and time to do this and overlooks the barriers to inclusion that this might create. Church asks whether there is a way we can allow people to delve into under-catalogued collections without putting the full onus of navigation upon them. Finally, she asks how exhibitions can be a part of the process of consolidating and sharing knowledge, while also recognizing that this is not a neutral activity.

Hence this chapter is not a history of the CPRE but an account of research engagement with its archival collections. In this chapter, Church adopts an autoethnographic approach to exploring the emotional components of undertaking research in a stored

---

5 For example, Oliver Impey and Arthur MacGregor, *The Origins of Museums: The Cabinet of Curiosities in Sixteenth and Seventeenth-Century Europe* (Oxford: Ashmolean Museum, 2017).

6 Dydia DeLyser and Paul Greenstein, " 'Follow That Car!' Mobilities of Enthusiasm in a Rare Car's Restoration," *The Professional Geographer* 67, no. 2 (2014): 255–68.

7 Hilary Geoghegan and Alison Hess, "Object-Love at the Science Museum: Cultural Geographies of Museum Storerooms," *Cultural Geographies* 22, no. 3 (2014): 445–65.

8 See Sharon Macdonald, *Behind the Scenes at the Science Museum* (Oxford: Berg, 2002); Geoghegan and Hess, "Object-Love at the Science Museum."

collection. The concept of the objective historical researcher has long given way to an interest in the positionality and emotional labour of research. This is a reflexive piece in which Church examines her own emotional journey in both encountering the archive and its collectors and in trying to communicate its significance to the wider world. In this she also looks back towards the emotional work that went into creating the archive and empathizes with its creators. As in Geoghegan and Hess's work,[9] this chapter suggests that new ways of working require new ways of writing, and hence this piece is intentionally reflexive and experimental in format. In this way we hope this chapter will provide some suggestions for both ways of thinking about and new ways of both doing and writing this kind of research.

CARE-FULL ACADEMIC LABOUR: ENCOUNTERING CARE IN COLLECTIONS-BASED RESEARCH

FRANCESCA CHURCH

Introduction: Care and the Archival Researcher

Reaching up to the catalogues on the reading room shelves, I lift the two heavy tomes from their space and take them to my desk; sometimes they sit next to me all day. On blue paper slips I make my selection; titles and references, dates and names. Occasionally, no matter how carefully I select the materials, their arrival at my desk is a surprise; books and records weightier than I had imagined, or booklets no more than a few slips of paper. Sometimes these are accompanied by the addition of book rests and paper weights; silently and kindly added next to my place by the reading room staff. It is at this juncture that I realize the weight of this moment—in the untying of ribbons knotted for decades, and in the opening of creaking minute books; I must be careful. A note on one of the pamphlets informs me that this is the only copy of the 1929 publication—simultaneously informative and burdensome. I become care-full.[10]

It is to this paused moment in the archive, this realization about and awareness of the complex layers of care that are bound up in archival practices, to which this chapter turns. As such, how might we define the concept of care? The *Oxford English Dictionary* provides a broad selection of ways with which to approach the term. This includes "to feel concern ... [to] trouble oneself," the lack of care or concern—"Who Cares?"—and also "to have a regard or liking for."[11] Already we can identify the possibilities of action and inaction, of an additional task or burden upon oneself, and of being fond of someone or something. Although we must note the distinction between what it means to care for and care of,[12] where care of or about something does not necessitate caring for it.[13]

---

9 Geoghegan and Hess, "Object-Love at the Science Museum."

10 The author's thoughts in the Reading Room at the Museum of English Rural Life.

11 Oxford English Dictionary (OED), "Care," www.oed.com/view/Entry/27902?rskey= hA4k2v [accessed July 5, 2019].

12 Sophie Bowlby, "Recognising the Time-Space Dimensions of Care: Caringscapes and Carescapes," *Environment and Planning A* 44, no. 9 (2012): 2101–18.

13 Bowlby, "Recognising the Time-Space Dimensions of Care."

Care has previously been framed as an "ethics of encounter"[14] that constitutes "a proactive interest of one person in the well-being of another and the articulation of this stance in practical ways."[15] As a result, care and practice are intertwined.[16] Care-taking involves physical and emotional labour[17] and is often emotionally demanding.[18] Indeed "emotional and practical relations often intersect in the provision of care."[19] As this chapter will demonstrate, archival research is full of moments of such care. Yet many of these practices, tensions, and emotions are often masked by a finalized piece of academic work,[20] whether in the form of a thesis, a publication, or other research outputs such as exhibitions. As such, Lorimer indicates the need for including "the context, encounters and events that constitute research practice."[21]

An archive is a "repository," which can be anything from a room or building, a storage box, a photograph album, or even a website.[22] An archive "holds or contains documents, which can take the form of written texts, photographs, sound recordings, postcards, medical records, printed materials, material objects"[23] that are "non-current records selected for permanent preservation."[24] Thus, broadly speaking, archival research "involves analysing and interpreting" these materials in order to "explore a particular topic or question or concern."[25] Yet this is not always straightforward; archives too can be "unloved." Indeed, materials can be "unloved" before they are encountered by archivists, who "rescue records from festering cellars, attics, etc., have them repaired when necessary, sort and catalogue them and make them available to the public."[26] Even

---

14 David Conradson, "Geographies of Care: Spaces, Practices, Experiences," *Social & Cultural Geography* 4, no. 4 (2003): 451–54 (508).

15 Janine Wiles, "Reflections on Being a Recipient of Care: Vexing the Concept of Vulnerability," *Social & Cultural Geography* 12, no. 6 (2011): 573–88 (574).

16 Christine Milligan and Janine Wiles, "Landscapes of Care," *Progress in Human Geography* 34, no. 6 (2010): 736–54.

17 Conradson, "Geographies of Care."

18 Graham Allan and Graham Crow, *Home and Family: Creating the Domestic Sphere* (Basingstoke: Macmillan, 1989).

19 Wiles, "Reflections on Being a Recipient of Care," 574.

20 Dydia DeLyser and Daniel Sui, "Crossing the Qualitative-Quantitative Chasm III: Enduring Methods, Open Geography, Participatory Research, and the Fourth Paradigm," *Progress in Human Geography* 38, no. 2 (2014): 294–307.

21 Hayden Lorimer, "Caught in the Nick of Time: Archives and Fieldwork," in *The SAGE Handbook of Qualitative Geography*, ed. Dydia DeLyser, Steve Herbert, Stuart C. Aitken, Mike C. Crang, and Linda McDowell (London: SAGE, 2009), 248–73 (249).

22 Niamh Moore, Andrea Salter, and Liz Stanley, "In Other Archives and Beyond," in *The Archive Project: Archival Research in the Social Sciences*, ed. Niamh Moore, Andrea Salter, Liz Stanley, and Maria Tamboukou (Abingdon: Routledge, 2017), 1–30.

23 Moore et al., "In Other Archives and Beyond," 1.

24 Michael Bottomley, "Conservation and Storage: Archival Paper," in *Manual of Curatorship: A Guide to Museum Practice*, ed. John M. A. Thompson (Abingdon: Routledge, 2012), 252–58 (252).

25 Moore et al., "In Other Archives and Beyond," 3.

26 Bottomley, "Conservation and Storage," 252.

after accession, previous damage or the fragility of the materials can provide difficulties regarding access and research. Of course, these issues are by no means confined to paper documents; digital collections face similar problems.[27] However, even the more easily accessed collections, or parts of them, might for a time be "unloved" due to their topic, technical nature, or even, perhaps, their "relevance." Storage boxes may sit in the archives gathering dust, unrequested and "unloved." And yet might we see this as part of the archive's allure? The excitement of calling up an item that may have been unrequested for years: What stories might it tell?

Archives are "the preserve of none because they are engaged with by many kinds of people, who use or create them in diverse ways."[28] This chapter represents not the archive as a whole but some of my personal archival encounters, the context of my research, and an account of care-full academic labour. In this way it suggests an emotionally engaged and reflective approach towards academic research. This chapter explores several forms of care that are bound up with collections-based research: care for materials, care as conceptualized by the collection's creators, care of the researcher for those represented in the collections, care for the researcher, and care through communication. While it does not focus on the subject in detail, it is also informed by the growing body of literature on enthusiasm.[29] Using examples from the Council for the Preservation of Rural England's (CPRE) archive, this chapter first explores the emotions and experiences bound up in working with archive sources and considers the ways in which scholars care for the material. Second, drawing on my own research experience, this chapter argues for the need to care for the researcher, to avoid getting lost in the archive, physically, and metaphorically. Third, this chapter then considers the role of care in communicating research, specifically, to be aware of the shadowy images that archives sometimes create, to recapture the textures of relationships and thus enter into a dialogue with the materials.

Drawing on examples from the CPRE archive, this section considers the ways in which researchers care for the archival materials with which they work and the emotional ties that scholars build with the individuals bound up in the histories held within an archive. While the researcher must be aware of the ways in which emotions can become a barrier to critical research, such emotional connections are also revealed as an important and attractive part of the research process, drawing the scholar back to the archive and providing inspiration for further research avenues.

---

27 Seamus Ross, *Changing Trains at Wigan: Digital Preservation and the Future of Scholarship* (London: National Preservation Office, 2000).

28 Moore et al., "In Other Archives and Beyond," 2.

29 Ruth Craggs, Hilary Geoghegan, and Hannah Neate, "Architectural Enthusiasm: Visiting Buildings with the Twentieth Century Society," *Environment and Planning D: Society and Space* 31 (2013): 879–96; Hilary Geoghegan, "A New Pattern for Historical Geography: Working with Enthusiast Communities and Public History," *Journal of Historical Geography* 46 (2014): 105–7; Geoghegan, "Emotional Geographies of Enthusiasm"; Geoghegan, " 'If You Can Walk down the Street and Recognise the Difference between Cast Iron and Wrought Iron, the World is Altogether a Better Place.' "

An Archive of Enthusiasm: The CPRE Archive

The CPRE was founded in 1926 by a group of influential and like-minded individuals keen to preserve and protect rural England. The CPRE was part of a wider preservationist movement that became "hegemonic within English culture in the late nineteenth and early twentieth centuries."[30] Among the early members of the CPRE were architects and planners, such as Professor Patrick Abercrombie, Guy Dawber, G. L. Pepler, Professor S. D. Adshead, and the Rt. Hon. Henry Hobhouse. Also represented on the Council were organizations such as the National Trust, the Commons Preservation Society, the Central Landowners' Association, and the Women's Institute, among many others. The CPRE has, since its creation, been through a number of name changes and is now called the Campaign to Protect Rural England, though still the CPRE.

The CPRE archive is now held at the Museum of English Rural Life (MERL) in Reading, along with a number of related archival collections regarding landscape preservation, planning, agriculture, and landscape architecture (among many others). The CPRE collection itself contains over 200 linear metres of archival materials and comprises a rich and varied array of items, such as correspondence, press cuttings, publications, photographs, and minute books, from their national headquarters as well as their county branches. Numerous scholars have used the CPRE archive, and the collection has provided a rich area for research into rural history as well as cultural and historical geography. Moreover, the contemporary CPRE continues to reflect on its history by engaging with the collection at the MERL, illustrated in the organization's recent publication, *22 Ideas That Saved the English Countryside*.[31] In the context of this volume, this archive also illustrates the potential of archival research for uncovering changing concepts and practices of "care" among activist and enthusiast movements.

Turning to the CPRE's first minute book, we can see that among its founding objectives was the intention to ensure "the protection of rural scenery and of the amenities of country towns and villages from disfigurement or injury."[32] Certainly, the CPRE had a wide range of things it wanted to protect: scenic views and landscapes, country lanes and footpaths, regional building materials and designs, wildflowers and trees, tranquillity, and enjoyment of the countryside (though this list is naturally not exhaustive). The members wished to preserve the England that they cared for, protecting it from ribbon development, unregulated building, disfiguring advertisements, and urban encroachment. They campaigned, displayed exhibitions, lobbied government, surveyed large areas, and published books and pamphlets. Each of these were acts of care; these proactive measures demonstrated their concern for a countryside they felt was in danger of being lost.

An interesting example of the motivations, practices, and products of such care can be seen in a county survey of the Thames Valley published in 1929.[33] Such surveys were

---

30 Jeremy Burchardt, *Paradise Lost: Rural Idyll and Social Change since 1800*, Vol. 23. (London: I. B. Tauris, 2002), 99.

31 Peter Waine and Oliver Hilliam, *22 Ideas That Saved the English Countryside* (London: Frances Lincoln, 2016).

32 SR CPRE A/1, Minute Book (1926–1930).

33 W. Mayo et al., *The Thames Valley from Cricklade to Staines: A Survey of its Existing State and Some Suggestions for its Future Preservation* (London: University of London Press, 1929).

part of a regional survey movement in the first half of the twentieth century, influenced by the planner and geographer Patrick Geddes,[34] which "embodied a particular kind of local knowledge that encompassed all the elements of the present, past and possible future of place."[35] The CPRE, keen to document the beauty of the countryside and fearful that large tracts of rural England would soon be lost to urban expansion and thoughtless development, encouraged the undertaking of these surveys by its members and local branches (the branches themselves were often mapped along county or regional lines). Turning the pages of this volume and unfolding the hand-drawn maps, I felt a great attachment to these individuals and their work. The result of possibly weeks of work (or more), the meticulously drawn maps, detailed and sometimes personal descriptions of towns and villages, and photographic records of tranquil scenes were all carefully collated to provide at the very least some physical evidence of the places and scenes they cared for. However, the survey books are a completed and finalized version of the survey, and while the time and effort expounded in collating the information is evident, they felt organized and contained. Direct engagement with the raw materials provoked a different kind of emotional response.

Experiencing Emotion in the Archive

A number of scholars have written about the emotions brought about through connections between researchers and the materials with which they work[36]—those emotional motivations behind our connections to things.[37] Some months after my experience with the surveys, I came across files relating to a separate set of surveys undertaken by the CPRE over a decade later.[38] Within these files were original maps, hand-drawn on tracing paper and covered in annotations and symbols. With the help of one of the reading room staff, I carefully opened out one of these maps, hoping that the tracing paper was not too fragile to unfold. The map was a detailed record of the amenities of East Riding in Yorkshire, and itself covered my small section of the reading room table (being around the size of twelve A4 pages). It included details on architecture, historical buildings and monuments, flora and fauna, agriculture, soil type and quality, topography, village names, local building materials, and noted areas of woodland or dense hedgerows. The care embodied in the map was astonishing, in the detail included, the scope of the survey, and the practical difficulties of undertaking such a survey.

---

34 David Matless, "Regional Surveys and Local Knowledges: The Geographical Imagination in Britain, 1918–39," *Transactions of the Institute of British Geographers* (1992): 464–80.

35 Catherine Brace, "Envisioning England: The Visual in Countryside Writing in the 1930s and 1940s," *Landscape Research* 28, no. 4 (2003): 365–82 (377).

36 Geoghegan and Hess, "Object-Love at the Science Museum"; Ludmilla Jordanova, *History in Practice* (London: Hodder Arnold, 2006); Leena Rossi and Tuija Aarnio, "Feelings Matter: Historian's Emotions," *Historyka. Studia Metodologiczne XXXVII–XXXVIII* 7 (2012): 165–85.

37 Geoghegan, " 'If You Can Walk down the Street and Recognise the Difference between Cast Iron and Wrought Iron, the World is Altogether a Better Place.' "

38 SR CPRE C/1/181/1, Landscape Survey of England and Wales (1941–1943).

To me, the map was a representation of the years of work undertaken by CPRE volunteers, their enthusiasm and passion often given freely. The map was signed in the bottom left hand corner by C. H. Drewry (a member of the East Riding Ramblers' Association, itself affiliated with the CPRE). This individual survey was one of a number carried out across the country by various individuals, which created, county by county, a personal and national record of England. Interested by the materiality and astounded by the care and consideration evident in this map, I continued to chat with the reading room assistant about it. Both of us were excited about being able to open out the map and realizing the level of detail, knowledge, and care that it embodied. Certainly, Mills notes that some materials have the ability to change the mood of a whole office.[39] A finding in the archive can reach beyond the researcher and can have an impact on others working in the reading room or museum.

As with an emotional response to the material, it is also important to note the place of emotional connections that researchers may have with the authors of work held in the archive or to those individuals documented within its pages. Indeed, as well as an emotive response to things and the research process itself, Rossi and Aarnio highlight that "persons, either present or absent, dead or alive, may arouse historian's emotions."[40] Certainly, a number of scholars have written about the emotional reactions that researchers have to the individuals and groups detailed within the pages of their research.[41] In fact, Bradley wrote about such attachments that the researcher may feel "as she 'uncovers' the history of her chosen group ... Identifying them as *hers*, she may slide towards identification *with* them, becoming in fancy 'one of the tribe.'"[42]

Some materials even seem to leave a lasting impact on the researcher; Hoeflich wrote of just such an experience working on the Lincoln Legal Papers project, recalling that "a number of years ago ... I was given the opportunity to hold in my hands a draft of the Emancipation Proclamation. That moment for me was the closest thing I have ever had to a religious experience. Certainly, it inspired me to do work on that project I had never done before. And the feeling of holding that document has never left me."[43] Duff, Craig, and Cherry maintain that a spiritual encounter such as this comes from a scholar's interaction with original archive materials; a "mystical experience that they traced to its union with the source."[44]

---

39 Sarah Mills, "Surprise! Public Historical Geographies, User Engagement and Voluntarism," *Area* 45, no. 1 (2013): 16–22.

40 Rossi and Aarnio, "Feelings Matter," 171.

41 Linda Bergmann, "The Guilty Pleasures of Working with Archives," in *Working in the Archives: Practical Research Methods for Rhetoric and Composition*, ed. Alexis E. Ramsey, Wendy B. Sharer, Barbara L'Eplattenier, and Lisa Mastrangelo (Carbondale: Southern Illinois University Press, 2010), 220–31.

42 Harriet Bradley, "The Seductions of the Archive: Voices Lost and Found," *History of the Human Sciences* 12, no. 2 (1999): 107–22 (110).

43 Michael H. Hoeflich, "Serendipity in the Stacks, Fortuity in the Archives," *Law Library Journal* 99 (2007): 813–27 (826).

44 Wendy Duff, Barbara Craig, and Joan Cherry, "Historians' Use of Archival Sources: Promises and Pitfalls of the Digital Age," *The Public Historian* 26, no. 2 (2004): 7–22 (19).

Nevertheless, this connection with the individuals whose letters, signatures, notes, and annotations fill the pages of the archives can also arguably become a barrier to critical reflection and interpretation. Bergmann argues that it is because of the "material reality of the archive" that as "one touches the actual paper and reads the actual words directly as they were written … it is hard not to feel drawn into becoming a part of the particular, personal audience for whom they are written."[45] Certainly there is "something very strongly appealing about … handling paper written or touched by the writers we study, the inkblots and cross-outs that went into their writing."[46] Ferguson echoes this warning, arguing that "when scholars find archives attractive, that too is coded as a kind of peril, suggesting we have fallen for their wiles: archives 'seduce'."[47]

Perhaps this goes some way towards shedding light on the fact that although research is shaped in part by "one's personal encounter with the archive," historians "rarely speak of them, and even more rarely do they do so in print."[48] Indeed, Rossi and Aarnio note that "even the historians, who write in the first person singular and strive after transparency in their research, hide their feelings."[49] In an effort to portray "good scholarly behaviour" or undertake objective and neutral research, "emotions must be wiped off from the research."[50] Yet can they ever be fully wiped away? It is the connections with individuals, the emotional ties formed, and the thrill of the archive that draw researchers back. As Bergmann writes, "the pleasures of that seduction, guilty pleasures or not, keep me returning to the archives."[51] We must then consider the researcher and the joys and perils of archival research.

Archive Fever: Care for the Researcher

Another place of care in working with archives, with which this section is concerned, is for the researcher. In other chapters in this book, authors have written about "object-love" and the inability of professionals to avoid falling in love with some items in their care. "Archive fever" is a comparable concept in academic research, and the term itself points to an underlying fear of "going native" and losing the desired detached objectivism. One has to avoid the very real danger of losing your way in the archives—not just for the sake of the research, but also because losing yourself is easily done—getting lost in the worry of all that material, of all those histories, and the absence of all those ideas. It is to be "plagued by patternlessness, by words and experiences being merely themselves,

---

45 Bergmann, "The Guilty Pleasures of Working with Archives," 230.

46 Bergmann, "The Guilty Pleasures of Working with Archives," 230.

47 Kathy E. Ferguson, "Theorizing Shiny Things: Archival Labors," *Theory & Event* 11, no. 4 (2008). https://muse.jhu.edu/article/257578/summary [accessed July 5, 2019].

48 Antoinette Burton, "Introduction: Archive Fever, Archive Stories," in *Archive Stories: Facts, Fictions, and the Writing of History*, ed. Antoinette Burton (Durham: Duke University Press, 2005), 1–24 (8).

49 Rossi and Aarnio, "Feelings Matter," 171.

50 Rossi and Aarnio, "Feelings Matter," 172–73.

51 Bergmann, "The Guilty Pleasures of Working with Archives," 230.

and by a facticity unrelieved by meaning."⁵² This idea of patternlessness chimed with my own experience of archival work: reading page after page with the hope of a "eureka moment" and a portion of text leaping from the page. This separation of what we need to know from what we do not know has been described as one of the most delicate tasks of archival work; a task that "has no explicit guidelines."⁵³

It is this search for meanings, patterns, and origins that Derrida refers to when describing what it is to suffer from "archive fever"; "it is never to rest, interminably, from searching for the archive right where it slips away. It is to run after the archive, even if there is too much of it … It is to have a compulsive, repetitive, and nostalgic desire for the archive."⁵⁴ While Derrida spoke of archive fever as a feeling of yearning or a compulsion, a number of academics have written about the physical effects of such a fever. Indeed, the archive can keep you awake at night,⁵⁵ induce motion sickness,⁵⁶ bring on a "vague weariness,"⁵⁷ and it is made manifest in my ever-increasing habit of writing lists. As with many aspects of academic work that seep into the "other time-spaces of our everyday lives,"⁵⁸ here too we find the effects of the archive. Arriving home after a day in the archive, the mind continues to disassemble and reassemble the concepts, ideas, and fragments of materials that you have industriously copied out.

And so I sat in the archives day after day, note-taking, reference-making, and list-checking. Frustrated and impatient, I could not understand my lack of progress. After all, I had a thesis to write! It was at this point that I realized how out of sync I was with the archive. The archive has its own rhythm, its own tempo. It is when you tap into this, or along with this, that you begin to see the real headway that you are making. When you give yourself the time to take notes, think, search, interpret, you also give the archive the time to open up, to reveal its histories. The German concept *sitzfleisch*, "the ability to sit long hours poring over often boring documents,"⁵⁹ captures this aptly. It takes time to carry out the "slow and unrewarding artisanal task of recopying texts, section after section."⁶⁰ There is no fast-forward, no Ctrl+F to find that quote that is just right. But even if this were the case, Underwood suggests that such a "full-text search can confirm almost any thesis you bring to it" or, worse still, "filter out all the alternative theses you

---

52 Susan Scott Parrish, "Rummaging/in and out of Holds," *American Literary History* 22, no. 2 (2010): 289–301 (1–2).

53 Laura Cameron, "Oral History in the Freud Archives: Incidents, Ethics, and Relations," *Historical Geography* 29 (2001): 38–44 (43).

54 Jacques Derrida, *Archive Fever: A Freudian Impression* (Chicago: University of Chicago Press, 1996), 91.

55 Carolyn Steedman, *Dust: The Archive and Cultural History* (Manchester: Manchester University Press, 2001).

56 Parrish, "Rummaging/in and out of Holds."

57 Arlette Farge, *The Allure of the Archives*, translated by T. Scott-Railton (New Haven: Yale University Press, 2013), 12.

58 Mills, "Surprise!", 20.

59 Hoeflich, "Serendipity in the Stacks, Fortuity in the Archives," 827.

60 Farge, *The Allure of the Archives*, 17.

didn't bring."[61] And so we must be wary of this, regardless of whether an archive is in paper form or digitized. As Susan Scott Parrish has put it, "if you go to the past with a list of what you are looking for, you will never get out of the present."[62]

How, then, might we find what we need if we don't know what we are looking for? Perhaps the concept of serendipity can offer some direction. There is a large body of literature that highlights the importance and influence of serendipity on archival research.[63] In its dictionary definition, serendipity is the "faculty of making happy and unexpected discoveries by accident. Also, the fact or an instance of such a discovery."[64] Serendipity has been argued to include three key features. Firstly, accident—an advantageous chance happening. Secondly, the "ability, comprised of intellect, learning, experience, and awareness, to recognize the accident when it occurs."[65] Thirdly, opportunity—the space, time, and possibility for such a happy accident to take place.[66] Parrish recommends "[getting] inside an archival starting place and then, without a strict research map or "plot" ... let your archive teach you ... Follow it, in and out of holds."[67] This parallels the inherently "emergent" nature of the research process[68] and excitingly enables "archives [to] suggest a relationship to the future" where anything might happen.[69]

And yet we must take care to remember the researcher. How can we balance the timescales of academic pressures against the stubborn and slow pace of the archive? Is it possible to have truly serendipitous moments with such constraints? Embarking on a project with little scope or definition of its aims or objectives may not be a concept with which many would be comfortable,[70] and should they even be? A doctoral project is structured by milestones such as annual reviews, confirmation of registration, and

---

61 Ted Underwood, "Theorizing Research Practices We Forgot to Theorize Twenty Years Ago," *Representations* 127, no. 1 (2014): 64–72 (66).

62 Parrish, "Rummaging/in and out of Holds," 6.

63 Bradley, "The Seductions of the Archive"; Cameron, "Oral History in the Freud Archives"; Duff et al., "Historians' Use of Archival Sources"; Karen M. Morin, "Unpopular Archives," *The Professional Geographer* 62, no. 4 (2010): 534–43; Jane Taylor, "Holdings: Refiguring the Archive," in *Refiguring the Archive*, ed. Carolyn Hamilton, Verne Harris, Jane Taylor, Michelle Pickover, Graeme Reid, and Razia Saleh (London: Kluwer, 2002), 61–82; Charles W. J. Withers, "Constructing 'the Geographical Archive'," *Area* 34, no. 3 (2002): 303–11; Tara Woodyer and Hilary Geoghegan, "(Re) Enchanting Geography? The Nature of Being Critical and the Character of Critique in Human Geography," *Progress in Human Geography* 37, no. 2 (2013): 195–214.

64 Oxford English Dictionary (OED), "Serendipity," www.oed.com/view/Entry/176387?redirected From=serendipity#eid [accessed July 5, 2019].

65 Hoeflich, "Serendipity in the Stacks, Fortuity in the Archives," 814.

66 Hoeflich, "Serendipity in the Stacks, Fortuity in the Archives," 813.

67 Parrish, "Rummaging/in and out of Holds," 11.

68 Natascha Klocker, "Doing Participatory Action Research and Doing a PhD: Words of Encouragement for Prospective Students," *Journal of Geography in Higher Education* 36, no. 1 (2012): 149–63.

69 Ferguson, "Theorizing Shiny Things," 11.

70 Paul Ashmore, Ruth Craggs, and Hannah Neate, "Working-with: Talking and Sorting in Personal Archives," *Journal of Historical Geography* 38, no. 1 (2012): 81–89.

regular supervisory sessions. Such a relaxed approach to research does not seem to fit particularly well in this scenario.

Understanding the singularities of the archive has often been described as a rite of passage or an initiation.[71] Yet if practices and conduct are often shaped by unwritten rules,[72] where should those new to the archives find such tacit knowledge? Lorimer has written about the profound silences regarding the practices and processes of collections-based research; it is often assumed that the researcher will naturally know what to do on arriving at the archives.[73] However, such work is anything but straightforward. Hoeflich suggests, then, that in teaching archival research skills, it is possible to create the conditions and space for serendipity. This includes encouraging students to be discerning and to take notes of possible leads and stressing the importance of being flexible and open to new or unpredicted research paths.[74] We must therefore take care to place the researcher at the heart of the research. It is by fully acknowledging the role of the researcher within archival work that we can more thoroughly explore the care bound up in academic work, encourage truly reflexive approaches, and provide more conscientious, critical, and considerate accounts of collections-based research.

Communication as Care

> Above and behind them a fire is blazing at a distance, and between the fire and the prisoners there is a raised way; and you will see, if you look, a low built wall along the way, like the screen which marionette players have in front of them, over which they show the puppets ... And do you see, I said, men passing along the wall carrying all sorts of vessels, and statues and figures of animals ... And of the objects which are being carried in like manner they would only see the shadows ... To them, I said, the truth would be literally nothing but the shadows of the images.[75]

The Spanish term *archivo* means "a person to whom is entrusted a secret or private knowledge."[76] Those who use the archives are entrusted with its knowledge. Of course, there are important issues of power, access, and forms of knowledge. But here I want to ask: what do we mean by entrusted? If care is characterized by trust and vulnerability,[77] we are not only trusted with the archives and its contents but charged with its care too; care in how the collection is represented, communicated, and displayed. This section considers forms of care through communication in collections-based research. Indeed, this section highlights the importance of seeing the archive as a place of interchange

---

71 Bradley, "The Seductions of the Archive."

72 Ashmore et al., "Working-with."

73 Lorimer, "Caught in the Nick of Time."

74 Hoeflich, "Serendipity in the Stacks, Fortuity in the Archives."

75 Plato's Allegory of the Cave from Book VII, *The Republic*, in Samuel Wells, *Christian Ethics: An Introductory Reader* (Bognor Regis: Wiley, 55.

76 Withers, "Constructing 'the Geographical Archive.'"

77 Conradson, "Geographies of Care."

and thus entering into a dialogue with a collection, listening more keenly to the ways in which archival materials might tell their histories while also enabling us to notice the ways in which they stay silent. Such silences can be continued beyond the archive itself, and thus it is important to consider these gaps when displaying materials and communicating research.

A set of interview recordings and transcripts within the CPRE collection captures this particularly well. The interviews, undertaken in the 1980s, were conducted with a number of CPRE employees and covered their memories of campaigns, other individuals involved in the preservationist movement, and the day-to-day practices of the CPRE. The following excerpt is taken from an interview with Max Nicholson, conducted by Robin Grove-White:

> RGW: There is an archive at Reading—Reading University ... At the Museum of English Rural Life ... there's some very, very interesting material ...
>
> MN: I think this is terribly important because I think in another ten years or so an awful lot of people ... [will] have no idea about anything that we've been talking about, no idea, and will find it very difficult to get it from the papers, because the papers of the time took it for granted.
>
> RGW: ... it's as much as anything the texture of the relationships.[78]

Interpretation and representation are interwoven in the texture of relationships. Therefore, in examining individual threads of meaning, how do we make sure we don't lose sight of the whole, as both a collection and in a wider historical context? These issues are relevant at all scales, from large museum displays to pop-up exhibitions or archive material demonstrations. Two examples from my research provided me with an opportunity to reflect on these issues of understanding, representation, and communication. The first was in curating an interactive exhibition for members of the CPRE, and the second was in collating materials for a workshop for doctoral students, both based on archive materials from the CPRE's collection at the MERL.

Within the CPRE collection is a set of exhibition panels from the Council's *Save the Countryside* exhibition that toured the country during the 1930s. The panels often include a set of photographs that distinguish good development from bad development, the ugly from the beautiful, and between selfish and neighbourly acts, as well as providing examples of positive planning and design. However, these exhibition panels suffered water damage before arriving at the MERL, and this, coupled perhaps with the bulkiness and awkwardness of the panels, means that they are rarely viewed or exhibited. However, the panels are a rich illustration of the CPRE's work at this time and are important to an understanding of the Council's motivations and practices. As such, photographic reproductions have been made of each of the panels that can be accessed next to the collection's catalogue in the reading room, without the panels being called

---

78 SR CPRE DX 151/10, Shell/CPRE Oral History Archive: Transcript of an interview with Max Nicholson (1989).

up from the storerooms, and are a source that I have returned to a number of times throughout my research.[79]

In putting together the catalogue for the interactive exhibition, however, was I to include all of the reproductions that I could fit neatly on to one table or in one folder or include a selection of the original panels, which, while limited in number, might provide additional elements that the copies could not capture? Certainly, it has been argued that being in contact with original sources allows the viewer to "be more fully in touch with the material and documentary contexts of the historical period."[80] I decided to include the reproductions in the exhibition, as by including the full set of panels, the range and scope of the CPRE's work at this time could be better conveyed. Certainly, the CPRE was not only comprehensive in its geographic reach, covering all of England,[81] but in the issues it addressed and campaigned for. Thus, alongside the reproductions, additional context and information regarding the panels could be provided by other sources, such as photographs of the exhibition on display at the time.

Yet Macdonald observes that "the assumptions, rationales, compromises and accidents that lead to a finished exhibition are generally hidden from public view."[82] We must, then, take care to understand not only the gaps within the archive but those gaps and silences that continue beyond the confines of the archive within our understanding and interpretation of their histories, and inevitably within our communication of the archive in research outputs such as exhibitions, workshops, or publications. This necessitates an increased reflexivity, encourages an opening-up of the research processes or the practices involved in designing an exhibition, and urges us to communicate this rather than falling silent. Of course, "like any reflexive text these reflections can only be treated as the things that we believed to be true of ourselves at a given moment,"[83] but it is in the willingness to discuss such reflections that a wider opening up of research can be achieved.

The archive is a place of dialogue. The researcher must ask questions of the archive, sift through layers of meaning, and in so doing, perhaps, reanimate the archive. Yet the researcher must also listen—to the questions that the materials pose, to the directions they give, and even to those points on which they lie silent. At the workshop—though I had outlined the themes I wanted to address when looking at the materials—the group was animated by the items on display, and conversations soon spun off onto topics that were inspired by the photographs and texts in front of them. The materials spoke of a meaning that I had not preformed. Therefore, while the archives are indeed a *"centre of interpretation,"*[84] they are also a centre of interplay where the relationship between

---

79 SR CPRE F/1–48, Exhibition Panels and Posters (1920s and 1930s).

80 Duff et al., "Historians' Use of Archival Sources," 19.

81 Matless, "Regional Surveys and Local Knowledges."

82 Sharon Macdonald, *The Politics of Display: Museums, Science, Culture* (Hove: Psychology, 1998), 2.

83 Adrian R Bailey, Catherine Brace, and David C. Harvey, "Three Geographers in an Archive: Positions, Predilections and Passing Comment on Transient Lives," *Transactions of the Institute of British Geographers* 34, no. 2 (2009): 254–69 (266).

84 Thomas Osborne, "The Ordinariness of the Archive," *History of the Human Sciences* 12, no. 2 (1999): 51–64 (52, original emphasis).

the researcher and the researched is defined by an ongoing exchange of questions and challenges. Bradley proposes that "in that endeavour of writing history we also inevitably rewrite history, that is, re-create the past in new forms."[85] However, this is not solely the work of the historian or researcher but instead results from an interchange between researcher and archive, at once illuminating the histories within its pages and, together, creating these histories anew.

Conclusion: Who Cares?

> Leaning back from the desk and stretching, I wonder if it's time to call it a day? The notebook, laptop, and archive files scattered around me are evidence of a productive but long afternoon. The other readers around me continue to focus on the materials in front of them, undeterred by there being just half an hour left until the reading room closes, and undisturbed by my beginning to shuffle papers together. I make a note of the point I have reached, perhaps a page number or the date and correspondents of a particular letter, underneath which I note the files that I have yet to look at, or possible themes to investigate at my next visit. Carefully I place the files back in the box which I had carried to my desk earlier that day. Then begins the quiet ferrying of items; archival weights and rests back on top of the cupboard, both catalogue volumes back on the shelf, and the box of archival items to the reading room staff at the desk. I book myself in to the reading room for the following day, ready to begin the process again.[86]

As Rossi and Aarnio declare, "feelings matter!"[87] This chapter's venture into the reading room at the MERL has attempted to explore this notion, focusing particularly on the role and importance of care in collections-based research. This chapter has shed light upon the ways in which care shapes archival practices and has brought to life the emotions bound up in encounters with archival collections.

Emotional reactions to archival materials and connections with the individuals mentioned within the pages of the archive are an important and natural part of collections-based research. Of course, we must take care not to be seduced by the archive, not to be fooled into forgetting our critical stance. Yet if we attempt to detach ourselves from an emotional interaction or connection with the archives, then we risk detaching ourselves from our research and the practices, experiences, and encounters that are its constituent parts. Indeed, as this chapter has shown, we must take care not to detach the researcher from the research. While the place of serendipity in archival research is acknowledged, we must be wary of assuming that an experience or a particular "find" is down to pure chance and not the intuition or methodical workings of a persistent researcher. A continued search for serendipity masks the ordinary and time-consuming practices of archival research, discourages self-reflexivity, and places unrealistic expectations of archival research on those new to the reading room and the materials called up from the storerooms. If we are to encourage a greater and wider

---

85 Bradley, "The Seductions of the Archive," 109.

86 Author's thoughts in the Reading Room at the Museum of English Rural Life.

87 Rossi and Aarnio, "Feelings Matter," 185.

engagement with collections, particularly those that may seem "hidden," "forgotten," or "unloved," then we must provide directions by which others may be able to follow. We must demand of ourselves a greater reflexivity and a more detailed discussion of academic practices from those involved in archival research, so that this knowledge is no longer tacit or assumed. We must tell our "archive stories."[88] Such reflexivity enables the researcher to understand and care about the gaps inherent not only within the archive itself but in the ways in which research is communicated or displayed; to better mediate between interpretation and representation. Yet it also reveals the ways in which researchers already care.

Working with archives involves moments, practices, and emotions of care. We can see snapshots of these when we identify with those groups and individuals bound up in the histories of the archive, in experiencing those emotions so intertwined with archival research—anxiety, doubt, "fever," attachment, patience, excitement, and joy—or even in that brief pause before opening a book or file that has, until now, gathered dust upon a shelf. The practices of collections-based research—requesting, reading, note-taking, reference-making, and interpreting—each of these is a careful act by a researcher, which works to regain something of a lost past, holding on to the archive's "promise (or illusion?) that all time lost can become time regained."[89] Perhaps the original meaning may never be regained in full, but in seeing the archive as a place of dialogue and interchange, we might begin to unearth each layer of meaning through the practice of careful academic research. In providing an account of care in collections-based research, this chapter contributes to discussions on archival research practices and, it is hoped, encourages care-full academic labour.

Archival Materials

The following archival sources are from the Council for the Preservation of Rural England's (CPRE) archive collection held at the Museum of English Rural Life, Reading.

SR CPRE A/1, Minute Book (1926–1930).
SR CPRE C/1/181/1, Landscape Survey of England and Wales (1941–1943).
SR CPRE DX 151/10, Shell/CPRE Oral History Archive: Transcript of an interview with Max Nicholson (1989).
SR CPRE F/1–48, Exhibition Panels and Posters (1920s and 1930s).

Bibliography

Abercrombie, Patrick. *The Presevation of Rural England*. London: Hodder & Stoughton, 1926.
Allan, Graham, and Graham Crow. *Home and Family: Creating the Domestic Sphere*. Basingstoke: Macmillan, 1989.

---

88 Burton, "Introduction."
89 Bradley, "The Seductions of the Archive," 119.

Ashmore, Paul, Ruth Craggs, and Hannah Neate. "Working-With: Talking and Sorting in Personal Archives." *Journal of Historical Geography* 38, no. 1 (2012): 81–89.

Bailey, Adrian R., Catherine Brace, and David C. Harvey, "Three Geographers in an Archive: Positions, Predilections and Passing Comment on Transient Lives." *Transactions of the Institute of British Geographers* 34, no. 2 (2009): 254–69.

Bergmann, Linda. "The Guilty Pleasures of Working with Archives." In *Working in the Archives: Practical Research Methods for Rhetoric and Composition*, edited by Alexis E. Ramsey, Wendy B. Sharer, Barbara L'Eplattenier, and Lisa Mastrangelo, 220–31. Carbondale: Southern Illinois University Press, 2010.

Bottomley, Michael. "Conservation and Storage: Archival Paper." In *Manual of Curatorship: A Guide to Museum Practice*, edited by John M. A. Thompson, 252–58. Abingdon: Routledge, 2012.

Bowlby, Sophie. "Recognising the Time-Space Dimensions of Care: Caringscapes and Carescapes." *Environment and Planning A* 44, no. 9 (2012): 2101–18.

Brace, Catherine. "Envisioning England: The Visual in Countryside Writing in the 1930s and 1940s." *Landscape Research* 28, no. 4 (2003): 365–82.

Bradley, Harriet. "The Seductions of the Archive: Voices Lost and Found." *History of the Human Sciences* 12, no. 2 (1999): 107–22.

Burchardt, Jeremy. *Paradise Lost: Rural Idyll and Social Change since 1800*, Vol. 23. London: I. B. Tauris, 2002.

Burton, Antoinette. "Introduction: Archive Fever, Archive Stories." In *Archive Stories: Facts, Fictions, and the Writing of History*, edited by Antoinette Burton, 1–24. Durham: Duke University Press, 2005.

Cameron, Laura. "Oral History in the Freud Archives: Incidents, Ethics, and Relations." *Historical Geography* 29 (2001): 38–44.

Conradson, David. "Geographies of Care: Spaces, Practices, Experiences." *Social & Cultural Geography* 4, no. 4 (2003): 451–54.

Craggs, Ruth, Hilary Geoghegan, and Hannah Neate. "Architectural Enthusiasm: Visiting Buildings with the Twentieth Century Society." *Environment and Planning D: Society and Space* 31 (2013): 879–96.

DeLyser, Dydia, and Paul Greenstein. " 'Follow That Car!' Mobilities of Enthusiasm in a Rare Car's Restoration." *The Professional Geographer* 67, no. 2 (2014): 255–68.

DeLyser, Dydia, and Daniel Sui. "Crossing the Qualitative-Quantitative Chasm III: Enduring Methods, Open Geography, Participatory Research, and the Fourth Paradigm." *Progress in Human Geography* 38, no. 2 (2014): 294–307.

Derrida, Jacques. *Archive Fever: A Freudian Impression*. Chicago: University of Chicago Press, 1996.

Duff, Wendy, Barbara Craig, and Joan Cherry. "Historians' Use of Archival Sources: Promises and Pitfalls of the Digital Age." *The Public Historian* 26, no. 2 (2004): 7–22.

Farge, Arlette. *The Allure of the Archives*. Translated by T. Scott-Railton. New Haven: Yale University Press, 2013.

Ferguson, Kathy E. "Theorizing Shiny Things: Archival Labors." *Theory & Event* 11, no. 4 (2008). https://muse.jhu.edu/article/257578/summary [accessed July 5, 2019].

Geoghegan, Hilary. "Emotional Geographies of Enthusiasm: Belonging to the Telecommunications Heritage Group." *Area* 45, no. 1 (2013): 40–46.

——. " 'If You Can Walk down the Street and Recognise the Difference between Cast Iron and Wrought Iron, the World is Altogether a Better Place': Being Enthusiastic about Industrial Archaeology." *M/C Journal: A Journal of Media and Culture* 12, no. 2 (2009): unpaginated.

——. "A New Pattern for Historical Geography: Working with Enthusiast Communities and Public History." *Journal of Historical Geography* 46 (2014): 105–7.

Geoghegan, Hilary, and Alison Hess. "Object-Love at the Science Museum: Cultural Geographies of Museum Storerooms." *Cultural Geographies* 22, no. 3 (2015): 445–65.

Hill, Kate. *Women and Museums 1850–1914: Modernity and the Gendering of Knowledge.* Manchester: Manchester University Press, 2016.

Hoeflich, Michael H. "Serendipity in the Stacks, Fortuity in the Archives." *Law Library Journal* 99 (2007): 813–27.

Impey, Oliver, and Arthur MacGregor. *The Origins of Museums: The Cabinet of Curiosities in Sixteenth and Seventeenth-Century Europe.* Oxford: Ashmolean Museum 2017.

Jordanova, Ludmilla. *History in Practice.* London: Hodder Arnold, 2006.

Klocker, Natascha. "Doing Participatory Action Research and Doing a PhD: Words of Encouragement for Prospective Students." *Journal of Geography in Higher Education* 36, no. 1 (2012): 149–63.

Lorimer, Hayden. "Caught in the Nick of Time: Archives and Fieldwork." In *The SAGE Handbook of Qualitative Geography*, edited by Dydia DeLyser, Steve Herbert, Stuart C. Aitken, Mike C. Crang, and Linda McDowell, 248–73. London: SAGE, 2009.

Macdonald, Sharon. *Behind the Scenes at the Science Museum.* Oxford: Berg, 2002.

——. *The Politics of Display: Museums, Science, Culture.* Hove: Psychology, 1998.

Matless, David. "Regional Surveys and Local Knowledges: The Geographical Imagination in Britain, 1918–39." *Transactions of the Institute of British Geographers* (1992): 464–80.

Mayo, Walter Longley Bourke, Patrick Abercrombie, Stanley Davenport Adshead, and William Harding Thompson. *The Thames Valley from Cricklade to Staines: A Survey of its Existing State and Some Suggestions for its Future Preservation.* London: University of London Press, 1929.

Milligan, Christine, and Janine Wiles. "Landscapes of Care." *Progress in Human Geography* 34, no. 6 (2010): 736–54.

Mills, Sarah. "Surprise! Public Historical Geographies, User Engagement and Voluntarism." *Area* 45, no. 1 (2013): 16–22.

Moore, Niamh, Andrea Salter, and Liz Stanley. "In Other Archives and Beyond." In *The Archive Project: Archival Research in the Social Sciences*, edited by Niamh Moore, Andrea Salter, Liz Stanley, and Maria Tamb</br>oukou, 1–30. Abingdon: Routledge, 2017.

Morin, Karen M. "Unpopular Archives." *The Professional Geographer* 62, no. 4 (2010): 534–43.

Osborne, Thomas. "The Ordinariness of the Archive." *History of the Human Sciences* 12, no. 2 (1999): 51–64.

Parrish, Susan Scott. "Rummaging/in and out of Holds." *American Literary History* 22, no. 2 (2010): 289–301.

Ross, Seamus. *Changing Trains at Wigan: Digital Preservation and the Future of Scholarship.* London: National Preservation Office, 2000.

Rossi, Leena, and Tuija Aarnio. "Feelings Matter: Historian's Emotions." *Historyka. Studia Metodologiczne XXXVII–XXXVIII* 7 (2012): 165–85.

Steedman, Carolyn. *Dust: The Archive and Cultural History.* Manchester: Manchester University Press, 2001.

Taylor, Jane. "Holdings: Refiguring the Archive." In *Refiguring the Archive*, edited by Carolyn Hamilton, Verne Harris, Jane Taylor, Michelle Pickover, Graeme Reid, and Razia Saleh, 61–82. London: Kluwer, 2002.

Underwood, Ted. "Theorizing Research Practices We Forgot to Theorize Twenty Years Ago." *Representations* 127, no. 1 (2014): 64–72.

Waine, Peter, and Oliver Hilliam. *22 Ideas That Saved the English Countryside*. London: Frances Lincoln, 2016.

Wells, Samuel. *Christian Ethics: An Introductory Reader*. Bognor Regis: Wiley, 2010.

Wiles, Janine. "Reflections on Being a Recipient of Care: Vexing the Concept of Vulnerability." *Social & Cultural Geography* 12, no. 6 (2011): 573–88.

Withers, Charles W. J. "Constructing 'the Geographical Archive.'" *Area* 34, no. 3 (2002): 303–11.

Woodyer, Tara, and Hilary Geoghegan. "(Re) Enchanting Geography? The Nature of Being Critical and the Character of Critique in Human Geography." *Progress in Human Geography* 37, no. 2 (2013): 195–214.

VOLUME CONCLUSION: HOW TO PUT A LITTLE LOVE IN YOUR STORED COLLECTION

WHAT WE AIM to have achieved by bringing these diverse contributions together around the idea of "unloved" collections is to stimulate questions on the overlapping themes: collecting, emotion, care, and enthusiasm. We have been particularly interested in applying this in relation to institutional practices within museums and museum storerooms. Each of these themes has an established or emerging legacy of its own elsewhere, but they haven't necessarily been brought together and explored at the points of connection as we have started to do here. In order to tie together the various threads of discussion, we return briefly to the opening questions posed in the introduction to this volume to outline our concluding thoughts.

1. What Are Unloved Collections and Who Cares for Them?

The term "unloved" collections is a useful prompt for discussion; however, it is very hard to define and comprises within it many potential strands of enquiry and reasons for becoming "unloved." As our interest is in the meeting point of practice and theory, we have not delved too deeply here into the theoretical investigation of value within material culture and museum/heritage studies, although questions of value are implicit across the volume. In relation to the process of devaluing objects or museum storage areas, some of our authors have made suggestions as to why this occurs in relation to the cases presented, including shifts in taste and fashion, changing research cultures, changing notions of aesthetics, or certain policies which might marginalize specific objects and spaces. For example, the refocusing of the museum as an agent of social change may render repetitive research collections a "luxury." They may become framed as a "burden," inherited from historic collecting practices, and indicate the need for more thematic collecting that can respond quickly to changing collecting needs.[1] This volume has interrogated what happens to objects that were collected under different traditions and how these can maintain a sense of value, although there is certainly more work to be done on understanding this subject.

---

1 Nick Merriman, "The Future of Collecting in 'Disciplinary' Museums: Interpretive, Thematic, Relational," in *The International Handbooks of Museum Studies, Volume 2: Museum Practice*, ed. Conal McCarthy, series ed. Sharon Macdonald and Helen Rees Leahy (Oxford: Wiley, 2015), 283–301.

What the discussions in the preceding chapters have highlighted is that these collections might not actually be "unloved" by the majority of people; they might simply require specialist skills or knowledge in order for their significance to be understood. This does not deny the value of plural interpretations of objects, but it does suggest that if collections are placed in storerooms which cannot be readily accessed or viewed, then we are never giving those who don't care the opportunity to love these objects. This research also suggests that museums are failing the existing "lovers" of these collections. Various chapters emphasized the quality of collections knowledge and different perspectives on so-called "unloved" collections held by nonprofessional experts. Our discussions with experts suggested that they feel their concerns are not necessarily important to collections staff or to policy- and decision-makers. These experts are often keen to visit stored collections (see discussions in Hess's chapter, this volume), and they may also be keen to contribute their expertise. However, this isn't always possible when difficult decisions have to be made around investment of resources, and the individuals or communities themselves have singular interests, as we have seen from some of the "enthusiast" groups discussed here. Externally funded co-curation projects in galleries are becoming commonplace, so how might we introduce co-curation as a sustainable method into behind-the-scenes processes of collections management?

There is no simple answer to this question, but seeing the problem less as an insurmountable cataloguing and conservation need and more as an intersection between research and engagement (as we did with "Who Cares?" and "Energy in Store") might open up new forms of funding, collaboration, and access to expertise. The relevance of museum objects is intrinsically tied into the museum's ability to connect to, access, and understand the significance of diverse forms of knowledge around them. Looking at everyday practices in museums helps us to understand how the cultural ecologies[2] of these organizations function and suggest new ways of working. The emphasis here is on building sustained relationships across different actors in order to help reinvigorate collections.

We have argued that it is not just certain kinds of objects but certain kinds of spaces which are overlooked within heritage and museum studies. "Behind the scenes" areas in museums, as a subject of research, hold their own interest, and after years of being seen as an embarrassing secret, a new understanding of museum storage seems to be in the process of developing. This is not without its own problems, and researchers such as Nicky Reeves have critiqued the concept of open storage areas by interrogating the material performances of transparency and museum labour which go on within them.[3] As more museum storage areas become the subject of grand architectural plans and are subsequently asked to deliver on investment in terms of public benefit, it will become

---

2 Defined by as "the complex interdependencies that shape the demand for and production of arts and cultural offerings." In Ann Markusen, Anne Gadwa, Elisa Barbour, and William Beyers, *California's Arts and Cultural Ecology* (San Francisco: James Irvine Foundation, 2011), 8, as cited in John Holden, *The Ecology of Culture* (Swindon: Arts and Humanities Research Council, 2015), 2.

3 Nicky Reeves, "Visible Storage, Visible Labour?" in *Museum Storage and Meaning: Tales from the Crypt*, ed. Mirjam Brusius and Kavita Singh (London: Routledge, 2018), 55–63.

all the more important to research these spaces and consider the different working practices and experiences that take place within them.

2. How Does Emotion Help Us to Understand "Unloved Collections"?

Despite a turn towards emotions and affect in museums, there is a lack of literature regarding the role of emotions in "behind the scenes" work with collections. This is particularly the case in relation to the way that emotions influence, and are influenced by, daily practices of care. What this volume indicates is the need for more reflection on how emotions impact practice and vice versa.[4] An awareness of this aspect of museum work needs to be integrated more strongly into practice so that we can understand how both professionals and publics may be turned towards or away from certain subjects or objects.

Certain aspects of professional practice arguably limit engagement with emotions or employ a logic of "flattened emotion." As the museum is envisaged as an agent of social change, a focus on those with specialist knowledge might be framed as a drain on precious resources, space, and time for marginalized audiences who we assume do not have an interest in the minutiae of object analysis. However, we should not assume that certain audiences will naturally dislike certain collections, as this does a disservice to both. Assumptions about likability and display-versus-storage potential are often made by higher-level decision-makers and museum designers, and not always by those who work daily with these objects. The structure of museum management also means that professionals working on research, engagement, and collections management might rarely come into contact with each other. Hence "unloved" collections are often framed purely as a collections management problem to be solved through collections management practices, not as a potential engagement opportunity. In this volume we hope to have illustrated what happens when these different forms of expertise come together.

In simple terms, putting an object into storage makes emotional and intellectual engagement more difficult. In addition, the design of storerooms (open or closed, near to the main museum site or far away from it) and decisions around whether to box rather than to display on shelves might make exploration, browsing, or "rummaging" (see Woodall, this volume) impossible. These are key methodologies for enabling emotional engagement, in part because they connect with a childlike sense of play. At a more fundamental level, the idea of the expert as dispassionate and all-knowing might make it hard to express emotion or engage with playful methods of engagement such as constructing imaginary back stories for objects (see Woodham and Kelleher, this volume).

Finally, for many curators lack of time, lack of expertise, and overwork might make it hard to spend time getting to know these collections and to experience positive emotional states from this activity. Yet it might not just be due to increasing demands and

---

4 See, for example, Jane Henderson, "Managing Uncertainty for Preventive Conservation, Studies" in *Conservation* 63, supplement 1 (2018): 108–12, with regards to how conservators may deal with issues of uncertainty in their daily practice.

decreasing resources, for as one museum practitioner pointed out to us: "they clearly didn't spend all day in the storerooms in previous eras or the stuff wouldn't be so poorly documented." We need to think about what we collect and why we collect. We need to recognize and interrogate the more "distanced" emotions that have come to typify professional practice (see Watson's and Church's chapters in this volume). At the same time, we must acknowledge that emotional responses and affect are influenced by culture, socioeconomic background, context, and personal experience. Research is desperately needed that further explores the implications of these on emotional responses in "behind the scenes" heritage contexts; the contributions in this volume are just a starting point.

3. How Do Different Kinds of Carers Express and Share Their Love for Collections?

Chapters in this volume also indicated that our consideration of some groups who care about museums, such as "enthusiasts," risks taking us down the wrong path. The term *enthusiast* suggests a heightened emotional state that was frequently lacking in face-to-face encounters. Many of our participants were quite reserved in describing their feelings for the objects in collections, but others felt comfortable connecting their personal stories and expertise to "unloved" collections (see Macleod, this volume). Often, however, their practices of care expressed the depth of their emotional attachment better than their interview statements. This may be indicative of a largely male, retired group of skilled workers. It may also be down to personality traits such as introversion or to do with the construction of a professional persona. However, the lack of demonstrative emotion doesn't mean that it's not there, just that it might be harder to find. The task of uncovering these emotional states may require messy methodologies to discover and understand.

"Energy in Store," the follow-up project to "Who Cares?" defined all participants as "experts," recognizing that different forms of expertise might exist, which could be controversial. The professionalization of the museum sector sought to raise standards, to recognize skills, and to secure wages. As with all processes of professionalization, this has led to gate-keeping, where those who will offer unpaid or lower-paid labour are seen as a direct threat to paid staff. Barriers to who can undertake certain tasks are constructed on the grounds of maintaining reputation and standards, and within museums there may be different kinds of professionalism with different concepts of care either working together or in conflict with each other. Beyond the museum, this process also has the outcome of excluding those who do not have access to the financial, social, and educational capital to professionalize. The groups in our project were not overly marginalized and used different kinds of capital and "sharp elbows" to gain access to collections. However, the difficulties in gaining access experienced by even these highly motivated and organized groups should be a warning. Can a focus on the care of objects be a way of removing care from people? We need to think about how we balance the needs of both, even in places such as museum storage where the object is given primacy.

For collections professionals and audiences alike, it might be difficult to perform or catalyze strong positive emotions where they are lacking. The idea of emotional "ruts" was raised directly and indirectly in some of the chapters. If an object doesn't instantly offer visual appeal or connect to specific memories, do museum professionals themselves overlook it and make judgements as to its significance? This has obvious implications for how objects are interpreted. It is important to understand that the conditions under which we value things are political and relational. Therefore, knowing how to "jump out of the ruts" and create different emotional responses is about recognizing how and why we have come to value things in certain ways. If we can question what lies behind these valuations and look at these objects in new ways, we may come to value them as much as, if not more than, objects which are "easy to love." This process will not always be straightforward or very comfortable, raising the question: what forms of practice in museums can aid this exploration? How might we see things with new eyes? Something this volume hopes to have revealed is that understanding the significance of the emotional experiences of "day-to-day" heritage is as important as research into "difficult" heritage.

4. Are There Ways in Which Different Kinds of Carers Can Work Together?

Some of our chapters (see sections 1 and 2 in this volume) suggested methods which may assist with "jumping out of ruts" through collaborative and creative practice. Humour, sociability, and play seemed to offer useful strategies; so too did the use of social media (see Carnall, and Woodham and Kelleher, this volume). Equally, the darker side of heritage—for example, the full realities of physical labour during the industrial and agricultural revolution (see Smith, this volume) and at different periods of history (see Watson, this volume)—could to a degree also provide a way in through empathy and respect. As part of the "Who Cares?" project, creative practitioners were also employed as consultants, and the ability to create something new in response to an object or storeroom seemed to enliven both professionals and novice audiences (see Woodham and Kelleher, and Woodall, this volume). Finally, for enthusiasts, experts, and novices alike, the chance to handle objects, as seen in Macleod's chapter, seemed to create an emotional reaction in a way which is well evidenced by wider research on this theme.[5]

To come back to the issue of professionalization, we might also think about how noncuratorial expertise is incorporated into working practices. In Hess's chapter the curator was willing to allow experts from beyond the museum to tinker with objects in order to gain further knowledge about their make and construction. The "Energy in Store" project took this to a further level by engaging different enthusiasts in the Science Museum's stored collections with the aim of exploring how they might inform practice within the museum.[6] As resources and expertise are threatened, we must be careful not to suggest that museums can all be volunteer run, but we must also, by necessity, engage

---

5 Helen J. Chatterjee, "Introduction," in *Touch in Museums: Policy and Practice in Object Handling*, ed. Helen J. Chatterjee (Oxford: Berg, 2008), 1–8.

6 See the "Energy in Store" project report, available via: https://group.sciencemuseum.org/project/energy-in-store [accessed July 5, 2019].

with those who would volunteer their time and knowledge out of love for these objects. The need to engage in this kind of work is pressing, as the generations who know these objects are dying out and new enthusiasts are in many cases not stepping forward.

What Next for "Unloved" Collections?

The concept of "unloved" collections has allowed us to interrogate the very nexus of collections, emotion, and care to explore new ideas and stimulate critical pathways into museums. For example, how can a more emotionally informed museum practice help stimulate greater use of currently stored collections? How does the concept of "care" in the context of collections shed new light on the barriers to wider engagement? Could a more nuanced understanding of "enthusiasm" help us to reconsider how we imagine expertise and engagement? And how can we start to reveal the "caring practices" embedded in existing institutional practices and professional standards in order to enable broader articulations of "care" to be understood?

As is often the case when complex topics are brought together, the discussions prompt and reveal a number of additional areas that are ripe for further exploration that we were unable to cover here. A key area for us were questions around how we conduct emotional research, and there are many more directions to take in order to address this than we have touched upon. When somebody chose to collect these items, they took time and care over it, so they must have had a reason, and working with these collectors or their contemporary counterparts might help us recapture that magic. Thus the exploration of "unloved" objects has started to reveal which objects have become "lost," "invisible," or "detached" from original contexts, within which they prompted an emotional response, and the processes that have led to this loss. However, our research also suggests some ways to revive or create new emotional connections.

We conclude that "unloved" collections could be better integrated with a rich alternative set of historical, artistic, and heritage practices, in particular with the diverse forms of "love" and "care" demonstrated by collectors, researchers, artists, enthusiasts, and other audiences. This is not at odds with the idea of the museum as an agent of social change, but museum storage areas are rarely seen in this way. As outlined above, we suggest that all the groups discussed within this volume can, in distinct ways, act as formal and informal trustees of "unloved" material culture, playing a key role in the reinvigoration of stored collections as more dynamic, affective, and haptic resources. In a time of diminished resources, we consider that developing a better understanding of those who can "care" and of potential "caring practices" will be of direct benefit to the sector and allow for more instances of the "triangulation" described in the opening paragraph to this volume to occur.

INDEX

Printed and bound by CPI Group (UK) Ltd, Croydon, CR0 4YY

23/04/2025

14661021-0003